Anti-Jewish Violence

Anti-Jewish Violence

Rethinking the Pogrom
in East European History

Edited by

JONATHAN DEKEL-CHEN
DAVID GAUNT
NATAN M. MEIR
ISRAEL BARTAL

INDIANA UNIVERSITY PRESS
Bloomington and Indianapolis

This book is a publication of

Indiana University Press
601 North Morton Street
Bloomington, Indiana 47404-3797 USA

www.iupress.indiana.edu

Telephone orders   800-842-6796
Fax orders   812-855-7931
Orders by e-mail   iuporder@indiana.edu

⊗ The paper used in this publication meets the minimum
requirements of the American National Standard for Information
Sciences—Permanence of Paper for Printed Library Materials, ANSI
Z39.48-1992.

Manufactured in the United States of America

Library of Congress Cataloging-in-Publication Data

Hughes, Aaron W., [date]
The invention of Jewish identity : Bible, philosophy, and the art of
translation / Aaron W. Hughes.
p. cm.
Includes bibliographical references and index.
ISBN 978-0-253-35537-9 (cl : alk. paper) — ISBN 978-0-253-
22249-7 (pb : alk. paper) 1. Bible. O.T.—Translating. 2. Bible.
O.T.—Versions. 3. Jews—Identity. 4. Translating and interpreting.
5. Language and languages—Philosophy. 6. Jewish philosophy. I.
Title.
BS1132.H84 2010
221.4—dc22
2010015225

1 2 3 4 5 15 14 13 12 11 10

CONTENTS

Part 3. Regional Perspectives

John Doyle Klier (1944–2007)

PREFACE: A TRIBUTE TO JOHN DOYLE KLIER (1944–2007)

John Doyle Klier was the Sidney and Elizabeth Corob Professor of Modern Jewish History at University College, London. He began his university teaching career at Fort Hays State University, Kansas. John moved to University College, London in 1990 and rose to the rank of Professor in 1996.

For anyone engaged in the study of modern European history during the past two decades, familiarity with John Klier's scholarship was a rite of passage. His seminal works—*Russia Gathers Her Jews* (DeKalb, 1986) and *Imperial Russia's Jewish Question, 1855–1881* (Cambridge, 1995)—are required reading in university courses around the globe. Scholars in the field had been waiting anxiously for the publication of his newest (and tragically, last) monograph. In the last few months of his life, John neared the completion of the manuscript for this book, titled "Russians, Jews and the Pogroms of 1881-1882," to be published by Cambridge University Press. Following his death, Lars Fischer, François Guesnet and John's widow, Helen Klier, took up the completion of that long-awaited project.

John was fond of saying that the work of Hans Rogger sparked the reassessment of relations between the late Imperial Russian state and its Jews. It is equally true for anyone who knew his work that John Klier gave this revision its scholarly "teeth." He was among the first pioneering Western scholars to work in the Soviet archives in the 1980s. As a result, John quite literally reshaped the way that scholars and laypeople thought about the behavior of the Russian state and its peoples toward their Jewish subjects and neighbors during the nineteenth century. Most notably, he helped to change the way recurring anti-Jewish violence was understood and allowed other scholars to question many assumptions about the connection between the Imperial Russian regime and the pogroms. The importance of this cannot be overstated, given the centrality of anti-Jewish violence in the varieties of national narratives of the Jewish people and the mark these have left on the popular memory about the Russian Empire. John helped to turn the study of pogroms and anti-Jewish violence into a field of study in its own right.

For anyone who had the good fortune to know him, from the first meeting it was obvious that John was much more than a brilliant scholar. His unique blend of intellect, earthly common sense, and warmth made it possible for him to bridge generations and geographical barriers among colleagues—young and old—in our profession. Younger scholars among us know from firsthand experience that John was an extraordinarily gracious and helpful man who continuously went out of his way to assist aspiring scholars from around the world.

All of these skills and qualities made John an axis of activity in our field. Jonathan Dekel-Chen met John Klier for the first time in 2004 while planning for the conference in Stockholm that formed the backbone of this volume. He recalls:

> Until then, John was for me little more than the author of landmark publications. But from that moment onward, I learned to trust John's keen judgment and intuition in administrative affairs as well as in the more subtle aspects of the "human condition." John Klier's boundless energy, marvelous sense of humor, welcoming spirit, and integrity are a model for all who worked with him. Beyond all these, however, I remember John at his most human moments, like stopping to smile and straighten my jacket collar as we were about to enter a formal reception in Jerusalem or laughing together as we noticed some of the contradictions of life in Russia today.

Natan Meir met John Klier while working on his doctoral dissertation, and immediately experienced the senior scholar's generosity personally as Klier sent him photocopies of handwritten notes that he had taken when going through decades of issues of newspapers in libraries in Ukraine—thus saving Meir weeks or even months of research.

> My most cherished memory of John is from Moscow, 2004, when we were attending the SEFER conference of Jewish Studies. As we traveled together one evening from the conference site back to the hotel, John's joy at being "back in the USSR," as it were, was plainly evident. Even slipping and sliding on the black ice that is a fixture on Russian sidewalks in the winter was part of the fun. Rather than take taxis everywhere and eat in Western-style restaurants, John relished immersing himself in the "authentic" experience of riding the metro and buying fresh *pirogi* at a sidewalk stand. Attending SEFER was very much part of this mindset: John was one of the few Western scholars to attend the conference regularly and always found the presentations and, most of all, the interactions with fellow scholars fascinating and invigorating. He always treated even the most junior of graduate students with great respect—and of course, despite what he himself acknowledged was a fairly heavy American accent, *always* gave his talks in Russian.

John Klier's influence can be felt on every page of this book. Together with David Gaunt (Stockholm), Israel Bartal, the late Jonathan Frankel, Oleg Budnitskii (Moscow), and Jonathan Dekel-Chen, John organized an international academic conference in Stockholm in May 2005, titled "Anti-Jewish Violence: Reconceptualizing 'the Pogrom' in European History, 17th–20th Century." The articles in this book are a product of that conference. Given John's expertise in this subject, and his boundless goodwill and energy, he took the lead in the editorial process. Following John Klier's tragic passing, it has been our honor to move forward toward publication of this very important volume and to dedicate it to John's memory. We wish to express our deep gratitude to Helen Klier, whose gracious assistance at the hardest of times made possible the completion of this volume. The volume reflects in many ways one of the most profound of John's gifts to our profession—the ability to bring together, and then bring out the best, in scholars from across generational and geographic boundaries. More than most, John Klier embodied this gift; we miss him, and it, greatly.

THE EDITORS

ACKNOWLEDGMENTS

The idea for this book originated at an international academic conference held in Stockholm in May 2005, titled "Anti-Jewish Violence: Reconceptualizing 'the Pogrom' in European History, 17th–20th Century." The articles in this book are a product of that conference. The partners in its organization included the International Center for Russian and East European Jewish Studies, Moscow; the Forum for Living History, Stockholm; the Swedish Committee against Antisemitism; the Baltic and East European Graduate School at Södertörn University, Stockholm; and the Leonid Nevzlin Research Center for Russian and East European Jewry at the Hebrew University of Jerusalem.

The editors would like to thank the following institutions for their generous support of this volume: the Leonid Nevzlin Research Center for Russian and East European Jewry at the Hebrew University; Södertörn University, Stockholm; the Harold Schnitzer Family Program in Judaic Studies at Portland State University, Portland, Oregon; and the Foundation for Baltic and East European Studies.

ABBREVIATIONS

Archives
Archival Notations (R = Russian, U = Ukrainian, E = Estonian)

d.	delo (file) (R)
f.	fond (collection) (R, U)
k.	korobka (box) (R)
l., ll.	list, listy (folio, folios) (R)
l.	lehekülg, leheküljed (page, pages) (E)
ob.	oborot (verso) (R)
op.	opis' (inventory) (R, U)
RG	record group
s.	säilik (inventory or storage unit) (E)
spr.	sprava (file) (U)
zv.	zvorotnyi bik (verso) (U)
AJA	American Jewish Archives, Cincinnati
AVPRI	Arkhiv vneshnei politiki Rossiiskoi imperii (Foreign Affairs Archive of the Russian Empire), Moscow
CAHJP	Central Archives for the History of the Jewish People, Jerusalem
GAARK	Gosudarstvennyi arkhiv pri Sovete Ministrov Avtonomnoi Respubliki Krym (State Archive of the Council of Ministers of the Autonomous Republic of Crimea), Simferopol'
GAIO	Gosudarstvennyi arkhiv Irkutskoi oblasti (State Archive of Irkutsk Oblast'), Irkutsk
GAKK	Gosudarstvennyi arkhiv Krasnoiarskogo kraia (State Archive of Krasnoiarsk Region), Krasnoiarsk
GARF	Gosudarstvennyi arkhiv Rossiiskoi Federatsii (State Archive of the Russian Federation), Moscow
GAVO	Gosudarstvennyi arkhiv Vitebskoi oblasti (State Archive of Vitebsk Oblast'), Vitebsk
GAZK	Gosudarstvennyi arkhiv Zabaikal'skogo kraia (State Archive of Transbaikal Region), Chita

IR TsNB	Manuscript Division of the Vernadsky National Library of Ukraine, Kiev
JDC	American Jewish Joint Distribution Committee Archive, New York
NARA	United States National Archives and Records Administration, Washington, D.C.
NAUK FO	National Archives of the United Kingdom, London: Foreign Office
NARB	Natsional'nyi arkhiv Respubliki Belarus' (National Archive of the Republic of Belarus), Minsk
NARBu	Natsional'nyi arkhiv Respubliki Buriatiia (National Archive of the Republic of Buriatiia), Ulan-Ude
NIAB	Natsional'ny istoricheski arkhiv Belarusi (National Historical Archive of Belarus), Minsk
RGAE	Rossiiskii gosudarstvennyi arkhiv ekonomiki (Russian State Archive of the Economy), Moscow
RGIA	Rossiiskii gosudarstvennyi istoricheskii arkhiv (Russian State Historical Archive), St. Petersburg
RGVIA	Rossiiskii gosudarstvennyi voenno-istoricheskii arkhiv (Russian State Military Historical Archive), Moscow
TsDIAU	Tsentral'nyi derzhavnyi istorychnyi arkhiv Ukraïny, Kyïv (Central State Historical Archive of Ukraine, Kyiv)
TsGIA SPb	Tsentral'nyi gosudarstvennyi istoricheskii arkhiv Sankta-Peterburga (Central State Historical Archive of St. Petersburg)
VOANPI	Vologskii oblastnoi arkhiv noveishei politicheiskoi istorii (Vologda Oblast Archive of Modern Political History)
YIVO	Archives of the YIVO Institute for Jewish Research, New York

Anti-Jewish Violence

Sites of Major Pogroms
1881-1884 and 1903-1906

*St. Petersburg

KOSTROMA

ESTONIA

ST. PETERSBURG

NOVGOROD

IAROSLAV

BALTIC SEA

LIVONIA

RUSSIAN

Volga

Iaroslav

•Ivanovo-Voznesensk Nizhnij Novgorod

TVER

Riga

Rezhitsa

PSKOV

VLADIMIR

Oka

COURLAND

Daugava

VITEBSK

•Velikie Luki

MOSCOW

N

KOVNO

Polotsk Gorodok

•Moscow

•Egor'evsk

Nemunas

VILNA

Minsk

Vitebsk

Orsha

Dnepr

SMOLENSK

Viaz'ma

Riazan'

RIAZAN'

Tana

GERMAN EMPIRE

SUWALKI

MOGILEV

Berezina

KALUGA

TULA

TAMBOV

Bialystok

Surazh

•Briansk •Orel

OREL

Klintsy

Novozybkov

•Starodub

Voronezh

GRODNO

MINSK

Gomel'

Pripiat'

Zlynka Semenovka

Kursk

Don

Warsaw

W. Bug

Nosovichi

Repki

Gorodnia Novgorod-Seversk

Sednev

Kyl'sk

Sejm

KINGDOM OF POLAND

Chernigov

Berezna

Putivl'

KURSK

VORONEZH

CHERNIGOV

Konotop

VOLHYNIA

Oster

Nezhin

Nosovka

Kozelets

Romny

Gadiach

Khar'kov

Gostomel'

Priluki

KHAR'KOV

Vistula

AUSTRIA-HUNGARY

Dnestr

Miropol'

Kiev

Borispol'

S. Bug

Belaia Tserkov

Pereiaslav

Drabovo •Khorol'

Zolotonosha

POLTAVA

Donets

Vinnitsa

KIEV

Smela

Chigirin

Kremenchug

Kobeliaki

Novomoskovsk

Lisichansk

Bakhmut

Luugansk

DON MILITARY

Kamenets-Podol'skii Mogilev-na-Dnestre

Zhmerinka

Vapniarka

Verkhnedneprovsk

Elisavetgrad

Ekaterinoslav

•Igren'

Iuzovka

EKATERINOSLAV

Don

Tisza

BESSARABIA

Bogopol'

Golta

Krivoi Rog

Aleksandrovsk

Rostov-on-Don

Balta

Ol'viopol

Nikopol'

Orekhov

Kamenskoe

Mariupol'

Birzula

Anan'ev

KHERSON

Berdiansk

Prut

Kalarash

Strasheny

Kishinev

Severinovka

Nikolaev

TAURIDA

KUBAN

Razdel'naia

Kherson

Genichesk

Odessa

Kuban'

Olt

Akkerman

ROMANIA

Izmail

Danube

Simferopol'

BLACK SEA

•Feodosia

Nemunas

Dnepr

Legend:

• Site of a major pogrom, 1881-84 and/or 1903-06

✶ Other cities

International border

Provincial border

The Pale of Settlement is shown in white.

0   50   100 miles

0   50   100 km

Cartography by Margaret Seiler. Adapted from *The YIVO Encyclopedia of Jews in Eastern Europe,* ed. Gershon David Hundert (New Haven, Conn.: Yale University Press, 2008).

Introduction

DAVID GAUNT, JONATHAN DEKEL-CHEN,
NATAN M. MEIR, AND ISRAEL BARTAL

In the history of Europe, the anti-Jewish pogroms of the late nineteenth and early twentieth centuries have been overshadowed in importance by the horrors of World War II and the Holocaust. This is a reasonable valuation given the relatively limited nature of the pogroms and the universal destructiveness of the Holocaust. However, the pogroms that erupted in late imperial Russia were, at the time of the events themselves, unrivaled episodes of ethnic violence and tended toward increasing levels of destruction with each new outburst. The enormous international interest expressed through extensive press coverage and the activities of humanitarian organizations created widespread sympathy for the plight of Jews inside the Russian Empire. At the same time, the repeated need for foreign outcries that ultimately did *not* ignite diplomatic intervention accustomed world opinion to high levels of racial violence and raised suspicions in Russia that governments could be benefiting from ethnic conflicts. The first great waves of migration of Jews from Eastern Europe, the politicization of the Jewish masses, together with the rise of the Zionist movement took place against the background of the pogroms. And as some of the articles in this volume show, the pogroms also formed the context in which the idea of combating "Judeo-Bolshevism" had its origin.

With the disintegration of the Soviet Union in the early 1990s came the opening of hitherto inaccessible archives and library resources in Russia and the various East European successor states. This new material enabled many pioneering advances in the study of pogroms. Some of these results are presented in this volume. No less significant, a number of the contributors present their unique findings here for the first time in English. These deal with the increasing geographic spread of pogroms throughout tsarist Russia, the continuation of pogroms through World War I, the Bolshevik Revolution, and the Civil War. Several researchers follow up recent observations that pogroms were closely related to the degree to which a locality was affected by modernization, urbanization, industrialization, and economic competition. Notwithstanding the importance of the archival "turn" in East European Jewish studies over the past two decades, like any other research tool, archives taken by themselves are no guarantor of historical accuracy or structural continuity. Hence, we hope that the essays in this volume achieve a balance between the availability of great quantities of new data and strong contextualization and analysis.

Another factor that encouraged new investigation of pogroms is the recent development of comparative studies of genocide, genocidal activities, ethnic cleansing, and other forms of interpersonal attacks. Until now, pogroms have seldom been a major part of these comparative analyses because their extent and multiple forms have not been fully understood. Most comparative studies until now have used the relatively mild and spontaneous 1881–1882 pogroms as a basic model and have ignored the much more violent and politically rooted pogroms of the Civil War period. While shocking in their day, the pogroms of 1881–1882 paled in comparison to the destructive power of the latter attacks. Moreover, the existing research tends to focus exclusively on events in and around the Pale of Settlement. While research since the 1980s has made clear that the pogroms of 1881–1882 were spontaneous rather than orchestrated, the pogroms of World War I and the Russian Civil War period undoubtedly had a systematic and officially sanctioned nature. In going beyond the geographic and even the chronological boundaries normally associated with pogroms in Eastern Europe, this volume seeks to describe them as a transitional form of ethnic violence. Pogroms can, therefore, be seen in a number of ways: as last emanations of ancient religious-based hatred; as early signs of officially sponsored racial warfare; and as precursors to full-scale genocide.

Historiography of Anti-Jewish Violence

As a stateless, diasporic people, traditionally lacking formal political power and representation, European Jews have had their history described by some scholars as a series of reactions to the interventions of dominant rulers and populations. Discriminatory legislation, prohibitions, geographic exclusion, expulsions, expropriations, and ritual violence intertwined with limited privileges and socioeconomic opportunities. This version of Jewish history is the sorrowful "lachrymose" story of martyrdom and victimization based on religious difference and rivalry. It differs greatly from a competing interpretation of Jewish history, which focuses on the agency, initiative, and creativity that enabled Jews to survive—and even flourish—despite harsh environments.

The nature of anti-Jewish violence changed as a result of develop-ments in the societies where Jews lived. Violence intensified and was chan-neled into new forms as economic competition evolved and as nationalism and ideologies targeted newly defined "national" and "racial" minorities. As new types of hostility emerged, older ones did not completely disappear; rather, old and new merged into a complex web of activities and motives. Thus, observers could speak of the continuous role of centuries-old reli-gious hatred, or anti-Judaism.[1] But at the same time, scholars could point to totally new economic, racial, or political motivations that became part of Europe's modernization.

Religions normally develop an everyday tolerance at the local level for other faiths, while preserving rivalries and maintaining a level of hate-speech. There is always a suppressed latent potential, as David Nirenberg has shown for medieval Spain. Here, ritual forms of violence on Good Fri-day were normally contained and seldom resulted in physical damage.[2] For violence to become widespread, there must be a way of legitimizing it in the social sphere through the spread of myths and other means. One out-standing example of this is the medieval "blood libel," the accusation that Jews would abduct and kill Christian children before the Passover holiday in order to use their blood in preparing ceremonial food (*matzot,* or un-leavened bread).[3] This legend formed the incitement for many anti-Jewish riots throughout the Middle Ages and up to the trial of Mendel Beilis in Kiev in 1913. Even though the government was directly active in the Beilis case, as a rule the individual and spontaneous incidents reflected the ten-sion between religious groups in local societies.

Many riots and massacres in modern European history have targeted Jews. Among the more notable of these occurred in the years 1789–1790, 1819, 1830–1831, and 1848. The pogroms of Odessa in 1821, 1859, and 1871 are particularly relevant for Russia. Those that erupted in the late nine-teenth century were qualitatively and quantitatively different. Conse-quently, the pogroms of 1881–1882 have been seen as a major break in the history of Jews in tsarist Russia.[4] Until then, there was an unchallenged be-lief that conditions for the Jews were progressively improving with the rise in their integration into the social fabric of the empire. After this wave of violence swept over large parts of Russia, the strategy of Jewish assimilation no longer seemed to be the only viable way forward. Moreover, the Jewish street experienced a rapid flood of pressures toward emigration and politici-zation. Jonathan Frankel concluded, "In essence what the crisis of 1881–1882 did was to deal a heavy blow to the hitherto prevailing faith in the onward march of liberalism as the natural solution to the Jewish question."[5]

Historical interpretations have shifted over time. The first Jewish analyses of the pogroms indicated official involvement. How else would it have been possible in the tsarist police state for so many destructive riots to occur simultaneously over such a wide geographic area?[6] Most of the earliest historiography accepted the view that Jews were scapegoats in the pogroms because of the blatant antisemitism present in all strata of tsarist society, particularly among high officials. Only much later did researchers revise this first impression: the pogroms were actually confined to certain parts of southern Russia and did not spread to the rest of the empire. They also argued that it was impossible to confirm the participation of high officials in the planning of the riots and that, in fact, a great number of perpetrators were punished.[7] The regime even created commissions to investigate the causes of the violence.

What Were the Pogroms?

Although pogroms could affect any targeted group, in normal usage the word has come to denote an anti-Jewish riot. One assertion in this volume is that during the period under investigation the pogrom was transformed from sporadic, spontaneous acts of mob violence with some government collusion into government-sponsored actions, if not policy, implemented by mechanisms of the state. The early pogroms (of which the 1881–1882 pogroms are the foremost example) targeted Jews as such, but did not aim to eradicate the Jewish people; thus, they fall outside the category of genocide. These riots caused greater loss of property (shops, warehouses, and homes) than deaths. The motivating factors here were socioeconomic, in particular the disruption caused by industrialization. Thus, these pogroms were not "interpersonal," but rather targeted wealth and property as symbols of economic injustice. Later waves of pogroms, however, can be described as "genocidal behavior" in that they involved mass murder of significant Jewish groups that were delimited by residence patterns, occupation, wealth, or visibility.[8]

Differences between pogroms in the nineteenth and twentieth centuries warrant more detailed exploration. As a first step, we must reassess the role of the perceived threat. Pogroms occurred throughout the nineteenth century in peaceful times as well as in times of severe crisis, like the assassination of Tsar Alexander II. But even then, no one perceived the state as being at risk from the Jews. However, the latter pogroms dealt with in this volume—those that broke out during the Russian Revolutions

(1905 and 1917), World War I, the Civil War, and the Russian–Polish War—transpired in periods when the state was threatened by international pressure. At these moments Jews were targeted as disloyal tools of foreign powers or as subversive revolutionaries plotting to topple the regime. By the time the pogroms had subsided in the 1920s, Jews were perceived as a major threat to the state (whether "Red" or "White") and had become a vulnerable civilian population.

Another difference is the extent of the violence. The early pogroms affected limited geographic regions and could be seen as an urban phenomenon—an unfortunate part of the processes of industrialization and modernization. Later, destruction became more systematic, often planned by state bodies (such as the military) or state-sponsored organizations, and even affected traditional rural villages. From their beginnings as isolated, sporadic incidents, pogroms were transformed into systematic sweeps instigated for military and political purposes. In their final stages, pogroms closely resembled full-scale ethnic cleansing of entire regions.

A third difference, not often explored in studies of anti-Jewish violence before the Holocaust, is the diverse array of Jewish responses to violence. These ranged from mass migration away from Eastern Europe to assimilationism to traditionalist quietism to politicization to organized self-defense. Also of crucial importance were the responses of Jews in other lands—especially Western Europe and the United States—to the pogroms perpetrated against their coreligionists in Eastern Europe.

Some of the chapters in this volume challenge the underlying assumption of the collection itself: does it really make sense to group all of these phenomena together under the somewhat reductionist rubric of "pogrom"? A central question within the historiography of the Holocaust is whether the anti-Jewish violence that occurred across East-Central and Eastern Europe before World War II was a "prelude" of sorts to the Nazi genocide. Phrased somewhat differently, this question can also be asked of any of the episodes of anti-Jewish violence studied in this volume: did the so-called "excesses" of each incident—many of them carried out with impunity—ease the way for the next swell of violence? There is no gainsaying the fact that a fateful consequence of the pogroms was that Jews had so clearly been victims of the preceding waves. The awareness of past violence and, in some cases, mass murder made it possible for later perpetrators to consider renewed targeting of this particular group. The success of the previous pogroms increased the vulnerability of the Jews as future victims. It seems to us that this factor alone would legitimate the grouping together of so many different kinds and scales of mass violence. Also, international opinion had become accustomed to see governments or political leaders as the organizers of mass murder for political reasons.

Two questions reappear throughout chapters in this volume in subtle and more explicit forms. Both questions require a cautious approach and have contemporary implications. First, while these and other research efforts may help to decode the sources of anti-Jewish violence, an equally intriguing question exists: is there a calculable formula for the prevention of such violence in situations that seem to portend the worst? The second question is more specific to the decades following the disintegration of the Soviet Union: how must historical analysis balance between accurate study and the needs of newly independent nations in Eastern Europe to construct their national narratives?

As originally conceived, the volume was to include an article by John Klier titled "Were the Russian Pogroms a 'Deadly Ethnic Riot'?" Klier presented an early version of this paper at the conference in Stockholm in 2005 on which this volume is based. Tragically, he was unable to complete this important contribution before his untimely death. Even in its unfinished form, however, the article raised a number of critical points. Perceiving the pogrom as a transitional phase, Klier turned our focus away from comparison of pogroms with its successor, genocide, and instead made his comparison with the more widespread premodern "deadly ethnic riot." This is a term developed by Donald Horowitz to cover "an intense, sudden, though not necessarily unplanned, lethal attack by civilian members of one ethnic group on civilian members of another ethnic group, the victims chosen because of their group membership. So conceived, ethnic riots are synonymous with what are variously called 'communal,' 'racial,' 'religious,' 'linguistic,' or 'tribal' disturbances."[9] Klier applied this concept to the case of the 1881–1882 pogroms—in his words, "the first outbreak of modern, wide-scale anti-Jewish violence in the Russian Empire"—and found it of great value in identifying the background factors and motives of those who participated in the pogroms. Klier's discussion pointed to the importance of political crisis as a trigger factor—the assassination of the tsar, World War I, and the Civil War. He also turned our attention toward the rise of accusations that the growing Jewish population, some of them in newly dominant roles introduced by new capitalist structures in the Russian Empire, many others impoverished and "flooding" into the cities in search of employment, threatened to take over, consume, or "swallow up" the dominant group; hence, the cries that could be heard during pogroms that "the Jews are sucking our blood." (This also jibes well with

Horowitz's observation that the deadly ethnic riot, whether in East Africa, South Asia, or elsewhere, is often explained by a threat of being literally "eaten" by the victimized group.)

Klier's examination confirmed the recent research that exonerated Russian officials from having planned the pogroms of 1881–1882. He did show, however, that many officials "certainly empathized with [the pogroms]," had sympathy for the perpetrators, and agreed to legal discrimination against the victims, such as the "May Laws" enacted in the wake of the pogroms. In this sense, government officials clearly approved of the pogrom as (in Horowitz's words) "a form of shadow legal redress," when the mob took things into its own hands in order to set things right, as it were. Klier also showed the applicability to the Russian pogroms of Horowitz's theory of the "cumulative effect" of ethnic violence over time; because the pattern and the expected outcome of a pogrom had already been set, each outbreak was both more violent than the one before and at the same time (and somewhat paradoxically, given the increasing level of violence), less unpredictable. The pogrom "became an integral part of the Russian discourse of violence, easily remembered and easily provoked." Klier also showed that, contra previous analyses that saw the perpetrators of the largest pogroms—those in the cities—as rootless mobs of poor migrant workers, the ringleaders of the pogroms were usually *local* townspeople who managed to stir up large crowds of peasants. Indeed, he concluded, "most *pogromshchiki* were from the Pale, and probably the majority were local people," in many cases egged on by the approving and legitimating presence of large numbers of educated society who gathered to watch the "entertainment." (As with all of his scholarship, Klier supported his conclusions with a rigorous scholarly framework, here in the form of extracts from numerous archival records in Russian and Ukrainian repositories.) Klier ended with a paradox: although the model of the "deadly ethnic riot" is very useful in determining the outcome of a pogrom once it begins, the pogroms of 1881–1882 were not particularly deadly, certainly not when compared with later eruptions of anti-Jewish violence in the Russian Empire.

Our volume opens with a comparative essay by David Engel on the meaning and definition of the term *pogrom*. Engel looks deeply into European modernity and the rise of the *Rechtsstaat* in order to try to explain the roots of modern anti-Jewish violence across the continent. Using the accounts of contemporary observers as a point of departure, he shows the various instances in which the concept was used—from May 1871 riots until the bloodbath of Kielce in July 1946. Unfortunately, the term was applied to so many differing cases that a clear definition based on usage alone is nearly impossible. A fascinating result is that the political application of the word *pogrom* was at times—as was the case for anti-Jewish attacks in Polish Lwów in 1919—just as controversial as the term *genocide* is today. There was, in effect, "pogrom denial" on the part of government officials and even some investigating diplomats, such as the American statesman Henry Morgenthau. This dispute suggests that pogrom and genocide are potentially twin concepts. Both are used to indicate crimes of exceptional mass violence, and both build on the fact that perpetrators saw their victims as a separate category of people whose threatening behavior "justified" attack. Moreover, both concepts impute intentions to the perpetrators and imply some sort of government involvement, and, finally, both can be seen as outgrowths of modern civilization.

Engel's case-by-case investigation leads him to question the innocence of governments, which other recent historians have taken pains to prove. Instead, he finds that states were indeed major players and that the era of the pogrom circa 1860–1940 coincided with the modernization of European states. Before this period, violence against Jews was rare and not connected to a belief that the state should protect the majority against what they perceived as a dangerous ethnic threat. As a state developed a judiciary system and the rule of law, it of necessity became the ultimate legal authority that regulated conflicts between citizens belonging to different ethnic groups. The modernizing Russian state created and implemented laws that restricted the activities, economy, occupations, residence, education, and cultural life of Jews. The legal representatives of the state, the administrators, judges, and police were integrated as agents into the big picture of collective violence between Christians and Jews in tsarist Russia.

Part 1 of this volume deals with pogroms during World War I and the Russian Civil War. These are under-researched events that fell under the deep shadow of the war and 1917 Revolutions. Eric Lohr deals with the anti-Jewish violence that accompanied the attempt by the Russian army to deport suspect populations away from the frontline. Suspected of disloyalty and even spying for the Germans and Austrians, the Jews were forcibly expelled from the western provinces. As Cossack detachments were often assigned to implement the orders, the expulsions became violent, particularly during the great Russian retreat from April to October 1915. Approximately one hundred pogroms erupted during these months, and once the Cossacks deployed outside a village, neighboring peasants would also join in. Lohr employs the concept "war pogrom" given that the army played a direct role. Orders for mass expulsion came from military leadership, and troops committed the violence. The dominant role of the army was a major feature, and Lohr can identify several high military and civil officials who shared the ultimate responsibility for instigating the wave of pogroms. Peter Holquist follows up Lohr's investigation with a detailed study of antisemitism in the General Staff during the Russian occupation of Austrian Galicia and Bukovina in 1914 and 1915. Chief of Staff General Nikolai Ianushkevich and Commander in Chief Grand Duke Nikolai Nikolaevich were particularly noted for pursuing a "targeted, systemic, and far-reaching antisemitic program" with repeated pogroms; this must be set against a backdrop of the "maelstrom of violence" sweeping through the region during the war years, including random pillaging by military units and the punitive (and often anti-Jewish) policies put in place by the military. Suspected of collective treason, the Jews were often attacked in the wake of rumors about shots fired at Russian troops from inside Jewish houses. This violence at first lacked structure and focus. As time passed, however, it became systematic and was accompanied by the expropriation of all Jewish landholdings and the removal of Jews from civil office. Holquist demonstrates that the role of specific individuals—in this case, high-level officials in the tsarist army who gave specific directives on the persecution of Jews—played a crucial role, in addition to the existing antisemitic attitudes ingrained in the Russian military, and the numerous political, social, and economic factors that contributed to the policy of violence and expulsion.

Russian society, then, became accustomed to military pogroms early in World War I. Previous research by Oleg Budnitskii has shown that the incidence of army pogroms increased exponentially during the Civil War period (1918–1921). He found evidence of more than a thousand pogroms and similar incidents in Ukraine alone, and estimated the number of Jewish deaths from a low of 50,000 to a high of 200,000. In addition, thousands of women were raped. His research showed that *both* the White Army and the Red Army perpetrated anti-Jewish pogroms. This indicates that any soldier who had previously served in the imperial army had been subjected to a heavy dose of antisemitism and had likely had the opportunity to participate in earlier pogroms.[10]

Anti-Jewish violence, including pogroms, continued even after the Russian Revolution and the collapse of the tsarist army. Using newspaper accounts and new archival materials, Vladimir Buldakov assembled a database of 320 reports of all sorts of anti-Jewish violence during 1917 and 1918. Some of these were cases of mass violence; others involved only individuals.

The data encompasses ninety full-scale pogroms, most of which occurred in August–October 1917 and March–May 1918. Much can be attributed to the aggression of retreating soldiers, food riots, and shop plundering that spun out of control, as well as the rapid emergence of "Judeo-Bolshevik" accusations. The largest pogrom of this period took place at Glukhov (in present-day Ukraine), resulting in an estimated four hundred Jewish deaths.

Jewish Responses

Organizing a Jewish response was problematic, especially because the causes of the first pogroms were unclear. From the start, the pogroms were welcomed by leading factions in radical political groups such as Narodnaia volia (The People's Will). They viewed the pogroms as a sign of the coming revolution and interpreted the violence as the people's retribution against Jewish exploitation.[11] For its part, the Russian government linked the pogroms to the assassination of Tsar Alexander II and saw revolutionary "anarchists" as the cause. Other interpretations, strongly represented in the international press, accused the reactionary tsarist government of instigating the violence. Inside Russia there was a widespread rumor that the new tsar had issued a decree for collective punishment of the Jews: "Beat the Jews." This caused deep spiritual crisis among groups such as the Society for the Spread of Enlightenment among the Jews of Russia, which had preached adaptation to Russian life.[12] In this climate of contradiction, Jews who supported revolutionary parties, as well as those Jews who strove for assimilation with Russian society, were placed in a similar quandary. Both of these groups had to make difficult choices: Should they remain loyal to, or reject, revolutionary politics? Should they remain inside or reject assimilation to Russia?

The Jewish ideological response had to account for the seeming dead-end of previous hopes for improvement in Russia. Given the rise in official antisemitism and new repressive legislation that made them legally inferior and vulnerable, Jews needed to reevaluate their position, whatever their social status. The available solutions, however, varied greatly.[13] The aristocratic approach favored appeal to Western countries for diplomatic intervention that would force Russia to take responsibility for the safety and welfare of its Jewish population. Traditionalists maintained their quietism, avoided conflicts with authorities, accepted the increased suffering, and abandoned the quest for improvement. The Russian-oriented modernist intelligentsia lost its bearing and the Jewish masses simply migrated in great numbers, millions to the West and an undetermined number to the growing cities of Russia. The stream of emigrants gave rise to philanthropic projects to direct the flow and to organize the resettlement of Jews. The dynamism and mobility of these decades in turn gave rise to questions of nationalism and political action, producing the evolution of the Zionist movement and the politicization of the Jewish street, embodied by, among the many political movements of the late nineteenth century, the General Jewish Workers Union in Russia and Poland (the Bund).

Traditionally, Jews had remained passive in the face of antisemitic violence. One way forward was to create self-defense units. The Bund, established in 1897 as a social-democratic party, formed such groups (called *kamf-grupe*) in the wake of pogroms at the start of the twentieth century, of which the 1903 Kishinev pogrom was the most violent. Jewish, and some non-Jewish, volunteers were armed with revolvers, knives, whips, and the occasional homemade bomb. In the city of Gomel, in Belarus, self-defense played a significant role in limiting damage during the pogrom in that city. Resistance was greatest in places where the Bund was strong; self-defense units operated in one-third of the 1903–1904 pogroms. The arming of Jews and the success of their defense could backfire, however. While primarily formed to protect property, the *kamf-grupe* resistance increased the brutality of the attackers, thus raising the number of deaths. In addition, armed self-defense groups provoked right-wing racist extremists to accuse them of insolence, insubordination, impudence, and contempt of Christians. Russian officials, police, and military, seeing signs of rebellion, grew increasingly suspicious of Jewish links to subversion, particularly when the Bund emerged as the largest socialist party in the Russian Empire. Unsubstantiated fears were widespread that the Jews were preparing anti-Russian pogroms, thus legitimizing anti-Jewish violence by loyal Russians. In Gomel, the police arrested not only those who rioted, but also some of the Jewish defenders. The governor of Mogilev summed up the aggressive reactionary attitude when he declared to a Jewish delegation, "Jews arming themselves and firing upon troops who are there to protect them—has there ever been anything like it? Under such circumstances it is not for us to defend you; we must defend ourselves against you."[14]

By the end of the nineteenth century, issues of human rights had become part of international politics, ironically propagated foremost by Tsar Nicholas II. Since the Russian government, led by Interior Minister Viacheslav von Plehve, was widely held responsible for encouraging the violence, it could be expected that international reactions to the brutal pogroms of the early twentieth century would have had diplomatic repercussions. In Britain and the United States vociferous groups lobbied their governments to deliver formal protests against the anti-Jewish sentiments in a Russia that was increasingly seen as brutal and barbaric. Efforts to influence foreign governments were, however, to no avail.[15] After decades of antagonism, Britain was trying to woo Russia as an ally, eventually culminating in the Anglo-Russian Agreement of 1907. Hence, it was unwilling to disturb relations. In the United States, the Kishinev pogrom caused the first major breach in relations with Russia. For the two decades from the pogroms of 1881–1882 until Kishinev, masses of Russian Jewish immigrants had been arriving on America's shores, most of them highly critical of the tsarist regime. They supplied information and advocated for philanthropic relief to be sent to their brethren who remained behind in Eastern Europe. Because of the growing public outcry to intervene on behalf of Russia's Jews, the U.S. government came close to sending a note of protest, as President Theodore Roosevelt had initially promised to Jewish leaders. In the end, however, no formal protest was lodged. The relatively weak governmental responses to antisemitism in Russia enhanced the impression that anti-Jewish violence might indeed be inevitable, given the environment of ethnic intolerance pervading the region. This generated doubt and disillusion over the fate of Russia's Jews.

Vladimir Levin's study of Jews as active agents responding to violence against them focuses on Jewish political activity in the wake of pogroms in the early twentieth century. These, he finds, were not far-reaching strategies to save the Jewish people as a whole but short-term efforts to deter further pogrom violence. The specific strategies that he outlines include intercession, self-defense, and anti-defamation (the systematic struggle against antisemitism). Intercession, the modern version of the age-old Jewish practice of *shtadlanut,* could be practiced on both local and national levels but almost always by the *individual*—and was thus considered by many nationalist-minded Jewish leaders and activists to be a controversial retreat to the traditional, and now scorned, creeping through the corridors of power. Self-defense, by contrast, was considered a much more appropriate response for those for whom national pride was a central virtue, though its effectiveness was debatable. Interestingly, it was not only revolutionary and nationalist groups that organized self-defense activities but also otherwise unaffiliated Jews who were determined that a pogrom not occur in their town. The third type of response surveyed by Levin, anti-defamation, was by its very nature less spontaneous and more of a long-term effort conducted (mostly) by Jewish liberals to discredit antisemitic forces within the Russian Empire. In parallel, they aimed to disseminate "correct information" about Jews among the local population. Even if none of these strategies was successful in the end, the choices made by Jewish leaders reveal much about the inner dynamics of Russian Jewish society and the nature of Jewish–Christian relations in the Russian Empire.

Natan Meir examines the threat of pogrom as a factor in everyday Russian Jewish life, using Kiev as a case study. Counter to commonly held views, Meir finds that the 1881–1882 pogroms seem to have had little long-term impact on Jews' sense of security in the city. Rather, the real threat to Jewish life in Kiev in the last two decades of the nineteenth century was the possibility of roundup and expulsion. While Kiev's situation was unique in some respects, there were many Jews throughout the Russian Empire who faced a similar threat, whether because they lived in areas designated as part of the countryside within the Pale of Settlement, or in cities outside the Pale that were off-limits to all but specific categories of Jews. After the upheaval of 1905, by contrast, when violence—organized and planned, not spontaneous—threatened to break out on a very regular basis, Jews "lived with a sword hanging over their heads" until the fall of the tsar's regime. There are signs that the moderate measure of integration that had been achieved within the city's civil society and associational life was dealt a serious blow as Jews stopped attending mixed groups and retreated into themselves. The near-pogrom after Prime Minister Petr Stolypin's assassination and the Beilis Affair only aggravated this trend. Indeed, it was likely that the increased Jewish integration into imperial life was a main stimulus for the conservative and xenophobic backlash against the empire's Jews in 1905. The charge of sedition heard in 1905—that Jews wanted to overthrow the tsarist regime—turned out to be much more serious and far-reaching than the nineteenth-century accusation of economic exploitation.

Regional Perspectives

Part 3 of this volume challenges what have become the commonly accepted geographic and chronological boundaries of pogroms, usually assumed to be in the Ukrainian lands of the tsarist empire. Lilia Kalmina investigates disturbances that have been called "pogroms" in Siberia, a vast expanse with very sparse Jewish settlement. The pogroms in Irkutsk (1905) and Krasnoiarsk (1916) were, as might be expected, part of larger disturbances expressing discontent with the authorities in periods of turmoil and social unrest (the Revolution of 1905 and World War I, respectively). In contrast to the very visible Jewish presence in the Pale of Settlement, Jews in Siberia were few and far between, and often lacking in religious or ethnic organization. Thus, as Kalmina shows, "Jews were not singled out as revolutionaries" as they so often were in areas of dense Jewish settlement. The coordinated attack against Jewish shops and traders in Krasnoiarsk, by contrast, was far more similar to a typical pogrom, but this may well have been due to the influence of antisemitic tendencies within the Russian army filtering through to Siberia by way of soldiers returning to the front. There are striking similarities to pogroms in the Pale of Settlement embodied by negligent officials and Judeophobic policemen sympathetic to the *pogromshchiki*, but also uniquely Siberian characteristics such as the high proportion of criminals among the perpetrators of the violence. Kalmina's research seems to show that, as scholars have suspected, the very high proportion of Jews within the total population of the empire's western borderlands played a crucial role in interethnic tension and hostility and, ultimately, in the outbreaks of violence. Where Jews were fewer and far less visible, as in Siberia, they were more likely to be better integrated into society and thus less likely to be attacked.

The somewhat peculiar case of Lithuanian Jewry is treated by Vladas Sirutavičius and Darius Staliūnas. They attempt to explain the stark contrast between the relatively infrequent episodes of anti-Jewish violence in the late nineteenth and twentieth centuries (which, as the authors show, were not quite as infrequent as has been assumed) and the brutal assistance rendered by a significant number of ordinary Lithuanians to the Nazis during the Holocaust. The authors provide a schematization of Lithuanian antisemitic attitudes (elite, popular, and governmental), and analyze the influence of traditional religious sentiments, Lithuanian nationalism, and Nazi policies by turn. They also consider the role that the various Soviet occupations played, as well as the complex economic relationships that bound Lithuanians and Jews throughout the period. Not surprisingly, they conclude that no one factor can explain either the relative paucity of anti-Jewish violence or the attacks that did occur, a supposition that serves to remind students of history that pogroms can never be studied in isolation from the often extremely complex political, social, and economic contexts in which they occurred.

Another seeming exception to pogrom violence, the relatively untroubled provinces of historic Belorussia, is considered by Claire Le Foll. She explains that the absence of pogroms in Belorussia in 1881–1882 cannot be attributed to a positive predisposition toward Jews on the part of the local intelligentsia, who, along with local bureaucrats and publicists, were rather conservative and tended to accept wholesale the official line on Jewish exploitation, fanaticism, and benightedness. Rather, the low level of violence can be attributed to the relative lack of urbanization and industrialization in Belorussia; compare the high concentration of pogroms in areas of Ukraine and territories of New Russia, which had recently experienced rapid in-migration to cities such as Odessa, Elizavetgrad, and Kiev by both Christians and Jews in search of jobs in the rapidly industrializing economy of the region. The provinces of Vitebsk, Minsk, and Mogilev would not experience industrialization on such a scale until the 1890s. Moreover, an array of socioeconomic and political factors ensured that the Belorussian provinces did not experience urbanization in the same way as those in Ukraine and Lithuania; market towns became overwhelmingly Jewish in population as Christian peasants either stayed on the land or migrated to other regions of the empire. Belorussia remained something of a backwater where the old economic order was little affected by the emancipation of the serfs. This underdevelopment insulated the region from the upheavals that accompanied the coming of modernity and a new economic order in other regions, especially Ukraine. The relative underdevelopment of Belorussian nationalism also contributed to the lack of active hostility between the two groups.

The last two chapters treat a chronological period that is usually considered to be "pogrom-free": the Soviet era. Arkadi Zeltser shows us a Belorussia four decades beyond that discussed in Le Foll's article, and substantially transformed in the intervening years. In the 1920s and 1930s, Jews and Belorussians competed to enter the Soviet middle class, which generated tensions between members of the two groups. Large-scale urbanization and industrialization meant that many Belorussians found themselves in the city for the first time, unfamiliar territory for them to which Jews were, of course, much more accustomed. Soviet policy gave official status to both Belorussian and Yiddish, stirring up resentments about who would have to learn whose language. On one side, Jews took exception to being forced to learn a supposedly "peasant" language that would probably be of little use in the long run. For their part, Belorussians did not want Yiddish—the language of a minority that was unintelligible to them— being used in official arenas. While Soviet authorities would not tolerate violence against Jews on any level whatsoever, the success that Jews experienced within the Soviet system gave rise to tensions that smoldered under the surface, especially during the 1920s. These seemed to diminish significantly in the 1930s, however, thanks to an array of factors specific to interwar Stalinism (e.g., concerns for physical survival and a decrease in unemployment mitigating interethnic tensions). As in the Lithuanian case, historians must ponder the question of how this relatively peaceful period was followed by large-scale Belorussian collaboration with Nazi mass murder of Jews after 1941.

Another arena notable for its lack of anti-Jewish violence is that of the agricultural colonies in interwar Soviet Crimea and southern Ukraine, explored by Jonathan Dekel-Chen. This chapter not only presents the historical context for that relative interethnic harmony that we find here, but also attempts to extrapolate in order to reach some tentative conclusions on the preconditions for intergroup violence in the Soviet Union. In the first two decades of Soviet rule, tens of thousands of Jewish agricultural settlers, with aid from agencies created by the state and by western Jewish philanthropic organizations, moved from towns and cities in the former Pale of Settlement to colonies in southern Ukraine and the Crimean peninsula. The complex ethnic mixture of Crimea, combined with competing claims over the lands of the peninsula, could easily have proved dry tinder for a firestorm of violence against Jewish colonization. In actuality, however, the colonies "became a respected part of the rural landscape within a few years." To be sure, an anti-antisemitic attitude was fostered by the Soviet state to defuse this potentially violent scenario. But Dekel-Chen shows that it was pure pragmatism that proved to be the decisive factor in the thaw, and even warming, in relations between the Jewish settlers and local farmers. The former needed their neighbors' help, while the aid provided to the Jewish colonies by Western philanthropies was *designed* to benefit not only the Jews themselves but also local Tatars, Russians, and Germans. A crucial aspect of this was the technical expertise provided by Western agronomists. While violent attacks against the Jewish colonies were not unknown in this period, they can be ascribed to "rural hooliganism" or to acts of protest against Moscow, rather than to classic antisemitism. Indeed, the less "malevolent" character of anti-Jewish attacks in these specific circumstances may help us better to understand the nature of quotidian Jewish–Christian relations elsewhere in Eastern Europe, and in other periods; in Dekel-Chen's words, "understanding the real quality of Jewish life in Eastern Europe calls for a delicate tallying of the cooperation and rancor that merged in everyday life wherever Jews interacted with non-Jews." Moreover, this historical episode shows the power of philanthropy in defusing ethnic tensions; it was the non-state actors—the NGOs of their day—who really ensured that Jewish settlement could occur with a minimum of resentment and a maximum of cooperation.

Notes

1. Léon Poliakov, *History of Anti-Semitism*, 4 vols. (London: Elek Books, 1966–1985); Gavin Langmuir, *History, Religion and Anti-Semitism* (Berkeley: University of California Press, 1990).

2. David Nirenberg, *Communities of Violence: Persecution of Minorities in the Middle Ages* (Princeton, N.J.: Princeton University Press, 1996).

3. R. Po-chia Hsia, *The Myth of Ritual Murder: Jews and Magic in Reformation Germany* (New Haven, Conn.: Yale University Press, 1988).

4. Theodore R. Weeks, *From Assimilation to Antisemitism: The "Jewish Question" in Poland, 1850–1914* (De Kalb: Northern Illinois University Press, 2006), 85; Benjamin Nathans, *Beyond the Pale: The Jewish Encounter with Late Imperial Russia* (Berkeley: University of California Press, 2001); Israel Bartal, *The Jews of Eastern Europe, 1772–1881* (Philadelphia: University of Pennsylvania Press, 2005).

5. Jonathan Frankel, "The Crisis of 1881–82 as a Turning Point in Modern Jewish History," in *The Legacy of Jewish Migration: 1881 and Its Impact,* ed. David Berger (New York: Brooklyn College Press, 1983), 9–22.

6. The landmark early work was Simon Dubnow, *History of the Jews in Russia and Poland* (Philadelphia: Jewish Publication Society, 1916).

7. I. Michael Aronson, *Troubled Waters: The Origins of the 1881 Anti-Jewish Pogroms in Russia* (Pittsburgh: University of Pittsburgh Press, 1990); John D. Klier and Shlomo Lambroza, eds., *Pogroms: Anti-Jewish Violence in Modern Russian History* (Cambridge: Cambridge University Press, 1992); Hans Rogger, *Jewish Policies and Right-Wing Politics in Imperial Russia* (Berkeley: University of California Press, 1986); Arkadi Zeltser, "Pogrom v Balte," *Vestnik Evreiskogo universiteta v Moskve* 13, no. 3 (1996): 40–63.

8. Manus Midlarsky, *The Killing Trap: Genocide in the Twentieth Century* (Cambridge: Cambridge University Press, 2005), 10.

9. Donald L. Horowitz, *The Deadly Ethnic Riot* (Berkeley: University of California Press, 2001), 1.

10. Oleg Budnitskii, *Rossiiskie evrei mezhdu krasnymi i belymi* (Moscow: Rosspen, 2005).

11. Claudio Sergio Ingerflom, "Idéologie révolutionnaire et mentalité antisémite: les socialistes russes face aux pogroms de 1881–1883," *Annales: Économies, sociétés, civilisations,* xxxvii, no. 3 (1982): 434–453; David Vital, *The Origins of Zionism* (Oxford: Oxford University Press, 1975), 56–57; Jonathan Frankel, *Prophecy and Politics: Socialism, Nationalism, and the Russian Jews, 1862–1917* (Cambridge: Cambridge University Press, 1981), 97–108; Stephen M. Berk, *Year of Crisis, Year of Hope: Russian Jewry and the Pogroms of 1881–1882* (Westport, Conn.: Greenwood, 1985); Moshe Miskinsky, "Black Repartition and the Pogroms of 1881–1882," in Klier and Lambroza, *Pogroms,* 62–90.

12. Erich Haberer, "Cosmopolitanism, Antisemitism and Populism: A Reappraisal of the Russian and Jewish Response to the Pogroms of 1881–1882," in Klier and Lombroza, *Pogroms,* 98–134.

13. David Vital, *A People Apart: The Jews in Europe 1789–1939* (Oxford: Oxford University Press, 1999); Bartal, *The Jews of Eastern Europe.*

14. Hans Rogger, "Conclusion and Overview," in Klier and Lambroza, *Pogroms,* 341–343.

15. Eliyahu Feldman, "British Diplomats and British Diplomacy and the 1905 Pogroms in Russia," *Slavonic and East European Review* 65 (1987): 579–608; Philip E. Schoenberg, "The American Reaction to the Kishinev Pogrom of 1903," *American Jewish Historical Quarterly* 63 (March 1974): 263–283; Talor Stults, "Roosevelt, Russian Persecution of the Jews, and American Public Opinion," *Jewish Social Studies* 33 (January 1971): 13–22.

~~ 1 ~~

What's in a Pogrom?
European Jews in the Age of Violence

DAVID ENGEL

A historian of Poland once took me to task in print for having reported in my 1987 book, *In the Shadow of Auschwitz*, that information about mass killings of Jews by Poles in Galicia and the
Russo-Polish borderlands during the months following the end of World
War I, and the large-scale protests by Jews abroad that ensued, prompted
the U.S. and British governments, during the second half of 1919, to dispatch special investigating commissions to probe the extent and causes of
the violence. To be sure, this critic did not dispute that such information had
in fact circulated in the West at the time in question, or that the United
States and Britain had thought the reports sufficiently credible to warrant
official efforts at verification, or even that many Jews had died violently at
Polish hands. What bothered him was rather that I had "fail[ed] to add
that [the American and British] observers, upon reflection, refused to characterize as 'pogroms' these disorders, which occurred in the context of
military operations against Ukrainian and Bolshevik forces and claimed at
least as many gentile as Jewish victims."[1]

As it happens, the criticism was factually incorrect. In truth, although
two of the five investigators noted that—as one of them, former U.S. ambassador to Turkey Henry Morgenthau, put it—"no fixed definition" of the
word *pogrom* "is generally understood," only Morgenthau himself explicitly avoided using the term; and he did so, he said, *only* because of the term's
imprecision. In contrast, his British counterpart, the MP for Whitechapel,
Sir Stuart Samuel, showed no such reluctance: for him, the deadly ram-
pages that took place in Lwów on 21–23 November 1918, Lida on 17 April
1919, and Wilno two days later "c[a]me under the head of pogroms in the
sense generally understood in England"—that is, "excesses organized by
the Government against a portion of the population, or when the authorities took no steps to restrain those perpetrating the excesses, or intervened
at a period too late to be effective in preventing the loss of human life."[2] In
Poland, Samuel commented, a more expansive usage of the word prevailed,

according to which "a 'pogrom' is understood to be an excess against a certain section of the population" no matter what the degree of government involvement. By that standard, attacks upon Jews in Kraków between 9–20 November 1918 and Łódź on 16 July 1919, of which he took special notice, also qualified as pogroms, even though they claimed no lives.[3] The occurrences in these two cities, together with deadly attacks in Kielce on 11 November 1918, Kołbuszowa on 7 May 1919, and Częstochowa on 27 May 1919, all cited by Morgenthau, also cast doubt upon the claim that the disorders were all connected with Polish military actions against Bolshevik and Ukrainian enemies.[4]

Moreover, it turns out that officials of the *Polish* government demonstrated no compunction at all, at least initially, about using the term when discussing the events in question among themselves. Long before Morgenthau and Samuel arrived on the scene, the Polish Foreign and Justice Ministries had each sent investigating commissions of their own to Lwów in December 1918 and January 1919, respectively, and each had referred unabashedly to the killing and plunder of Jews by Poles in that city as "the November pogrom."[5] It was only in public statements that Polish spokesmen found it preferable to speak of "alleged" or "so-called pogroms," no doubt with the aim of keeping Western forces hostile to Polish national political aspirations from arguing that, as prominent Polish historian and political adviser Franciszek Bujak put it in a memorandum to the 1919 Paris Peace Conference, "the Poles are incapable and unworthy of an independent State existence, because their first steps [as a sovereign people] were an outbreak of racial hatred."[6] It was in the context of such political efforts that Polish representatives abroad found it useful to propagate the myth about the American and British investigators' rejection of the "pogrom" label. To the same end, those representatives also employed the oft-practiced tactic of semantic reversal—that is, they imposed a highly restrictive definition upon a phenomenon commonly understood in broader terms in order to suggest that if one of the restrictive conditions had been violated, the phenomenon itself could not have occurred in the first place.[7] Thus, for example, Bujak insisted that the label *pogrom* was appropriate only to "systematically organized massacres and robberies carried out with the aid of an indifferent attitude, or even of a co-ordinate action of the police authorities, as was the case in Russia."[8] On the basis of that definition, he could state emphatically that "there ha[s] never been any pogrom at all, or even serious riots, in Poland"; indeed, for him and others pogroms were by definition exclusively a Russian, not a Polish, phenomenon.[9] Others explicitly or implicitly attached even further restrictions:

pogroms had to be directed only against Jews as such, not against them in any socioeconomic or political role; they could not occur together with any other disturbance of the public order; they had to be motivated entirely by groundless, unprovoked religious or ethnic hatred; the victims had to be entirely defenseless; and casualties needed to run into at least the thousands.[10]

Of course, if consistently and universally applied these restrictions, taken together, would effectively bar use of the word *pogrom* in virtually any of the cases in which it has commonly been employed, from the May 1871 riots in Odessa through the bloodbath in Kielce in July 1946—not to mention its increasing appearance in both scholarly and public discourse as a designation for certain episodes of ethnic violence in which Jews are not involved at all.[11] Indeed, all of those incidents fail on at least one count. But consistent, rigorous application of a technical term was not what those who objected to its use in reference to post–World War I Poland were after; they sought rather to persuade others that what actually happened in places like Lwów, Częstochowa, Lida, and Wilno was far less serious than the images the word *pogrom* commonly aroused in the public mind, or even that, as a 1919 memorandum issued in the name of the Polish Governing Commission in Lwów declared, "there are no grounds to speak here of an organized pogrom or of a violent hostile stirring of the masses against the Jews."[12] They assumed, no doubt, that a pogrom by some other name would smell less foul. Yet although what was at stake for those who quibbled over the applicability of the word was never denotative historical precision, three generations of historians have been persuaded that whether or not the term was actually employed reveals something of significance about the events in question themselves.

No doubt many will contend that this history suggests the need for a serious attempt to clarify what a pogrom is or is not. In the event, however, no such clarification is possible, for "pogrom" is not a preexisting natural category but an abstraction created by human beings in order to divide complex and infinitely varied social phenomena into manageable units of analysis. As a result, in the absence of universal agreement concerning the specific behaviors to which the word refers or of some supreme authority to whom the power of definition has been delegated, there can be no logically or empirically compelling grounds for declaring that some particular episode does or does not merit the label.[13] Nevertheless, the repeated protests of some scholars that what happened in Lwów in November 1918 was not, strictly speaking, a "pogrom"—or similar claims about the killing of two Jews and one Pole in the townlet of Przytyk in March 1936, which became the subject of a similar bit of semantic legerdemain and on-going argument in Poland and beyond in 2001[14]—do raise an important question: What exactly is gained by grouping together under a single ru-bric such disparate occurrences as the killing of two Jews in Balta in March 1882, forty-five in Kishinev in April 1903, and upwards of fifteen hundred in Proskuriv in February 1919—all episodes to which the label *pogrom* has been widely attached? Are these events commensurable in any analytically useful way? Does speaking of them together under a single rubric, as what the great early twentieth-century Dutch historian Johan Huizinga called a *Ganzheit*, a self-contained whole,[15] enhance historians' ability to answer particular questions about past or present relations be-tween Jews and non-Jews with which they might productively occupy themselves? Or does it rather impede that ability?

The problem is thrown into even sharper relief when other incidents, also habitually tagged "pogroms," are added to the list: the riot in Warsaw on Christmas Day 1881, when street mobs took revenge on Jews for alleg-edly disrupting midnight mass in the Church of the Holy Cross, damaging much property but killing no one; the deadly confrontation between strik-ing factory workers and local Jews in Łódź in May 1892, in which the strikers killed three Jews while 140 Polish workers were shot by strike-breaking police; the riot of Russian and Ukrainian miners in the company town of Iuzovka in the Donets Basin three months later, in whose course 180 Jewish-owned shops and the local synagogue were burned, but no Jews lost their lives; the June 1898 plunder of the tavern of one Naftali Löw in the west Galician hamlet of Frysztak by a crowd of peasants com-ing to market, who caused no Jewish casualties and did minimal damage to property but who lost twelve of their own number when the Austrian police shot into the crowd in an effort to break it up; the punitive expedi-tion conducted by Russian military personnel against the Jewish quarter in Siedlce in September 1906 following the assassination of the local police chief, which claimed some thirty Jewish lives; the April 1919 execution by Polish soldiers in Pińsk of thirty-five Jews groundlessly suspected of abet-ting the Bolsheviks in the Polish–Soviet war; the so-called White Terror in Hungary of 1919–1920, which left perhaps as many as 3,000 Jews dead; the massacres of perhaps 60,000 Ukrainian Jews during the same years by armies competing for control of the territory; the repeated but nonfatal beatings of Jewish students in universities throughout Greater Romania between 1923 and 1928; the officially instigated *Kristallnacht* attacks upon synagogues and Jewish-owned property throughout Germany and Austria on 9 November 1938 in the wake of the shooting of a Nazi official by a Jewish teenager, in whose course ninety-one Jews were killed; the coordinated onslaught against the Jews of Iași by Romanian police, soldiers, and civilians on 29 June 1941, where the single-day death toll may have reached five thousand or more; or the slaughter of forty-six Jews in Kielce on 4 July 1946 in response to a blood libel. Do such disparate episodes really have anything in common significant enough to warrant placing all of them under a single analytical heading? Might greater insight into the dynamics of relationships between Jews and non-Jews in modern Europe, or of intercommunal relations more broadly, result from splitting these events into multiple categories, based upon the identity of the perpetrators; their expressed motives, charges, and demands; the means they employed; the processes by which the targets were selected; the extent of damage to life, limb, and property; the role of state authorities; the immediate historical background and context of the violence; or multiple combinations of these and other variables? Or might such insight be augmented more by casting an even wider net, lumping together not only those violent encounters between European Jews and their neighbors that *have* been called pogroms but also others bearing a generic similarity that do not usually receive the designation—the 1819 *Hep! Hep!* riots in Germany, for instance, or the disturbances in Budapest during the Tiszaeszlár ritual murder trial in 1883–1884, or the multiple assaults on Jews and their businesses that spread throughout France in conjunction with the Dreyfus Affair in 1898? Perhaps analysis should also incorporate generically similar events beyond Europe, or ones in which Jews were not involved, like the anti-Catholic riots that took place in Philadelphia in 1844, the assault upon the African American residents of Detroit in 1943, or the repeated murderous attacks by Hindus upon Muslims that have characterized intercommunal relations in several Indian cities since partition of the subcontinent in 1947.[16] Notice: the categories of analysis, the names and the scope assigned them, are matters of free choice; there is nothing in nature that obliges anyone to prefer one framework over another, no DNA tracers to establish irrefutable familial links and evolutionary affiliations. Scholars need only adduce cogent reasons for whatever arrangement of categories they prefer. Only once they do so can discussions about what belongs in and out of particular categories have any serious intellectual—as opposed to polemical—value.

This is not to say that historians are free to lump discrete events together or to split abstractions apart arbitrarily: there must be some common features that permit meaningful discussion of any aggregate as such. As it turns out, the large majority of the events or sets of events listed in the previous paragraphs, though manifestly dissimilar in detail, appear to display a surprising number of shared characteristics. To begin with, all took place in divided societies in which ethnicity or religion (or both) served as significant definers of both social boundaries and social rank. Moreover, all involved collective violent applications of force by members of what perpetrators believed to be a higher-ranking ethnic or religious group against members of what they considered a lower-ranking or subaltern group. Indeed, those against whom such force was applied were identified primarily on the basis of their group membership, not because of anything they might have said or done as ethnically or religiously unlabeled individuals; at most it can be said that the appliers of the decisive force tended to interpret the behavior of victims according to stereotypes commonly applied to the groups to which they belonged. Either during or following violence, perpetrators expressed some complaint about the victims' group, claiming collective injury or violation of one or more of their own group's cardinal values or legitimate prerogatives as a result of some action allegedly taken on behalf of the lower-ranking group by one or more of its members, or by that group as a whole. And, according to the perpetrators, the injured, higher-ranking group could be made whole only through violent action unmediated by the mechanisms that the state normally provided for resolution of disputes or redress of grievances. In other words, the episodes in question all seem to have embodied a fundamental lack of confidence on the part of those who purveyed decisive violence in the adequacy of the impersonal rule of law to deliver true justice in the event of a heinous wrong. In the perpetrators' hierarchy of values the transgressions of the lower-ranking group were of such magnitude that the legitimate order of things could be restored only when either they themselves took the law into their own hands or—as in Pińsk in 1919, Ukraine during the Russian Civil War, Kristallnacht, or Iaşi in 1941—instruments of the state or claimants to state power bypassed normal political and legal channels in favor of direct action against the offenders. Such a moral balance made perpetrators believe that what they had done was right, even where, as in the majority of the cases at hand, state authorities representing the community whose integrity they sought to defend told them the opposite by trying them for their misdeeds.

Please note: I do not claim that these features, taken together, constitute the essential defining characteristics of a "pogrom." My claim is merely that it is possible to identify a set of historical incidents that display all of those characteristics. For strictly denotative purposes it does not matter what name that set is assigned, if it is to be named at all. If a name must be given, that name could just as well be a letter of the alphabet or some other symbol, with each member of the set designated by a numerical subscript. A new term could also be coined to name it, as physicist Murray Gell-Mann chose the nonsense word *quarks* to refer to a set of subatomic particles that shared certain mathematically predicted peculiarities. In fact, there is much to recommend preferring such a practice in naming the category of incidents in question to employing any widely known existing word or phrase that seems to bear some lexical connection to the set's distinguishing properties. To begin with, it is virtually impossible, except in highly controlled disciplines like mathematics or law, to insist upon rigorous usage of words and phrases that are already employed in the common discourse in nonrigorous ways. Furthermore, many of the words or phrases that come initially to mind for the incidents that comprise the category carry strong judgmental overtones that make the words themselves an issue of contention. Indeed, it is precisely these properties of ordinary language that open the door to the sort of semantic red herrings observable in the discussion of the violent encounters between Poles and Jews in 1919. The less that door is left ajar, the less liable are discussions of either abstract analytical categories or the items they comprehend to be hijacked by debates over the appropriateness of a label. After all, what is most important in such discussions is the usefulness of analytical categories themselves, not the names given to them.

Moreover, even if additional research should reveal that one or another of the incidents mentioned in the previous paragraphs did *not* incorporate all of the characteristics ascribed to the as-yet-unnamed set, the definition of the set itself need not become an issue. As long as it is possible to identify a set of incidents that *do* share the attributes enumerated, the only question that need be discussed is to what extent thinking about those incidents together, as part of a single analytical category, offers insight into matters of concern that would not be as easily achieved were what Huizinga called "the eternal flux of disparate units" divided up in some other way.[17]

It seems to me that a broad analytical category that incorporates all incidents sharing the features identified can indeed potentially help formulate valuable insights about at least one matter of broad contemporary concern—the ways in which different political and economic arrangements promote or threaten the physical security of traditionally subaltern social groups. Such a category not only directs attention to people whose physical security is threatened or violated because of their membership in a subaltern group, but it also invites consideration of the complex ways in which state authorities figured in relations between the threatened and those who threatened them. To be sure, suggesting that state authorities might be a useful focus of analysis in discussing events often labeled "pogroms" may seem somewhat ironic in light of the effort scholars have invested over the last two decades and more in countering the popular notion that the archetypical pogroms, those of Imperial Russia, were deliberately instigated at the highest levels of government. Yet it turns out that states were indeed major players in nineteenth- and twentieth-century collective anti-Jewish violence, although in ways not immediately obvious. In the event, the violent episodes considered here all seem to have taken place during a particular interval in the long-term historic evolution of public attitudes toward the modern state and its role in society in different places around the globe. And grasping the nature of that interval turns out to be crucially important in understanding where, when, and how such episodes are most likely to occur.

That instances of the category of violent events in question were largely concomitant with a particular stretch of historical development is suggested first of all by the fact that incidents directed against Jews that exhibit all five of its defining characteristics have virtually disappeared in Europe since the end of the first half of the twentieth century. Historians will be hard pressed to identify a similarly long period of time before the second decade of the nineteenth century when anti-Jewish violence of this type was so rare. In fact, from the 1860s through the 1940s, not even a decade passed without some notable episode of this sort. In contrast, although the centuries before the French Revolution saw numerous violent outbursts against Jews, only a few of them appear, as far as can be told from the generally scant evidence at the disposal of scholars, to display all of our category's features, and those that did, traumatic and catastrophic as they often were, seem to have occurred at widely dispersed intervals. In many such outbursts the element of impersonal, stereotypical selection of the victims on the basis of a generalized grievance against Jews as such appears to have been absent, and complaints about the failure of authorities to redress the perpetrators' grievances or to protect them from damage allegedly done them by their Jewish neighbors are not in evidence to nearly the extent that they are between 1800 and 1950.

Actually, it is to be expected that violence of the category that subsumes many of the incidents commonly labeled "pogroms" should have become significantly more frequent around the beginning of the nineteenth century. Indeed, it was only shortly before that time that European states managed to impose on their subjects a notion of law as a systematic, universal principle of government instead of as one of a number of accept-

able vehicles for mediating among competing claims of rights and prerogatives. The former conception, which was characteristic of Europe before
the modern era, represented law as something distinct from justice—a
separation that was actually institutionalized in medieval England with
the creation of a system of equity courts alongside courts of common law.
That conception held that establishing a just order was the function primarily of custom and tradition, whose guardians were in the first instance
men (in the gender-specific sense), not abstract rules to which all men (and
women) were subordinate. In pre-modern and even early modern times,
the administration and preservation of justice were thus highly personal
matters, often achieved less through formal, lasting institutions than by ad
hoc extrajudicial and infrajudicial vehicles for resolving conflicts—vehicles
recognized as entirely legitimate by the societies that employed them. Those
vehicles themselves often involved violent action, including duels, feuds
and vendettas, lynchings, physical intimidation, and pursuit by vigilante
forces.[18] One of the grand unifying themes in modern European history is
the effort by states to supplant these sorts of activities by their subjects with
permanent, impersonal mechanisms for adjudicating disputes, in order to
provide the long-term security of life, limb, and property whose scarcity
ultimately rendered the pre-modern system of personally administered justice untenable.

In order to accomplish this goal, states had to claim what Max Weber
called "the monopoly of the legitimate use of physical force within a given
territory"[19] and to make that claim stick. They could do so, of course, by
building up military and police forces of a size and firepower sufficient for
suppressing any unsanctioned use of violence by their subjects. That was
a costly strategy, however—one that most European states of the time simply could not afford. A strategy that *could* potentially be executed with
greater ease was to *persuade* subjects to renounce extrajudicial violence
voluntarily, to disavow the traditions that legitimated such violence, and to
entrust responsibility for maintaining the just order that those traditions
were supposed to establish to a fixed set of faceless officials representing a
distant sovereign. That was the strategy that underlay the concept of the
Rechtsstaat—literally both the "state of laws" and the "state of justice"—
that became the norm throughout Europe and its cultural extensions by
the final third of the nineteenth century: the notion that laws created by
rational human beings in accordance with universal philosophical principles, without necessary regard for time-honored local custom—a law to
which the creators themselves were subject—when administered directly
and impartially by agencies of the state that were themselves constituted

by those laws, offered a more effective guarantee of a just order than any pre-modern means to that end. Indeed, it was one of the great conceits of the Constitution of the United States that the seven articles composed in Philadelphia in 1787, which did nothing more than set forth new procedures and mechanisms for the enactment, interpretation, and enforcement of laws, would, in the words of that document's preamble, "establish justice"; and its promise to do so was one of the principal bases upon which it demanded (and continues to demand) acceptance by the citizenry. Tsar Alexander II expressed much the same notion following the reform of the Russian judiciary in 1864, when he indicated his wish "to establish . . . expeditious, just, merciful, and impartial courts for all our subjects; to raise the judicial authority by giving it proper independence; and, in general, to increase in the people that respect for the law which national well-being requires."[20]

Merely making the argument, though, was hardly sufficient by itself to overcome the weight of longstanding traditions that had entrusted justice to a very different set of agents. Popular resistance to the new system is not difficult to imagine: picture the embattled sheriff of the Hollywood western trying to persuade a mob of enraged ranchers and their hands not to hang the cattle rustler they have just apprehended but to hand him over for trial, probably before a circuit judge from some distant city who knew precious little of life on the range. In order to gain acceptance, by ranchers confronting a rustler or by anyone else, the state and its laws had to prove that they could deliver justice in fact—justice as understood by the people over whom the state sought to exercise its authority. As long as it appeared to be doing so—as long as courts in Hollywood's version of the American West made sure that rustlers were properly punished and the other traditional prerogatives of cattlemen were preserved—the state would have no need to enforce its monopolistic claims violently. But let a bunch of land-hungry sodbusters try to fence in traditionally free cattle range, and there was no way short of calling out the cavalry to keep hired gunslingers from settling the conflict with an old-fashioned shootout.

It turns out that in the history of virtually every modern state of any significant size it is possible to identify a period, sometimes lasting only a few years, sometimes a century or more, in which subjects put the state's ability to establish justice on trial, as it were. If states demonstrated that the new *Rechtsstaat* accorded with traditional notions of justice and helped to sustain a fundamentally moral social order, then subjects were by and large inclined to acquiesce as it steadily usurped the customary prerogatives of individuals and local nonstate institutions to control the conditions under which their communities lived. But whenever the *Rechtsstaat* appeared to be subverting the time-honored moral order, they were prepared to take to the barricades en masse to force its restoration. During these transitional periods, states had often not yet developed sufficient security forces to deter violent campaigns of this sort; even greater London had no regular police until 1829, and the first detail of Sir Robert Peel's "bobbies" created by Parliament in that year numbered only 1,000 officers for a municipal population of more than 1.1 million, or about one-fortieth the proportion of full-time sworn law enforcement officers to the total population of the United States in 2004.[21] Add to the mix the fact that such periods generally coincided—though not at all coincidentally—with times of rapid and far-reaching demographic, economic, and social change that swept away a host of traditional social frameworks and generated deep anxiety and insecurity among masses of people becoming less and less able to control their own situations, and it should come as no surprise that they were everywhere characterized by unprecedented levels of collective violence, even if little of it was of catastrophic proportions and most had nothing to do with ethnic or religious issues. In different parts of Europe, different parts of the eighteenth, nineteenth, and even early twentieth centuries constituted what might well be called the heyday of the aggressive crowd— that peculiar social configuration that historian George Rudé characterized in 1964 as "a mixed population of what in England were termed 'lower orders' . . . , [who] appear frequently in itinerant bands . . . , fired as much by memories of customary rights or a nostalgia for past utopias as by present grievances or hopes of material improvement, and [who] dispense a rough-and-ready kind of 'natural justice' by breaking windows, wrecking machinery, storming markets, burning their enemies of the moment in effigy, firing hayricks, and 'pulling down' . . . houses, farms, fences, mills, or pubs, but rarely by taking lives."[22] This era also generated a series of ideologies justifying these and other uses of violence precisely for the purpose of restoring the more just order imagined to have existed before the *Rechtsstaat* arrogated to itself the position of sole legitimate arbiter of rights and privileges. These developments are what led Jacob Talmon to label the entire stretch of European history since the French Revolution as "the age of violence"—an age catalyzed in the first instance by the broadening assertion that "there is no arbiter above the state" and in the second by the refusal of some elements of society to acquiesce to that assertion's consequences.[23]

To be sure, the bulk of the violent acts that typified this age differed from most of those directed against Jews who belong to the category under consideration here: in the latter instances the attackers came from more varied social strata and displayed more varied forms of organization; they held themselves of a higher, not a lower order than their targets; ranking was based on ethnoreligious, not socioeconomic criteria; and the taking of lives was more common than not. Yet it hardly seems accidental that anti-Jewish violence of this particular type reached its apogee precisely during a general European age of violence. There may not be a generic resemblance between those acts and the ones that have drawn the attention of scholars like Rudé, but there does appear to be—moving one level higher in the classical taxonomy of Linnaeus—a familial one. And the familial connection lies in the backward-looking, restorative purpose perpetrators routinely ascribed to their violent behavior.

European Jews became a frequent target for brutal, physical restorative action in the so-called age of violence as a result of their changing relation to European society during that era. In pre-modern times the Jews' social position vis-à-vis their non-Jewish neighbors was rooted in custom, sanctioned by religious teaching, and generally enshrined in contract. Both Christians and Jews themselves saw Jews as a people in exile, living out a divine punishment for misdeeds (although the two groups differed sharply as to what those misdeeds were). Jews thus merited, in their own eyes as well as those of the surrounding society, a degraded status, marked by whatever signs the surrounding society deemed appropriate. Such a state of affairs was seen by Christians and Jews alike as entirely just and proper, in full accord with the divinely sanctioned moral order of the universe. But that particular Christian–Jewish consensus broke down more or less concomitantly with the rise of the *Rechtsstaat,* as one European state after another—for complex, multiple reasons having to do with those same sweeping changes that ushered in the *Rechtsstaat* and activated the aggressive crowd to begin with—signaled its intention to explore ways of integrating Jews into the surrounding society on a more or less equal basis, and Jews were by and large happy to go along. As a result, from the beginning of the nineteenth century, in a wave generally moving from west to east across the European continent, Jews began to turn up in increasing numbers in places of residence and socioeconomic positions where they had not previously been noticeable to nearly the same degree. For large segments of the European population, the growing appearance of Jews in those physical and social spaces merely added to their overall mounting insecurity in a world where familiar frameworks were collapsing all around them. Moreover, such mounting Jewish visibility looked to be a violation of hallowed norms. Thus to the extent that any state promoted Jewish integration, or even failed to maintain customary Jewish–

Christian barriers and to force Jews to keep within their proper social boundaries, the state could be seen as a *cause* of that violation, as an agent if not actively fomenting then at least condoning a disgraceful injustice. And since one of the dominant modes of protest against such state misbehavior at the time was to reclaim local control over the administration of justice by force, violent opposition to the increased visibility of Jews and their expanding social role was to be expected.

And indeed, the details of the various occurrences of anti-Jewish violence that might productively be analyzed together reveal assorted variations on this single theme. For example, the first of the German *Hep! Hep!* riots, which broke out in Würzburg, then part of the Kingdom of Bavaria, on the evening of 2 August 1819, was triggered by a meeting between two prominent non-Jewish advocates of what was known at the time as "civil amelioration" for Bavaria's Jews. One of them, Professor Behr, pro-rector of the local university, was also a member of the newly established Bavarian Assembly, itself the creation of Bavaria's fifteen-month-old constitution, and had just returned from an assembly session in distant Munich, where he had made a pro-Jewish speech. The other, Professor Brendel of the Würzburg law faculty, had recently published a strong defense of expanding Jewish legal rights in a local journal. According to a contemporary newspaper account, the meeting between these two partisans and symbols of a Bavarian *Rechtsstaat,* which took place on a public street, "inflamed the emotions, [whereupon] a crowd formed, which approached the store of an Israelite near the bridge, smashed the windows, threw merchandise onto the street, and then went after more Israelites."[24] Another report explained the broader background of the violence: "For some time now a hidden dissatisfaction has reigned here over the marked increase in the number of Jews in town, where formerly not a single one of them would have been tolerated."[25] And indeed, Jews had been expelled from Würzburg in 1576 and had not reappeared in noticeable numbers until the town was annexed to Bavaria in 1803. Those who joined the crowd in Würzburg were thus inveighing against what appeared to them to be the failure of the Bavarian state to uphold their town's traditional exclusion of a social inferior—an exclusion that by moral standards in force for centuries was altogether just. That failure became immediately manifest in the public meeting of two representatives of the state who not only opposed the traditional ban but generally denigrated local custom in favor of positive law. The encroachment of the impersonal state upon an individual community's time-honored prerogatives demanded protest; the form chosen for protest was typical of the times.[26]

The Würzburg riot took place at a point in time when a local population was adjusting to new principles and instruments of government whose
legitimacy was contested and future still a matter of doubt. The same, it
seems, can be said, mutatis mutandis, of the so-called southern storms of
1881, which followed a period of some fifteen to twenty years in which
the visibility of Russian state agencies and the degree to which they im-
pinged upon the daily lives of former serfs and their traditional institutions had expanded notably—a result, inter alia, of complications in implementing the emancipation settlement of 1861 and the state's growing role
in promoting an industrial economy in which railroads altered traditional
production and distribution patterns. Among those former serfs the notion
had developed, as the French traveler Anatole Leroy-Beaulieu observed in
1881, that government officials who came to the countryside to administer
the emancipation statute were not *executing* the will of the tsar—the sole legitimate source of authority, which had not changed since time immemorial—
but *subverting* it, so that, in the words of one official, although they "submit
to the statute . . . , in their own hearts they remain deeply attached to their
own hopes, and it will be long before they give them up."[27] The dramatic
rise in the Jewish population of Imperial Russia during this interval, its
rapid migration to cities and towns (especially in Ukraine and New Russia),
and its increasingly visible role in new sectors of the economy all must
have seemed like yet further indications of the same subversion: when the
tsar had really been in control, Jews had maintained their proper place,
but when the tsar's indubitable will could be supplanted by a piece of
paper in the hands of some pen-pusher claiming to represent "the law,"
then Jews could threaten to swallow the cities and countryside, take away
jobs, and otherwise upset the economic and social order, and "the law"
could not be counted upon to prevent them from doing so. The presumed
antagonism between tsar and "law" and the danger when traditional
ways of doing things were abandoned came to a head in March 1881 with
Alexander II's assassination; the new tsar, Alexander III, now had to re-
assert control over a regime whose depersonalization and departure from
tradition had gotten out of hand. At their most basic level, the anti-Jewish
attacks of 1881 seem to have been aimed, however nonsensically, at helping the new tsar do so; hence the widespread belief among the pogromists
that the tsar had actually ordered them to rise up against the Jews (who
had become so impudent as to dare to kill his father).[28]

In both 1819 and 1881, collective violence was precipitated by widespread doubt over the state's *willingness* to establish justice. In other instances it reflected more a lack of confidence in the state's *ability* to do so.

Such appears to have been the case in the anti-Jewish actions perpetrated by military personnel during armed conflicts in ethnically mixed East European regions following World War I. Lwów, Proskuriv, Pińsk, and Wilno were all under martial law when Jews were killed there in 1918–1919; military forces were acting in loco civitatis because normal state mechanisms of justice had yet to be established, or wartime conditions prevented them from functioning. However, the commanders who either instigated the violence or allowed it to proceed unchecked had little knowledge of positive state law governing conduct in the situation they faced. Hence, when confronted by reports, rumors, or suspicions that local Jews had thrown potentially decisive weight behind their enemies, which is what precipitated anti-Jewish violence in these places, they responded with a purely intuitive sense of what justice demanded—death to the offenders, collectively identified on the basis of stereotypic associations. They thus permitted their own soldiers to play the part of the aggressive crowd and take the law into their own hands. Note: none of these actions was undertaken in the heat of battle; they were rather *punitive* expeditions carried out *after* the immediate threat of hostile takeover had passed. Despite emphatic denials by perpetrators when informed by state authorities that their acts actually constituted legal wrongdoings, their sole purpose was to restore what local custom regarded as a proper moral balance after Jews had upset it through allegedly treacherous behavior. Indeed, General Antoni Listowski, regional commander of Polish forces in Podlasie, declared in his order to the population of Pińsk of 7 April 1919 justifying the execution of thirty-five suspected pro-Bolshevik Jews two days earlier that the town's Jews as a whole were guilty of the crime of "blatant ingratitude" (*jaskrawa niewdzięczność*)[29]—hardly a precise legal offense, but surely a moral one.

There was an additional moral dimension to these violent incidents as well: they took place amid a mounting perception that Jews comprised a political force to be reckoned with—something that, by all traditional norms, should never have occurred. That it *had* occurred in spite of those norms posed a particularly serious problem for those European states that defined themselves as national—that is, as representatives of a particular ethnic community whose existence predated that of the state and to whom the state purportedly belonged. After World War I, such national states found themselves under mounting pressure from the communities they claimed to represent to reverse the supposed rise in Jewish power. Doing so, however, conflicted with the principles of universal applicability of law and its impersonal administration that were basic to the ethos of the

Rechtsstaat. Hence in some countries, defenders of those principles found their control challenged by political elements that, rejecting the *Rechtsstaat* ideal, demanded the state employ its monopoly on the use of physical force to restore its constituting ethnic group's historic prerogatives vis-à-vis Jews and to make certain that Jewish offenses to the proper moral order were punished swiftly and decisively. In Nazi Germany, as well as in Romania under the dictatorship of Ion Antonescu, these elements managed to gain the upper hand at certain points. That development is in the final analysis what produced the violence of Kristallnacht and Iaşi, when officials acting in the name of the state instigated the formation of aggressive crowds and encouraged them to chastise Jews mercilessly for their alleged collective misdeeds. The former was initiated by radical party formations, backed by Josef Goebbels, over the objections of Heinrich Himmler and others, who continued to argue that state law, not uncontrolled violence, was the proper instrument for solving Germany's so-called Jewish problem. The latter stemmed in large measure from a temporary *rapprochement* between Antonescu and his erstwhile allies in the Iron Guard movement following the outbreak of war between Romania and the Soviet Union. In each case, though, state sanction of crowd violence was short lived: both governments quickly turned from inciting the crowds to coopting them into a far more orderly, systematic, and ultimately lethal assault against the Jews that was carried out *within* the framework of state law.

Indeed, it was ultimately the ability of European states in the second half of the twentieth century to persuade their populations that they *could* effect justice with regard to Jews that brought about the virtual disappearance since the middle of the twentieth century of the particular sort of anti-Jewish violence under discussion here. Their success in doing so has not by itself brought Jews greater security, however: as the examples of Germany and Romania under Nazi impact show, one of the ways to bring populations behind state responses to threatening changes in the Jews' social or demographic profile—or to changes in the social or demographic profile of any subaltern group, for that matter—is, to borrow a phrase from Radu Ioanid of the United States Holocaust Memorial Museum, to turn violence from "a societal to a governmental enterprise,"[30] carried out not by enraged mobs but by formal, regulated, state-directed command structures. It thus appears that popular willingness to leave the matter of interethnic justice to an impersonal legal and administrative apparatus will enhance the physical safety of traditional subalterns only when states themselves are determined to promote that safety and their subjects acquiesce out of either agreement that the state's determination is in fact just or respect for state authority, or both. All of these conditions have in fact become the norm in Europe over the past fifty years, thanks largely, I suspect, to the ongoing revolution in communications technology, which so far has helped a liberal-minded cultural elite gradually wean ever-greater segments of European society from many (though hardly all) traditional ethnic prejudices, thereby raising the standing of many subaltern groups and mitigating social divisions as it has inculcated general respect for the rule of law. That process is hardly complete, however. Nor is it irreversible. Groups that have traditionally enjoyed significant advantages in societies divided according to social rank have much to lose when assertion of rank's privileges comes to be seen as unjust. Such losses may not be of great consequence in times of plenty nor generate much anxiety when states appear to provide generally stable environments. Let plenty vanish, though, or stability be threatened, and both the claim of traditional subalterns to scarce resources and state protection of that claim in the name of abstract notions of justice are liable to be contested with vigor.

Preventing that eventuality is a far more formidable challenge than explaining the dynamics of intercommunal violence in the era of the aggressive crowd, but perhaps the prospects for prevention will be enhanced by sustained effort at historical explanation. Historical explanation, though, depends in significant measure upon the analytical categories through which it proceeds. A category that incorporates the five elements that can be identified in most instances of anti-Jewish violence that have habitually been labeled "pogroms" (and many other instances of intercommunal violence, whether involving Jews or not, that have not generally been so labeled) appears to offer sufficiently intriguing insight into the problem to encourage its continued employment in the study of additional incidents, and not only those in which Jews have been victims.

Acknowledgments

To the memory of my teacher, Hans Rogger, and my colleague, John Klier.

Notes

1. Neal Pease, "New Books on Poles and Jews during the Second World War," *Polish Review* 33 (1988): 351.

2. National Polish Committee of America, *The Jews in Poland: Official Reports of the American and British Investigating Missions* (Chicago, n.d.), 22.

3. Samuel himself did not use the word *pogrom* to apply to these incidents; he labeled them "excesses" and indicated that "the military authorities endeavored to restrict the action of the [rioting] soldiers as much as possible." However, "excess" was the essential criterion he ascribed to what he called the Polish definition of *pogrom*.

4. Ironically, there is evidence to suggest that the Russian word *pogrom* (often in its perfective verbal form, *pogromit'*) was initially employed, beginning in the sixteenth century, to designate collateral violence accompanying military operations. See John D. Klier, "The Pogrom Paradigm in Russian History," in *Pogroms: Anti-Jewish Violence in Modern Russian History*, ed. John D. Klier and Shlomo Lambroza (Cambridge: Cambridge University Press, 1992), 34, n. 1.

5. "Raport delegacji Ministerstwa Spraw Zagranicznych R.P. w sprawie wystąpień antyżydowskich w Lwowie," 17 December 1918, in Jerzy Tomaszewski, "Lwów, 22 listopada 1918," *Przegląd Historyczny* 75 (1984): 281; David Engel, "Lwów, November 1918: The Report of the Official Governmental Investigating Commission," *Kwartalnik Historii żydów* 3 (2004): 387–395.

6. Franciszek Bujak, *The Jewish Question in Poland* (Paris: Imprimeris Levé 1919), 31.

7. On the notion of semantic reversal, see David Engel, *Semantikah u-folitikah be-te'ur ha-yehasim bein ha-Polanim la-Yehudim* (Tel Aviv: Tel Aviv University, 1990), 7–8.

8. Bujak, *Jewish Question*, 34.

9. Ibid., 32.

10. Engel, *Semantikah u-folitikah*, 8–10.

11. See, for example, Paul R. Brass, ed., *Riots and Pogroms* (New York: New York University Press, 1996); Donald L. Horowitz, *The Deadly Ethnic Riot* (Berkeley: University of California Press, 2001), 20.

12. "Mémoire sur les troubles contre les Juifs," n.d., United States National Archives and Records Adminstration, Washington (NARA), M1751 (Biuro archiwalne przy Komisji Rządzacej w Lwowie), microfilm reel 1.

13. For the theoretical basis of this claim, see David Engel, "Away from a Definition of Antisemitism: An Essay in the Semantics of Historical Description," in *Rethinking European Jewish History*, ed. Jeremy Cohen and Moshe Rosman (Oxford: Littman Library of Jewish Civilization, 2008), 31–35.

14. Piotr Gontarczyk, *Pogrom? Zajścia w Przytyku*, Biała Podlaska 2000; Jolanta żyndul, "Jeśli nie pogrom, to co?" *Gazeta Wyborcza* 8 March 2001, and subsequent exchanges. Several entries in the discussion have been published in English in *Polin* 17 (2004): 385–403.

15. Johan Huizinga, "The Idea of History," in *The Varieties of History*, ed. Fritz Stern (New York: Meridian Books, 1956), 291.

16. Michael Feldberg, *The Philadelphia Riots of 1844: A Study of Ethnic Conflict* (Westport, Conn.: Greenwood Press, 1975); Robert Shogun and Tom Craig, *The Detroit Race Riot: A Study in Violence* (Philadelphia: Chilton Books, 1964); Ashutosh Varshney, *Ethnic Conflict and Civic Life: Hindus and Muslims in India* (New Haven, Conn.: Yale University Press, 2002).

17. Above, n. 15.

18. For further development, see Julius R. Ruff, *Violence in Early Modern Europe 1500–1800* (Cambridge: Cambridge University Press, 2001), 73f.

19. Max Weber, "Politics as a Vocation," in *From Max Weber: Essays in Sociology*, ed. H. H. Gerth and C. Wright Mills (New York: Oxford University Press, 1946), 78.

20. Quoted in W. E. Mosse, *Alexander II and the Modernization of Russia* (New York: Collier Books, 1962), 74–75.

21. See the figures compiled by the Bureau of Justice Statistics of the United States Department of Justice, http://www.ojp.usdoj.gov/bjs/lawenf.htm (accessed 20 March

2008). For the initial size of the London metropolitan police, see David Thomson, *England in the Nineteenth Century* (London: Pelican Books, 1950), 66–67.

22. George Rudé, *The Crowd in History: A Study of Popular Disturbances in France and England 1730–1848* (New York: John Wiley, 1964), 5–6.

23. Jacob Talmon, *Be-idan ha-alimut* (Tel Aviv: Am Oved, 1977), 22–23.

24. Quoted in Jacob Katz, "Pra'ot Hep-Hep shel shenat 1819 be-Germaniyah al rik'an ha-histori," *Zion* 38 (1973): 67.

25. Quoted in Katz, "Pra'ot Hep-Hep," 66.

26. For more recent work on the 1819 riots, see Stefan Rohrbacher, *Gewalt im Biedermeier: Antijüdische Ausschreitungen in Vormärz und Revolution* (Frankfurt am Main: Campus-Verlag, 1993).

27. Quoted in Anatole Leroy-Beaulieu, *The Russian Peasant* (Sandoval, N.M.: Coronado Press, 1962), 31.

28. For supporting sources and analysis, see I. Michael Aronson, "Geographical and Socioeconomic Factors in the 1881 Anti-Jewish Pogroms in Russia," *Russian Review* 39 (1980): 18–31.

29. "Rozkaz Generała Listyowskiego w sprawie krwawych zajść w Pińsku," *Dziennik Nowy*, 9 April 1919, p. 4 (copy in NARA, M820, reel 226).

30. Radu Ioanid, *The Holocaust in Romania: The Destruction of Jews and Gypsies under the Antonescu Regime, 1940–1944* (Chicago: Ivan R. Dee, 2000), 109.

PART 1

Twentieth-Century Pogroms

~ 2 ~

1915 and the War Pogrom Paradigm in the Russian Empire

ERIC LOHR

The series of pogroms and riots that occurred in 1915 represents one of the most significant pogrom waves in Russian history, yet it has often been left out of broader generalizations and conceptual discussions on this topic. Drawing upon a large collection of reports on pogroms compiled by Jewish organizations and archival sources, this article analyzes this pogrom wave. It aims to identify similarities and differences by comparing the anti-Jewish violence to that of other such waves, and to a large anti-German pogrom in the same year. How did the context of war make this particular group of pogroms different from others, and in what ways was it nonetheless similar? There has been an emerging consensus among scholars in the last several decades that, contrary to the general impression, high-level government officials were not directly to blame for pogroms in Imperial Russia.[1] The government more often considered pogroms to be volatile and dangerous expressions of popular violence, and as such generally tried to restrain or prevent them.[2] One of the implications of this research is that broader parts of the population appear to have had greater agency in the violence than the older concept of the government-conjured pogroms implied.

As we shall see, popular participation was a significant factor in the 1915 pogroms—whether they were against Jews in the front zone or Germans in Moscow and other cities in the interior—and the upper levels of the government registered strong opposition to them. However, the 1915 pogroms are fundamentally different from any previous wave of pogroms in one crucial aspect: the role of the army. In fact, one of the most unequivocal findings from the field reports is the central role of the army (especially Cossack units) in nearly every pogrom during that year. In addition to establishing the crucial role of the army, I will argue that the war transformed the way people thought about the Jewish and German targets of popular violence, mainly by incorporating them into a new economic nationalist discourse that had broader appeal than the kind of reactionary antimodernism of the prewar decades described so well by Heinz Dietrich Löwe.[3] Economic nationalism provided a more ideologically coherent context for violence than had been present in any prior pogrom wave.

The Pogroms of 1915

The majority of pogroms during World War I were concentrated in the period of the great Russian retreat from April to October 1915, with roughly one hundred separate events that could be categorized as pogroms.[4]

The best available records of the pogroms were collected by the Collegium of Jewish Social Activists, a group of leading Jewish politicians and Duma deputies who collected copies of military and civilian deportation orders as well as reports from affected individuals and communities. Its collection of reports has not survived in full, but its published and unpublished records provide a large enough sample to allow for some generalizations.[5] The following discussion is based on reports of nineteen pogroms in Vilna province, thirteen in Kovno province, seven in Volhynia, and fifteen in Minsk province. In this sample of fifty-four cases, pogroms began only three times without soldiers present. The army clearly initiated the violence in nearly every case. More specifically, Cossack units appear to have instigated nearly all of the pogroms. More than four-fifths of the reports explicitly identify the appearance of Cossacks in the area as the key event spurring the pogrom. The pattern became widely known throughout the front zones; by summer, reports increasingly claimed that peasants were responding to even the rumor that Cossacks were coming by appearing on the edge of Jewish settlements with empty carts, waiting for the Cossacks to begin a pogrom, ready to join the looting. According to the reports, most of the physical violence was linked to attempts to extort payments from Jews. Rape was mentioned in one-third of the reports.

The pogroms in these reports were not always linked to explicit orders to expel or deport Jews from the areas where violence occurred. However, Cossack officers often used their power to order expulsions of Jews as an excuse to loot. In some cases, officers ordered Jews to leave their towns within hours or minutes, denied them access to carts, and beat and robbed Jews as they departed.

The predominant role of Cossacks in the wave of pogroms is striking, and it raises questions about the degree to which Cossacks were really under the army's control. The army command did, however, play an important role in creating the conditions for pogroms to occur. It certainly seems to have made little attempt to punish Cossack soldiers or their officers for violence and pogroms against Jews, Germans, or others.

Most important in creating the framework for the pogrom wave was the army's extensive program of mass expulsions and deportations of Jews, Germans, and foreigners from areas under military rule. These actions left all these populations vulnerable to looting. Conducted as a crude prophylactic against espionage and the potential enlistment of "unreliable populations" by enemy states, the mass forced expulsions affected roughly one million civilians during the war—with most occurring in 1915.[6] These operations clearly marked the targeted populations as pariahs outside the protection of the authorities. It was no great step to conclude that they could be plundered at will. In fact, local populations frequently appeared outside communities that had been forced by military order to leave their homes. While they sometimes waited for people to leave before sifting through the items left behind, in others they struck preemptively, violently looting the communities about to be deported or already on the road.

The army also developed the practice of hostage-taking as a policy of collective responsibility, ostensibly to prevent Jewish spying. On the ground, the army often simply legitimated extortion. According to the reports, officers (primarily Cossacks) would take prominent Jews "hostage" and threaten to kill them unless relatives or the community paid ransom. In one case, a Cossack officer systematically went through a town's residents, taking nearly every adult male "hostage" until the officer received ransom payments for the release of each.[7]

The "War Pogrom" and the "Prewar Pogrom Paradigm"

Having described the general characteristics of the war pogrom, I will now further develop the model by comparing and contrasting five of its key elements with those of the prewar paradigm: (1) the role of the army; (2) the attitude of the central government; (3) the role of religion; (4) economic tensions; and (5) the role of nationalism.[8]

The Role of the Army

The most significant difference between the two pogrom paradigms is the direct role of the army in the violence. There is no doubt that the War Ministry had more than its share of anti-Jewish officers in the prewar decades and that the elite of the ministry was close to the antisemitic far right.

In the Duma era, the far right conducted a campaign to expel all Jews from the army. In 1912, a secret questionnaire was circulated among the highest-ranking generals and War Ministry officers asking whether Jews should be expelled from the army. Among respondents, twenty-eight of forty-four argued in favor of expulsion.[9] But soldiers only participated in pogroms in isolated instances prior to 1914, and though more research needs to be done on the topic, one might even argue that there were more cases of the army intervening to stop pogroms than of participating in them before 1914.

The dominant role of the army in the pogroms of 1915 thus shows a remarkable departure from the prewar paradigm. How can one account for this? One major difference was the declaration of the so-called "War Statute" on the outbreak of the war in 1914. The statute granted the army nearly unlimited control over civilian affairs throughout the entire area declared under military rule. It forced civilian authorities to implement all military orders throughout the area and explicitly granted military commanders the right to deport individuals or groups.[10] The military most dramatically influenced civilian affairs in areas close to the front, where troops were present. However, army rule expanded far beyond these narrow zones through a network of regional military district commanders who exercised ultimate authority under the War Statute over most of Ukraine, Belarus, the Baltics, Poland, Finland, the Caucasus, Petrograd, and much of Central Asia and the Far East. Most significantly, nearly the entire area of legal Jewish residence came under military rule. The commander in chief (Grand Duke Nikolai Nikolaevich until his replacement by the tsar in August 1915) nominally held the highest authority over civilian affairs within this area. But in practice, his assistant, the commander in chief of army headquarters, managed civilian affairs. Nikolai Ianushkevich held this crucial position until his replacement by Mikhail Alekseev in August 1915. Ianushkevich expressed an intense personal dislike of Jews and, according to the Minister of Finance Petr L'vovich Bark, by the summer of 1915 had become "obsessed with the idea of spies and spying" by Jews, Germans, and foreigners within the empire.[11]

Ianushkevich's attitude was not extraordinary among the leading generals. In fact, a survey sent to the top army officials found that nearly all of them (including Alekseev) shared a presupposition that Jews were disloyal and should be treated as spies.[12] While the army elite had long been anti-Jewish, it had never had such institutional freedom to pursue whatever policies it chose. In fact, the contrast to 1905 is instructive. In the earlier period, according to William C. Fuller, the key point of contention between the military and civilian authorities centered on military discontent with civilian government use of the army to suppress riots, rebellions (and even occasionally pogroms) among the civilian population.[13] In contrast, during World War I, the army had a near carte blanche.

Related to the role of the military is the general feature of the prewar pogrom paradigm—that outside agitators played an important role in stimulating or organizing pogroms.[14] The sudden influx of millions of soldiers in 1914–1915 can be seen to some degree as an extreme case of this phenomenon. Memoirs of soldiers from the Russian interior often portray the process of crossing into the Pale and Poland as akin to entering a foreign country; the prejudices of these outsiders were often not tempered by familiarity.

The Role of the Central Government

While the role of the army sharply distinguishes the 1915 pogroms from earlier ones, the argument that the central government authorities did not conjure up or approve of prewar pogroms holds at least as strongly for 1915. The Council of Ministers and most other leading civilian authorities unequivocally opposed pogroms and the mass expulsions and hostage-taking policies in the front zones that facilitated pogroms. Their meetings in the summer of 1915, when the pogrom wave was at its worst, are full of complaints about the army and the inability of civilian authorities to stop the pogroms and expulsions. The reactionary Minister of Interior Nikolai Maklakov, in a May 1915 discussion of army orders to deport 300,000 Jews from Kurland and Kovno, made the case clearly: "I am not a Judeophile, but I cannot approve. The danger is internal—of pogroms and feeding a revolution."[15]

The contrast can also be seen in official reactions to the massive May 1915 pogrom against Germans in Moscow. It was the only pogrom in one of Russia's two major cities, and the estimated 70 million rubles in damages made it perhaps the most costly pogrom in Russian history to that date.[16] Afraid that society was about to descend into revolutionary chaos, local authorities hesitated for three days before the civilian city governor ordered the garrison troops to fire into the crowds and end the pogrom. But in the weeks following the Moscow riots, civilian authorities throughout the country acted energetically, and despite much evidence that pogroms were in the making elsewhere, managed to thwart other outbreaks of anti-German violence.[17] Thus the role of the central government does not distinguish the war pogrom from the prewar paradigm. The difference is that the War Statute created a huge zone under military rule where civilian authorities could do little to stop the violence when the military was involved.[18]

Religion

The third difference is the role of religion. Many of the prewar pogroms were associated with religious processions, rumors of ritual murder, intercommunal ethnic and cultural tensions, and the like. Traditional religious prejudice helps explain the disproportionate amount of violence directed against Jews as compared to other minorities, such as Germans, who were subjected to similar mass deportations and expulsions. But religious events and rumors do not appear to have directly instigated pogroms *during* World War I. Nearly every report indicates instead that the appearance of the military, in particular the Cossacks (or rumors of their imminent appearance), precipitated the pogrom.

The Role of Economic Tensions

Commercial competition was a crucial element from the very beginning of modern pogroms in Odessa, where Greek–Jewish competition in the city was a key to the outbreak of the first major pogroms as early as the 1870s. It also helps to explain why most pogroms began in urban areas and only later spread to rural regions. Commercial competition did not have such a direct correlation to the outbreak of pogroms in World War I. The predominantly urban basis of the violence typical of earlier waves did not apply in 1915. The geographic dispersion of pogroms had much more to do with the attitudes of the heads of military regions and the actions of individual commanders in the field than on the level of tension between local Jewish and other populations. In areas such as Riga, where the military authorities made it clear that pogroms would not be tolerated, they simply did not occur—even when tensions between Jews and Christians were quite intense.[19] At the same time, many towns with no significant commercial or trade activity suffered some of the most violent pogroms of all. In a number of cases, local peasants and townspeople, soldiers, and even Cossacks protected Jews from attacks.

However, economic motives did have an important role to play in World War I—from the very earliest expulsions. For example, on 14 October 1914, some 4,000 Jews were driven from their homes in a town outside Warsaw, and forced to make their way by foot to the city of Warsaw. They were denied access to carts for their belongings, and shortly after their departure, local Poles took over their vacated businesses and properties. When a few of the expellees were allowed to return a week later, local authorities refused to intervene to return properties and apartments to their Jewish owners.[20] As the expulsions increased in frequency in early 1915, the looting and takeover of Jewish property became increasingly common. The Council of Ministers expressed its concern at the blatant disregard for the most basic norms of private property, and imposed strict rules requiring *all* deportee properties (primarily German, enemy subject, and Jewish) to be sequestered by the Ministry of State Properties and protected by local authorities.[21] However, while local authorities did manage to bring looting and uncontrolled takeover of deported Russian-subject German and enemy-subject properties somewhat under control, they were unable or unwilling to do the same for Jewish property.[22]

When the expulsions of Jews reached a mass scale in April and May 1915, the looting and spontaneous takeovers of property shifted rapidly to full-scale pogroms during and before the actual orders for expulsion or deportation. In some areas, Jews were rounded up, loaded onto railroad cars, and deported in brutal but orderly fashion; in many others, the process was extremely violent and chaotic.

Where local populations joined in the violence and looting, nearly one-fifth of the reports indicate that rumors of Jewish coin hoarding and refusing to give coin change for paper currency provided an important stimulus for the outbreak of violence. The perception that Jews were hoarding coins was based in small part on reality. Given growing inflation, both Jews and Christians had a strong incentive to hold onto their precious metal currency and not exchange it for more rapidly depreciating paper banknotes.[23] Local newspapers spread rumors of Jewish hoarding and short-changing, and a number of pogroms began when a Cossack, soldier, or local resident went to a Jewish store and was turned down when demanding to change paper currency for precious metal coins.[24] In this and other ways, wartime inflation sharply exacerbated Christian–Jewish relations, which had already been tense in the immediate prewar period.

Nationalism and the War Pogrom Paradigm?

There is little doubt that socioeconomic factors added to the hostility of locals toward Jews, and that the dynamic of pogrom violence was significantly affected by the powerful motive of loot. But this hardly distinguishes the wartime pogroms from those prior to the war. If anything, the "war pogrom" is distinguished by the lesser role of socioeconomic tensions as a precipitating factor compared to the appearance of soldiers and Cossacks in a given locale.

Paradoxically, however, a strong case can be made that while socioeconomic factors did not *precipitate* pogroms, the war powerfully structured the context for pogrom violence, combining in a volatile mix with patriotic-nationalist mobilization. Thus, the war pogrom paradigm differs from the relative chaos and lack of structured meaning characteristic of the prewar paradigm.

The key to explaining this phenomenon is the socioeconomic position of Jews as a commercial diaspora.[25] The impression—and to a significant degree the reality—that Jews held positions in commerce, banking, industry, small business, insurance, and trade in numbers far exceeding their proportion in the population as a whole added a serious socioeconomic dimension to already existing anti-Jewish attitudes. In an era of rapid social change and rising national awareness, the competition of non-Jewish populations for these positions added a sharp new element to an old problem. The tensions were by no means simply along a Russian–Jewish axis. In fact, they were sharpest in the Polish parts of the empire, where an intense campaign to boycott Jewish businesses had been led by the Polish National Democratic Party shortly prior to the war. Similar developments were evident in the Baltics, Ukraine, and other areas.[26]

Such tensions intensified well before 1914 and were more closely connected to the pressures of modernization than war. The mobilization of the country, however, introduced several new elements that changed the dynamic. Most importantly, it suddenly transformed the other major commercial diaspora population of the empire, the Germans, from a privileged minority into enemy aliens. A major campaign against German and foreign commercial diasporas and their perceived economic "dominance" (*zasil'e*) over Russians and other "core" nationalities quickly became an obsession of the mass media, the Duma, and the Ministry of Interior. It resulted in radical legislation to liquidate large and small businesses and to nationalize landholdings and other properties owned by enemy aliens. Total war generally put pressures on the empire to mobilize around patriotic themes and around the "reliable" core populations of the empire. This created a heightened sense of tension with populations of the empire deemed to be unreliable. The rhetoric surrounding the implementation of anti-alien legislation tapped a powerful new emancipatory economic nationalism that came to the fore during the war. It appealed to a sense of the core Russian nation not as imperial overlord, but as disadvantaged underdog. It called for nationalist mobilization against "dominant" diasporas within the empire and the use of radical economic policies of expropriation and nationalization to achieve its goals. The program against Germans was very popular across a fairly broad political spectrum.[27]

The structural similarities between Germans and Jews in the empire were striking. While Jews were Russian subjects and thus not targeted by the laws on enemy aliens, the perception that the Jews were the most suspect enemy population in the empire was well established. It is easy to see how the themes, motives, and rhetoric of mobilization against enemy aliens spread to Jews (and vice versa). Articles in the press, denunciations, petitions, bureaucratic memos, and the correspondence of army commanders all freely mixed the language of "German *zasil'e*" with that of "Jewish dominance." The campaign encouraged the idea of expropriating the property of enemies, and, by redistributing the land of deported Germans to "core" national groups, created a strong sense that the property of the forcibly expelled minorities in the front zone was unprotected. A certain symbiosis emerged between the nationalizing agendas of Poles, Ukrainians, Lithuanians, and others on the one hand and the radical army and government policies of mass expulsion and expropriation on the other.

The wartime mobilization against commercial diasporas created a new context for pogroms. Ironically, while the 1915 pogroms invariably started because of Cossack and army presence, they also were more national and more part of a nationwide mobilizational context than any previous wave of pogroms. This perhaps is the most important paradigmatic difference that the war context brought to pogroms. They increasingly became conceived as a means to a larger nationalist end. The pogroms were closely linked to the targeted mass expulsions of Jews, Germans, and foreigners from the front zones. The simultaneous official permanent expropriation of the properties of Germans and foreigners, together with the official nature of the army-ordered expulsions, gave a sense that the policies in the front zone were more than temporary expedients or aberrational acts. They appeared to be closer to a program of permanent demographic change in the region, intended not only as an expulsion of unreliable populations, but also (most clearly for the Germans) as an attempt to transfer their properties and homes to others, to permanently remove them from the population.

Although these shifts in intention and result were by no means complete or without contradiction, they do suggest an important conceptual step toward the catastrophic linkage of the civil war pogroms to the larger national and social agendas of the White, Ukrainian, Green, Black, and Red perpetrators.

Notes

1. For a discussion of recent scholars' findings on the issue of government responsibility for pogroms in the Russian Empire before World War I, see John D. Klier and Shlomo Lambroza, *Pogroms: Anti-Jewish Violence in Modern Russian History* (Cambridge: Cambridge University Press, 1992), 315.

2. The most important exception was the massive wave of pogroms following the issuance of the October 1905 Manifesto, when Assistant Minister of Internal Affairs Dmitrii Trepov and several regional government officials played important roles in facilitating pogroms. See Shlomo Lambroza,"The Pogroms of 1903–1906," in Klier and Lambroza, *Pogroms*, 234–247.

3. Heinz Dietrich Löwe, *Antisemitismus und reaktionäre Utopie: Russischer Konservatismus im Kampf gegen den Wandel von Staat und Gesellschaft, 1890–1917* (Hamburg: Hoffmann und Campe Verlag, 1978); Löwe, *The Tsars and the Jews: Reform, Reaction and Anti-Semitism in Imperial Russia, 1772–1917* (Chur, Switzerland: Harwood Academic Publishers, 1993).

4. For a full account of army policies toward Jews in the front zone, see Eric Lohr, "The Russian Army and the Jews: Mass Deportation, Hostages and Violence during World War I," *The Russian Review* (July 2001): 404–419.

5. The collections of reports used for this article are found in Gosudarstvennyi arkhiv Rossiiskoi Federatsii (State Archive of the Russian Federation) (GARF), f. 9458, op. 1, d. 163; and the Archive of the YIVO Institute for Jewish Research, New York, Mowshowitz Collection, 13090–13245. The best published sources include [Maxim M. Vinaver, D. O. Zaslavskii, and G. M. Erlikh], "Iz 'chernoi knigi' rossiiskogo evreistva. Materialy dlia istorii voiny 1914–1915 g.," *Evreiskaia starina*, 10 (1918): 231–296, and "Dokumenty o presledovanii evreev," *Arkhiv russkoi revoliutsii* 19 (1928): 245–284. See also the memoir of a Jewish political activist who participated in relief efforts for Jewish expellees: Ia. G. Frumkin, "Iz istorii Rossiiskogo evreistva," in *Kniga o russkom evreistve ot 1860-kh godov do revoliutsii 1917g., sbornik statei* (New York: Soiuz russkikh evreev, 1960), 74–110.

6. For a collection of documents on the expulsions of Jews, see Eric Lohr, "Novye dokumenty o Rossiiskoi Armii i evreiakh vo vremena Pervoi mirovoi voiny," *Vestnik evreiskogo universiteta* 26 (Moscow, 2003): 245–268.

7. "Iz 'chernoi knigi'," 218–219.

8. For an account of the features of the pogrom paradigm, see Klier and Lambroza, *Pogroms*, esp. John Klier, "The Pogrom Paradigm in Russian History," 13–138.

9. Yohanan Petrovsky-Shtern, "The 'Jewish Policy' of the Late Imperial War Ministry: The Impact of the Russian Right," *Kritika: Explorations in Russian and Eurasian History* 3, no. 2 (Spring 2002): 248–250. A similar questionnaire distributed during World War I brought comparable results. See Rossiiskii gosudarstvennyi voenno-istoricheskii arkhiv (Russian State Military-Historical Archive) (RGVIA), f. 2005, op. 1, d. 155.

10. *Polozhenie o polevom upravlenii voisk v voennoe vremia* (Petrograd: Voennaia Tip. imperatritsy Ekateriny Velikoi, 1914); Daniel Graf, "The Reign of the Generals: Military Government in Western Russia, 1914–1815" (Ph.D. diss., University of Nebraska, 1972).

11. Bakhmeteff Archives, Columbia University, Bark Memoirs, chapter 14, p. 43.

12. RGVIA, f. 2005, op. 1, d. 155.

13. William C. Fuller, Jr., *Civil-Military Conflict in Imperial Russia, 1881–1914* (Princeton, N.J.: Princeton University Press, 1985).

14. I. Michael Aronson, "Geographical and Socioeconomic Factors in the 1881 Anti-Jewish Pogroms in Russia," *Russian Review* 39, no. 1 (Jan. 1980): 31. On the causes and spread of deadly ethnic violence in general, see Donald Horowitz, *The Deadly Ethnic Riot* (Berkeley: University of California Press, 2001), esp. 224–225, 395–407.

15. *Sovet ministrov,* 163.

16. "Zaiavlenie no. 174," in Gosudarstvennaia Duma, *Prilozhenie k stenograficheskim otchetam* 27 (1915), 2; GARF, f. r-546, op. 1, d. 1, ll. 105–108.

17. The case for this interpretation of the riots is made in Eric Lohr, "Patriotic Violence and the State: The Moscow Riots of 1915," *Kritika: Explorations in Russian and Eurasian History* 4, no. 3 (Summer 2003): 607–626.

18. Michael Cherniavsky, *Prologue to Revolution: Notes of A. N. Iakhontov on the Secret Meetings of the Council of Ministers, 1915* (Englewood Cliffs, N.J.: Prentice-Hall, 1967), 56–74; *Sovet Ministrov Rossiiskoi imperii v gody Pervoi mirovoi voiny: bumagi A. N. Iakhontova: zapisi zasedanii i perepiska,* ed. B. D. Galperin et al. (St. Petersburg: Dmitrii Bulanin, 1991), 169, 204–205.

19. YIVO, Mowshowitz Collection, 13214.

20. "Iz 'chernoi knigi,' " 233; "Dokumenty o presledovanii," 247.

21. RGVIA, f. 2005, op. 1, d. 24, l. 305.

22. Eric Lohr, *Nationalizing the Russian Empire: The Campaign against Enemy Aliens during World War I* (Cambridge: Harvard University Press, 2003), chapter 4.

23. On the problem of wartime inflation, with some discussion of its impact on relations between nationalities, see Iu. I. Kir'ianov, "Massovye vystupleniia na pochve dorogovizny v Rossii (1914–fevral' 1917 g.)," *Otechestvennaia istoriia* 1 (1993): 3–18.

24. YIVO, Mowshowitz Collection, 13197, 13200.

25. Specifically, see Eric Lohr, "Russian Economic Nationalism during World War I: Moscow Merchants and Commercial Diasporas," *Nationalities Papers* 31, no. 4 (Dec. 2003): 471–484. On the general problem, see Löwe, *Antisemitismus und reaktionäre Utopie* and his *The Tsars and the Jews.* See also, Yuri Slezkine, *The Jewish Century* (Princeton, N.J.: Princeton University Press, 2004).

26. Theodore Weeks, *From Assimilation to Antisemitism: The "Jewish Question" in Poland, 1850–1914* (Dekalb: Northern Illinois University Press, 2006), 165–168; Frank Golczewski, *Polnisch-Jüdische Beziehungen, 1881–1922: Eine Studie zur Geschichte des Antisemitismus in Osteuropa* (Wiesbaden: Steiner, 1981), 106–120.

27. Eric Lohr, "Russian Economic Nationalism during World War I: Moscow Merchants and Commercial Diasporas," *Nationalities Papers* 31, no. 4 (December 2003): 471–484.

~ 3 ~

The Role of Personality in the First (1914–1915) Russian Occupation of Galicia and Bukovina

PETER HOLQUIST

The Russian army during World War I engaged in a wide range of anti-Jewish measures. In occupied Galicia and Bukovina—where Jews comprised 11 percent and 12 percent of the population, respectively—its conduct was particularly brutal.[1] Of course, there were institutional, cultural, and political reasons for the Russian army's conduct.[2] Indeed, in certain respects the army's antisemitic violence was overdetermined. There were a variety of factors impelling the Russian army to engage in violence against Jews; any one of them would suffice to explain such conduct. In this article, however, I want to highlight the role of individuals in this process during the army's first occupation of Galicia. I will focus on two individuals in particular: General Nikolai Ianushkevich, chief of staff for the Supreme Commander in Chief, Grand Duke Nikolai Nikolaevich; and Court Chamberlain Valer'ian Nikolaevich Murav'ev, the Foreign Ministry's attaché on occupation issues in Bukovina.

Despite the structural foundations for violence against the region's Jewish population, it is nevertheless important to weigh the role of specific individuals on policy. Ianushkevich and Murav'ev were key figures in formulating a far-ranging and programmatic antisemitic agenda in Galicia and Bukovina. They failed to realize this agenda, however, due to the resistance of the region's military governor-general, Count Georgii Bobrinskii, and the lack of coordination within the Russian government. The case of the Russian army's conduct in occupied territories also underlines the fractured and polycratic nature of state policy under Nicholas II during the war years. Tellingly, the proposal leading to punitive measures against the Jewish population in Bukovina originated not in the normal chain of command, but through the emperor's endorsement of the extreme program of a low-ranking consular official.

Much of the information in this article comes from the diary of Vladimir Grabar', appointed by the Russian Foreign Ministry to General Headquarters (*Stavka*) to oversee issues of international law. He had been born in Vienna in 1865 to a Ruthene family—Hrabar—committed to pro-Slavic and anti-Habsburg politics.[3] Forced to emigrate, the family found a home in Russia and Russianized their name to "Grabar'." Vladimir pursued a degree in international law at Moscow University. In 1893 he received the appointment to the chair of international law at Iur'ev University. While impeccably qualified, his opportunity came as a result of Russification policies. The imperial government, seeking to accelerate Russification in the Baltic provinces, required that the German university of Dorpat—one of the three oldest in the entire Russian Empire—be called "Iur'ev" and insisted that the faculty should lecture in Russian. (Under Estonian rule it became, and remains, Tartu University.) Grabar' occupied the chair of international law previously held by scholars who wrote and lectured in German. In addition to his academic duties, for twenty-five years he served as a corresponding editor for and contributor to the prominent Brokhaus-Efron encyclopedia as well as the *Novyi entsiklopedicheskii slovar'*, thus widely disseminating his views on international law to the Russian educated public. He held liberal views and protested against reactionary policies in the universities.

During World War I, Grabar' put his training in international law to practical effect, when the Ministry of Foreign Affairs appointed him as legal adviser to the Diplomatic Chancellery at General Headquarters. One of his main tasks at Headquarters was to compile accounts of German atrocities—as he noted, "meaning, of course, only German and Austrian atrocities."[4] Soon officials at Headquarters were coming to justify their own cruel conduct as sanctioned by "military necessity" and by considerations of "security." Grabar' suspected that this argument served simply as a pretext to justify persecution. Ordered by General Ianushkevich to compile an account of German atrocities, Grabar' felt compelled to indicate cases where German conduct had been praiseworthy. Ianushkevich was so outraged by this action that he immediately had Grabar' dismissed. In April 1915, just as Russian forces were being driven from most of Galicia, Grabar' formally resigned his post "on grounds of health."[5] His account is especially interesting because Grabar' was himself a Ruthene and thus had a special interest in the Russian occupation of eastern Galicia, where Ruthenes comprised the bulk of the population. Equally significant, however, is his principled stand on issues of international law. He was one of the few critics of the atmosphere of pervasive antisemitism found at General Headquarters. His diary traces the evolution of antisemitic views there.

Typologies of Violence in the First Russian Occupation of Galicia

Galicia under the first Russian occupation experienced a maelstrom of violence. The violence committed by Russian forces in the 1914–1915 period can be divided into three general forms: first, widespread but unsanctioned marauding and pillaging by passing military units; second, a set of punitive policies that operated at the level of widespread military practices, particularly in regard to the Jewish population of Galicia and Bukovina; and, third, the attempt by General Nikolai Ianushkevich, the chief of staff for the Supreme Commander in chief, Grand Duke Nikolai Nikolaevich, and certain front commanders to pursue a targeted, systemic, and far-reaching antisemitic program.

Much of Galicia was devastated by autumn 1914, first by the fighting and then by the subsequent marauding of soldiers and civilians. Pillaging and pogroms were the most basic form of violence perpetrated by Russian troops upon the civilian population of Galicia. Vladimir Grabar', in his capacity as the Foreign Ministry's liaison to General Headquarters on issues of international law, testified that rape by Russian forces was common and extended even to young girls.[6] Grabar', in addition, heard "horrible accounts of looting by the Russian army." It seemed, he noted, that there was a total collapse of any sense of justice or law. The war, "which could have been holy and honorable, has instead become a raid of some wild horde, a mockery of all law and honor."[7] A young Roman Catholic priest with whom Russian officers were quartered in the winter of 1914–1915 observed:

> When you first arrived near Kraków, the entire population of Galicia welcomed you. You seized cattle, horses, oats, hay, grain. It was hard. But you treated us well. We understood: war is war. There was no point to bringing along hay and meat with you, when you could get it all in Galicia. So we gave it you, and for all of it you paid. Now [in December 1914] you have turned into robbers and pillagers. You take our last cow and condemn the little ones to starvation. Take a look at our children: they wander like shadows, hungry [and] poor. . . . They fade before our very eyes—and we are unable to help them. You snatch the last crust of bread from their mouths. You mock us. . . . Now all segments of the population hate you. You behave like wild beasts. In Dembits your soldiers raped sixty young girls. Those are no rumors. They brought them to Tarnów to testify as witnesses, and their shame

was then confirmed by your own doctors. Here in Ryglitsy nine soldiers in the course of one night raped a thirty-two-year-old woman;
by the morning she died, tortured to death by them.[8]

Cossack units were worse than all others. "To tell the truth," one Jewish
refugee explained to the erstwhile ethnographer of shtetl life Solomon
Rapaport-Ansky, "ordinary troops . . . seldom bother anyone. The real
problem is the Cossacks. The moment they ride in, they start shooting and
beating."[9]

All segments of Galician society suffered from the Russian army, but
Jews were particularly subject to this violence. They became targets because of a confluence of several factors: the spy hysteria sweeping the military, the belief that Galician Jews were hostile to the Russian occupation,
and the dissemination of antisemitic views among the troops by officers and
the nationalist press. But there can be no doubt that Jews were the primary focus of the Russian Army's violence.[10] In letters, Jewish soldiers in
the Russian army reported the massacres and pillaging committed by their
own units. One Jewish soldier recounted that

> when our brigade marched through one village, a soldier spotted a
> house on a hill, and told our commander that it was probably the home
> of Jews. The officer allowed him to go and have a look. He returned
> with the cheerful news that Jews *were* indeed living there. The officer
> ordered the brigade to approach the house. They opened the door and
> found some twenty Jews half dead with fear. The troops led them out,
> and the officer gave his order: "Slice them up! Chop them up!"

This soldier's experiences in Galicia eventually drove him insane.[11]

The Russian occupation of Galicia saw repeated pogroms. The largest
were in Brody, immediately upon occupation by Russian forces early in
the war, and in Lwów in late September 1914. The pogrom in Brody was
precipitated by the shooting of a Russian officer outside a hotel. The daugh-
ter of the hotel's owner, a Jewish girl, was seized as the perpetrator and
lynched. The troops then rampaged through the Jewish quarter and burned
down the synagogue, killing nine Jews.[12] The story was similar in Lwów:

> Early one afternoon a shot was heard in the middle of the Jewish
> quarter of the town. Immediately shooting began all over the town.
> Seventeen Jews were killed, as well as two Christians, and two Jew-
> ish houses were demolished. . . . Immediately after the pogrom, Jewish
> hostages were taken, and they have not yet [ca. mid-1915] been
> released.[13]

In his report on the Lwów pogrom, the military governor-general for occupied Galicia, Count Georgii Bobrinskii—based in Lwów—did not single out the Jews for culpability, and referred only to the fact that there
were shots from windows. Nevertheless, General Ianushkevich, in his
reply, insisted on the Jews' guilt and demanded "harsh reprisals, regardless of ramifications."[14] There were other pogroms, too. Every time Russian forces entered the city of Stri (Stryy, in modern Ukraine), which
passed back and forth several times, they pillaged and looted its large
Jewish population. The region around Sadagora, a town in Bukovina sto-
ried for its Hasidic court, also suffered repeated pogroms from Russian
forces.[15]

The violence of the German army during World War I was brutal in a
systematic and didactic way, favoring demonstrative execution.[16] In formal
terms, Russian military culture embraced deportation rather than execution. (There were institutional reasons: the guidelines for the governor-
general of occupied Galicia replicated the powers of governor-generals
within Russia—including the power to expel individuals by administrative order.) In contrast to German directives ordering collective executions
in Belgium and northern France for the actions of *francs-tireurs*, for instance, the Russian governor of Ternopil' ordered the deportation of civilians guilty of shooting at Russian troops.[17] The distinguishing feature of
Russian violence, however, was its lack of focus and structure. Ansky commented on this difference. He described the report of a Russian unit that
ordered the Jews of a shtetl near Wolkowisk to strip naked, dance with
one another, and then ride on pigs—before shooting every tenth person.
Ansky then recounted another report, this time of a German unit that
marched into the shtetl of Blonye, near Warsaw. It came upon a farm-
house that had been turned into a barracks for cholera patients whom the
Russians had been forced to leave behind. Concerned that the disease
might spread to their soldiers, the Germans surrounded the barracks with
straw and ignited it, burning all 192 patients to death. Ansky continues:

> I don't know what's worse: torching a barrack filled with sick people
> or making people strip naked, ride on pigs, and gunning them down.
> The barrack fire, no matter how inhumane, at least had a specific goal.
> With the Germans, you knew what you were dealing with. You knew
> that when it came to a necessary objective, they wouldn't stop at the
> worst cruelty. By the same token, you could be certain that if you
> didn't get in their way, they wouldn't lay a finger on you. But with
> Russians, you were never sure of your life, of your dignity. The Rus-
> sians were never guided by sound logic or practical considerations.[18]

This unstructured but widespread violence marked the first Russian occupation of Galicia (1914–1915) and remained a prominent factor in the second one (1916–1917).

The Army's Attitude toward Jews

In addition to general attitudes toward the ethnicities of Galicia—Poles, Jews, Germans, Ukrainians—Russian commanders' views of the population derived from the official General Staff studies of the region. Reporting possible routes of advance and regions for quartering troops, these studies also described the likely response of various segments of the population to Russian occupation. They predicted, unsurprisingly, that the German population would be hostile. The Polish segment, due both to its privileged position under Austrian rule and its "Catholic fanaticism," was "unreliable" and might even be "hostile." The majority of the population—Ruthenes, which Russian military studies described simply as "Russian" peasants—would welcome the Russian forces as liberators, except for the small Ukrainophile intelligentsia. (Grabar'—a Ruthene himself—was more skeptical of this portrayal of Ruthenes as being Russians at heart.) Jews, these studies predicted, "motivated by their own selfish interests," would "serve both sides, both by supplying goods but also by spying."[19]

Such accounts clearly were informed by antisemitic stereotypes. What is significant, however, is that such studies had not singled out the Jewish population as innately hostile and the primary foe of the Russian army. The shift to *this* view occurred in the first weeks of the war, when the army's generalized suspicion of Jews catalytically combined with a mood of fear and uncertainty. A British civilian working with a Polish relief agency for three months in occupied Galicia reported as follows:

> Thus a large hostile element was found by the Russians, a considerable percentage being Jewish. It was impossible that this element should not come into conflict with the invading forces, and the following history is said to have repeated itself in many places. The Cossack advance guards entering a town or village would enquire the direction or disposition of the Austrian forces from the Jews, these being indeed practically the only source of information as to the way to take, the nature of the countryside, etc. The Cossacks would make a mistake, or be misled, fall into what they believed was an ambush, lose some of their officers, come back furious and burn the Jewish quarter. It can hardly be doubted that on such occasions they used their

weapons on the wretched inhabitants. The Cossacks also raped Jewish women and pillaged freely.[20]

A Jewish physician serving in the Russian military reported that by mid-1915, "The ruin of the Jewish population of Galicia is almost complete—the houses are leveled with the ground and property destroyed. The methods were everywhere the same: after some provocative shot of a never disclosed person, came robbery, fire, and massacre."[21]

The prevalent antisemitism within the military as a whole obviously goes a long way in explaining the persecution of the Jewish population in Galicia. Yet this targeted persecution was not repeated during the second Russian occupation of 1916–1917.[22] The *general* antisemitism of the military was a necessary, but not sufficient, factor for targeted persecution. The true catalyst was a set of policy directives for the persecution of Jews and tacit sanction of antisemitic violence from the high command, a variable present in 1914–1915 but which was absent in 1916–1917. The high command began to issue directives singling out Galician Jews for persecution beginning in late September 1914. The first significant discussion of restrictive measures against Galician Jews is found in the memorandum of Nikolai Bazili, the vice-director of the Diplomatic Chancellery at General Headquarters (thus a civilian and Foreign Ministry official), who lobbied for the confiscation of Jewish landholding as an essential precondition for winning over the Ruthenian population. His antisemitic program, in other words, was a means to achieving the liberationist agenda for the region's "Russian" population, rather than a goal in itself.

For General Ianushkevich, the antisemitic program was an end in itself. Ianushkevich immediately seized on Bazili's report and submitted it both to Governor-General Bobrinskii and to the Imperial Council of Ministers, demanding the immediate seizure of all Jewish landholding in Galicia and Bukovina.[23] In forwarding Bazili's memorandum to the Council of Ministers, Ianushkevich observed that the questions Bazili had raised "can evidently be resolved only in the circumstance when the occupied territories are definitively united with us, that is, upon the conclusion of peace." "On the other hand," he continued, "the conditions of martial law permit us to take certain more decisive measures with greater ease than would be possible after the conclusion of peace." Austrian law permitted Jews to own land, and—according to the laws of war—these laws remained in force in the occupied territory. Ianushkevich continued by stating that in Galicia

> we will face a difficult struggle with Jewry. It would seem essential to
> employ for this end the possibilities that are granted us by martial

law. First and foremost the question of sequestering the property (and especially real estate) of individuals who have fled from Galicia. The employment of such an energetic measure against a Galician Jewry, which in any case is hostile to us, is justified as well by the necessity of demonstrating our decisiveness to protect our army by any means necessary from its [Jewry's] hostile actions.[24]

From late September 1914 until his removal in August 1915, Ianushkevich would energetically press both the Council of Ministers and his subordinates in the military to pursue a coordinated policy to seize all Jewish landholding and remove Jews from the judiciary and all civil posts.

Antisemitism totally pervaded General Headquarters, according to Vladimir Grabar', who was attached to it for more than nine months, from August 1914 to May 1915, as the Foreign Ministry's adviser on questions of international law. "Here at General Headquarters," he noted, "one word is absent: 'Jew' [evrei]. It seems I am the only one to use it. . . . Everyone else, including members of the [Foreign Ministry's] diplomatic chancellery . . . speaks only of 'kikes' [zhidy]." Over morning tea, members of the diplomatic and civil affairs chancelleries discussed programs for "exterminating" the Jews of Galicia [proekty istrebleniia "zhidov"]: some suggested mass expulsion to Austria, others called for the confiscation of all Jewish landholding, "and so on and so on."[25] One Constitutional Democrat reported that certain commanders in the field believed that "the center of Judeophobia is the General Headquarters. . . . The unnecessary and shameful pogroms and excesses derive from here, and not from the depths of the army."[26] In addition to Ianushkevich, General Nikolai Iudovich Ivanov, commander of the Southwestern Front, and General Aleksei Ermolaevich Evert, commander of the Fourth Army, were also known to be a radical antisemites.[27] In June 1915, one Constitutional Democrat reported that "in a train-car he heard a conversation between two officers, one of whom directly spoke in favor of resolving the Jewish question in the Turkish manner—intimating by this the pogroms against Armenians."[28] (By this date the Russian military and Russian educated society were quite aware of the Armenian genocide. On 24 May 1915, the Allied governments had issued their collective note threatening judicial sanction for its perpetrators.)

Many observers believed that the diffusion of such views to the lower ranks was the most significant factor influencing the conduct of Russian troops. One general addressed the soldiers of his division in December 1914 with the following speech: "Remember, brothers, that your first foe is the Germans. They have long sucked our blood, and now want to conquer our land. Don't take them prisoner, bayonet them—I'll answer for it. Your second foe are the kikes [zhidy]. They are spies and aid the Germans. If you meet a zhid in the field—bayonet him, I'll answer for it."[29] One Jewish military doctor wrote the following concerning his colleagues:

> That the army officers are antisemites is a commonly known fact. Everybody who had a chance of being in their society affirms it. I [the author of this letter, a military doctor, a Jew, and a well-known and very active social worker in Petrograd] once spent a night with a great number of officers of different ranks and regiments, and I am compelled, although with deep sorrow, to acknowledge that I have heard and seen things which surpassed all my fears. The "Jew" was the chief topic of all conversation, anecdotes, menaces, and songs. One young officer, whose only exploits had consisted in demolishing Jewish houses, gained the sincerest applause of the company by his very picturesque tales of his deeds of destruction in the numerous Jewish towns of Galicia which had been visited by him and his troops.[30]

This same doctor reported that the soldiers "naively reported what they had done, being sure that no wrong was committed by them, since it was permitted by the 'natshalstwo' [sic] [authorities]."[31] In his travels through Galicia, Ansky found that conscripts were less antisemitic than officers, "but hearing the venom spewed by their superiors and reading about Jewish treason day after day they too came to suspect and hate the Jews." In particular, soldiers received their views from antisemitic and hyper-patriotic newspapers that were distributed throughout the army.[32]

Ansky and the Constitutional Democrats, of course, wished to indict the ruling elites and exculpate the common soldier. But one Russian admiral serving at General Headquarters also noted with satisfaction that the occupation of Galicia was having its desired effect: all those participating in the occupation were turning antisemitic. "Upon the conclusion of this campaign," he observed, "the troops also will be disposed against the 'kikes.'"[33] His hope seems to have been fulfilled. The units retreating from Galicia in spring 1915 were "full of hostility to Austrian Jews" and in the course of their retreat they projected these views onto Russian Jews.[34]

Ianushkevich and those who shared his expansive programs, however, faced a dilemma. The laws of war permitted them to punish specific individuals, but—because the territory was occupied rather than formally annexed—they could not introduce major new economic or administrative laws. Yet, if they waited for peace, they would not be in charge of the legislation introduced into newly annexed Galicia: that task would belong to the Russian legislature, the State Duma. Officials at General Headquarters discussing the "Jewish question" expressed the conviction that it was best to slaughter the Jews now, while it was still possible. If the army temporized, "it will then be difficult, because 'Sir Duma' will not permit it."[35] The Russian nationalist Dmitrii Vergun, in his hyper-patriotic newspaper *Novoe vremia,* also counseled that "we should not forget that there are measures which can be taken only in wartime. In this sphere it is long past time to get to work."[36] In making a case for the expropriation of Jewish lands during wartime (a case very similar to Ianushkevich's)—and less than one month after the Council of Ministers had rejected Ianushkevich's plan—the Nationalist Party activist Dmitrii Nikolaevich Chikhachev stressed that the moment was propitious for "solving" the Jewish question in occupied Galicia. He argued that this solution should come during the war, since after the war the "philosemitic" stance of both Russia's allies and the liberals in the Duma would prevent any radical anti-Jewish measures.[37] Thus the desire to circumvent the new parliamentary organs drove right-wing activists and officials to embrace wartime as a favorable moment for implementing radical proposals that they would not be able to pass in peacetime.

Yet Russia remained an old regime political system. It lacked structures that could institutionally coordinate and ideologically inspire a major antisemitic program, such as the Committee of Union and Progress's Secret Organization in Ottoman Turkey, the Bolshevik Party, or the Nazi Party. Ianushkevich had intentionally created a disjointed system of command and administration. Yet the very polycractic structure he had helped create then prevented him from being able to pursue his program in any systematic way.

The Expulsion of Galicia's Jewish Population

One major aspect of warfare on the Eastern Front was the massive expulsion of civilian populations. The Russian Army alone expelled up to one million Jewish and German subjects over the course of 1915.[38] Although it is not commonly recognized, these operations began in Galicia and Bukovina—specifically, in Bukovina in January 1915.[39] Then, as the army retreated back into Russia throughout 1915, it continued the policy it had begun in Galicia and Bukovina of expelling Jews en masse from the front region.

Before September 1914, the Russian military had not particularly concerned itself with Galicia's Jewish population. After that time, those desiring a "radical" solution to the "Jewish question" pressed for the expropriation of Jewish landholding under cover of wartime. They did so out of fear that their wide-ranging program would be impossible after the peace, due to the anticipated interference of Russia's allies and the Duma. (In fact, both the Council of Ministers—on grounds of international law—and Governor-General Bobrinskii prevented the expropriation of Jewish landholding *during* the war, although they indicated that they would have no objections to doing so after its conclusion.) The military, gripped by spy hysteria, increasingly viewed Galicia's Jewish population as a security concern. But through January 1915 there were no concrete plans for deportation. When such plans did crystallize, the proximate cause was not—as is commonly believed—suspicions of "Jewish" espionage, but rather an attempt to practice something that might be termed "preemptive reprisals."

The policy began to evolve in late September 1914. The Foreign Ministry's attaché to the Southwestern Front, Court Chamberlain V. Murav'ev, traveled to Czernowitz, the capital of Bukovina, soon after its seizure by Russian forces. There he was to serve as a specialist on issues of occupation. He argued that Russia must be tactful regarding the claims of neutral Romania to the region. But he was already thinking in terms of population expulsion. Murav'ev pressed for Russian occupation of all of southern Bukovina since "the Balkan Wars give reason to believe that, in regions with a mixed Russian-Romanian population, we will not find one Russian community left after Russian forces depart." Murav'ev believed the city of Czernowitz's Jewish population was hostile to the occupying Russian forces.[40] Three weeks later, on 7 October, a sudden Austrian attack caused panic among the small Russian garrison, forcing it to flee across the Prut River.

Murav'ev's response to this event in October 1914 laid the groundwork for the deportations, which would begin in January 1915. Murav'ev first participated in an unsuccessful attempt to retake the city. He then traveled to Lwów to report on the city's loss to the Austrians, arriving in a hysterical state.[41] In his reports on the city's capture, he focused on the response of Czernowitz's Jewish population to the Austrian entry. In the surrounding region, "the Jews attacked Russian peasants who had welcomed our soldiers, beating them and stealing their property." He continued:

> This has set a difficult task before us—the trial and deserved punishment over those who bowed at our knees when we were there, but who revealed their true face when we left. We must be just but unyielding. If we make several examples, our authority, which has been shaken lately, will be established for the whole future. I think that these events are even useful, since now at least we know who are friends are and who are enemies in Bukovina.[42]

Over the next several days he bombarded his superiors with similar reports. He pleaded for permission to accompany the military detachment assigned to recapture Czernowitz, arguing that he had an important role to play: "we should take the most severe repressive measures toward those individuals—primarily Jews—who during our retreat openly mocked Russia and now persecute our supporters."[43] Murav'ev's superior, head of the Diplomatic Chancellery Prince Nikolai Aleksandrovich Kudashev, granted him permission to accompany the detachment assigned to seize the city. But he also lectured Murav'ev that "while I entirely acknowledge the necessity of firm measures in cases where there is no doubt, I nevertheless believe that we cannot establish our authority by relying on [firm measures] alone. A cool head and the observance of absolute impartiality are essential so that the population does not lose respect for us or lose faith in our fairness and might."[44] Murav'ev, in his reply, claimed that there were no grounds to fear superfluous cruelty, since the military "shows great humanitarianism." But, he continued, the lack of courts in the occupied region meant that those responsible for persecuting Russia's supporters would escape punishment. "The system of taking hostages has shown good results and we cannot proceed any differently when entire Russian communities remain in the hands of our foe. Experience has shown," he expounded, "that Jews and Ukrainians . . . in the abandoned territories can be restrained only . . . by fear of retribution upon our return. In any case," he assured his superior, "you should bear in mind that I accept the heavy moral burden."[45] Grabar' reports that the entire General Headquarters was well aware of Murav'ev's proposals "to punish the Jews, who had mocked Russians during the retreat . . . he argues for the necessity to orchestrate a pogrom of the Galician Jews."[46]

Russian forces soon retook Czernowitz but did not immediately target the Jewish population. Murav'ev, however, pursued his own personal "investigation" into their conduct during the Russian retreat in early October. He submitted two reports on the situation in Bukovina, one on 30 November 1914, and another on 1 January 1915.[47] In his November report, he again charged that the Austrians had practiced widespread repressions, although he had yet to complete his investigation on them. By early January, he had completed his personal "investigation of Austrian atrocities during our last retreat from Czernowitz." In the city itself, the Austrians had hanged four pro-Russian peasants for sympathizing with Russian forces. There were also executions in the surrounding towns. "Local Jews," he charged, "had indicated who should be hanged. . . . Interrogations have confirmed many cases of beatings at the order of gendarmes and acts of vengeance by the Jews on Russian and Rumanian peasants." Murav'ev concluded by noting that "the peasants *expect from us liberation from the Jewish yoke*" [italics in original]. For Russian officials, this argument had the added appeal of providing an explanation for the anemic response of the supposedly "Russian" peasants in Galicia and Bukovina to Russian rule: beaten down by decades of Teutonic dominance, they now lived in fear of Jewish denunciations to Austrian authorities.

So what? Court Chamberlain Murav'ev was not a military commander; he was a low-level Foreign Ministry official reporting to the Diplomatic Chancellery. His views, however, became significant not due to his institutional position, but due solely to the support his views received from Emperor Nicholas II. Kudashev, head of the Diplomatic Chancellery at General Headquarters, reported to Foreign Minister Sergei Dmitrievich Sazonov that Grand Duke Nikolai Nikolaevich, Ianushkevich, and the emperor himself were all very pleased with Murav'ev's 30 November report on Galicia and Bukovina, in which he had reported on his personal investigation into Austrian atrocities as well as the hostility of the Jewish population to Russian forces.[48] Kudashev also forwarded Murav'ev's report of 1 January 1915, containing the conclusions of his "investigation" and arguing for the need to "liberate" Russian peasants from the Jewish yoke, to General Ianushkevich, who read it with great interest. Ianushkevich penned a notation at the bottom of Murav'ev's note: "I propose that it would be very desirable to drive all the Jews to the Krauts."[49] This phrase— "drive all the Jews to the Krauts"—became one of Ianushkevich's favorite expressions.[50] Soon afterward, Kudashev again reported to his superior, Foreign Minister Sazonov, that "the Emperor asked about the tour of Court Chamberlain Murav'ev to Bukovina and used very warm expressions regarding his activity." Before the assembled personnel of headquarters, Nicholas II singled out Murav'ev for praise.[51] There could be no doubt by early January that the emperor and the commander in chief sanctioned his views.

This conviction that "the Jews" were terrorizing Russian supporters among the population in Galicia and Bukovina crystallized into a policy program, however, only in late January 1915. At that time an Austrian offensive threatened Czernowitz. By the end of the month, Russian forces were again forced to withdraw from the city. Less than a week before these forces abandoned the city, on 22 January, Ianushkevich issued an order sanctioning the deportations and hostage-taking that would continue for the next six months. It explicitly cited preemptive reprisal, rather than espionage, as its rationale:

The experience of the war has revealed the clearly hostile attitude of the Jewish population of Galicia and Bukovina toward us. Every adjustment in our lines that leads to a temporary withdrawal of this or that region is followed by brutal measures by our foe toward the portion of the population that is sympathetic to us and whom the Jews denounce to the Germans. In order to prevent atrocities against the population which is devoted to us—and [to protect] our forces from espionage, which the Jews pursue along the entire front—the Commander in Chief has ordered, beginning in Bukovina . . . to drive the Jews after the retreating foe and to seize hostages from among [them]. The Jewish population is to be warned that they are answerable for all violence perpetrated upon the civilian population at the Jews' instigation. In doing this, it is essential to instill in the population that this measure is taken for its own protection and is a measure forced on us by six months of restraint and the unshakable conviction of the disloyalty [of the Jews] and of [their] cruelty to the local population.[52]

Here Ianushkevich gave form to his desire, expressed in his notation at the end of Murav'ev's report of 1 January, "to drive the Jews to the Krauts." By mid-February 1915 the newspaper for the Southwestern Front was printing lurid reports of Austrian atrocities toward the pro-Russian population in Galicia and Bukovina, claiming that "bands of Austrians . . . slaughtered entire Slavic communities." A later report, in March, charged that "the Jews" were accompanying Austrian patrols and pointing out Russian sympathizers among the peasantry.[53] College Assessor Olfer'ev—another mid-level employee of the Ministry of Foreign Affairs, like Murav'ev, assigned to advise the military—continued through February to charge that the Jews had engaged in "systematic treachery and espionage, as a result of which the Austro-German forces have perpetrated executions and cruelties upon the Christian peasant population that has been unheard of in its cruelty."[54] Lest there be any thought that Ianushkevich was freelancing, in early March 1915 Nicholas II—who had been so impressed with Murav'ev's investigation of the "atrocities" in Czernowitz—issued an order directing that "those nationalities that are hostile to us will have to answer for atrocities . . . against the Slavic and Romanian population of Bukovina. This threat ought to be implemented immediately upon the occupation of even a portion of Bukovina, as soon as the atrocities which have been perpetrated are discovered."[55] (Note that Nicholas II was certain of the existence of "atrocities" that had yet to be "discovered"!)

From late January 1915, army commanders began expelling Galician Jews, both individually and in large groups, from areas of the front region.

The military dispatched hostages and those it suspected of espionage directly to Russia. But the military turned over the vast majority—Jews expelled en masse from the front region—to Governor-General Bobrinskii's occupation administration. By this time Bobrinskii had very strained relations with Ianushkevich. Bobrinskii had opposed and managed to block several components of Ianushkevich's antisemitic agenda: the sequestration of all Jewish landholding; the introduction of the Russian justice system in Galicia; and a proposed ban on Jews receiving philanthropic aid. On all these issues, Bobrinskii—by and large supported by the Council of Ministers—managed to blunt Ianushkevich's far-reaching proposals. An official of the old order, he did not do so out of any warm feelings toward Jews. Ansky recalled that representatives of the Jewish community of Lwów had a favorable impression of him. He seemed "a civilized European trying to live in peace with the people in the occupied region. . . . He was indeed highly educated and good-natured, striving to avoid violence, even toward Jews, whom he did not perhaps care for in his heart of hearts."[56] Ianushkevich reproached Bobrinskii for failing to support his energetic policies: "[I]t has been reported that Jews continue to terrorize the Russian and Polish population but nevertheless the handling of them continues to be too delicate. I order you to take measures for the strict fulfillment of the requisite orders, with no exceptions." While promising to prosecute any cases of Jewish persecution of Christians, Bobrinskii replied that he would pursue all cases of theft and looting "without regard to nationality."[57] In April 1915, at the time Ianushkevich was pressing his program for expelling Jews from Galicia, Bobrinskii pointedly noted in an interview with a prominent newspaper that he had no complaints regarding the conduct of the Jewish population in occupied Galicia.[58]

Nevertheless, Bobrinsksii had to confront the problem of dealing with the thousands of Jews expelled from the front region by military authorities. He could not send all these individuals into Russia, nor could he send them back to their place of residence. Instead, he took to settling the expellees in the eastern districts of Galicia, closest to the Russian border. (The western portion remained under direct military control.) In the Chortkiv district alone, he settled 4,000 Jews expelled from Bukovina. By early March, he was no longer able to provide for the more than 10,000 expellees in eastern Galicia and requested assistance from the Southwestern Front's chief of provisioning, who also served as Bobrinskii's superior. The latter told Bobrinskii that Galician Jews could no longer remain in Galicia and must be expelled to Poltava province in the Russian Empire.[59]

Until this point, few people outside Galicia and Bukovina knew of these policies. Under the field regulations hastily approved in July 1914, the region fell under military control. Ianushkevich's machinations had ensured that the civilian government was kept in the dark about the military's actions in the vast region declared to be "the front." Moreover, the military authorities had imposed a draconian pass system to control movement into and out of Galicia.[60] When Bobrinskii—at the direct order of his military superiors—contacted the governors of Russian provinces neighboring Galicia in order to coordinate the dispatch of more than 10,000 Galician Jews, he stunned the civilian authorities. For the first time they learned of the extent of the military's measures. Ironically, because of the manner in which the request proceeded, most officials thought the expulsion plan had originated with Bobrinskii himself. The Minister of Internal Affairs and the entire Council of Ministers opposed the plan. Not only was the government entirely unprepared to care for the 10,000 souls about to be dumped in various Russian provinces, but it also opposed the entry of any more Jews—and Austrian Jews at that—into the Russian Empire. After an extensive correspondence, Ianushkevich backed down. Military authorities would deport only hostages to Russia, not the entire suspect population.[61] Ianushkevich insisted, however, that military units continue to drive Jews before them toward the Austrian lines as they advanced. He was convinced that the measures against the Jews had been insufficiently firm, due to interference by the government.[62]

By the time the army command had relented, however, it was on the verge of the Great Retreat of 1915, in which the Russian Army lost much of Galicia and Poland. As the military abandoned most of Galicia in early June 1915, it ordered that all males between the ages of eighteen and fifty be removed to Russia, in order to deprive the Austrians the opportunity of conscripting them.[63] To this number was added a wave of peasant refugees fearing retribution from Austrian authorities. The total number of people who left Galicia with Russian forces was more than 100,000, half of them Jews removed as an "unreliable element."[64] In the course of the retreat, the Russian army passed through the Pale of Settlement, and in the process visited a string of pogroms and expulsions against its own Jewish population. Yet the Great Retreat had one other effect. It shattered faith in the military command, and General Ianushkevich and Commander in Chief Nikolai Nikolaevich first and foremost. By mid-summer they were removed. In the aftermath of their removal, both the Russian government and military undertook an investigation into what was already acknowledged to be the "failed" occupation of Galicia and Bukovina. One conclusion found in all their subsequent reviews was that the obsession with plans for the region's civilian population—to punish Jews and liberate Ruthene peasants—had been counterproductive.

* * *

It is becoming clear that many practices identified with World War II—population deportations, ethnic cleansing, genocide—were also present in World War I. The Russian military's policy of deportation and its widespread antisemitic measures certainly number among the worst cases of violence against civilians in World War I. It is not surprising, of course, that the military of the autocratic Russian empire should engage in anti-Jewish violence. This was the state that had orchestrated the Beilis case in 1911–1912 and whose attitude towards anti-Jewish pogroms was widely viewed as complicit. Certain currents in the government had embraced a policy in the years before the war of "Russia for Russians" (*Rossiia dlia russkikh*), a slogan with particular appeal among some segments of the military. So the violence against Jews, which rose as a crescendo in 1915, first within the occupied territories and then across the Pale of Settlement during the Great Retreat, had many causes—institutional, cultural, and political. Yet we are still left to explain why the violence came to a crescendo in 1915—and not earlier—and then why, in certain key respects, it abated. While raping and pillaging continued after 1915—affecting non-Jews as well—the type of targeted antisemitic violence evident in 1915 was no longer in evidence. The role of specific historical conjunctures, and the activity of key individuals—such as General Nikolai Ianushkevich and Court Chamberlain V. Murav'ev—are part of the explanation.

Notes

1. For treatments of the Russian occupation and its policies, see Mark von Hagen, "The Great War and the Mobilization of Ethnicity in the Russian Empire," in *Post-Soviet Political Order: Conflict and State-building,* ed. Barnett Rubin and Jack Snyder (New York: Routledge, 1998), 34–57, here at pp. 41–48; Aleksandra Bakhturina, *Politika rossiiskoi imperii v vostochnoi Galitsii v gody pervoi mirovoi voiny* (Moscow: AIRO, 2000); Alexander Victor Prusin, *Nationalizing a Borderland: War, Ethnicity, and Anti-Jewish Violence in East Galicia, 1914–1920* (Tuscaloosa: University of Alabama Press, 2005); Christoph Mick, "Natsionalisierung in einer multiethnischen Stadt: Interetnische Konflikte in Lemberg, 1890–1920," *Archiv für Sozialgeschichte* 40 (2000): 113–146, here at 128–138; Alexander Prusin, "The Russian Military and the Jews in Galicia, 1914–1915," in *The Military and Society in Russia, 1450–1917,* ed. Eric Lohr and Marshall Poe (Leiden and Boston: Brill, 2002); and V. N. Savchenko, "Vostochnaia Galitsiia v 1914–1915 godakh: Natsional'no-politicheskaia situatsiia i politika rossiiskoi administratsii," *Otechestvennaia istoriia* 5 (2002): 76–89. The most important eyewitness account is by the

Jewish ethnographer and activist S. Ansky, *The Enemy at His Pleasure: A Journey through the Jewish Pale of Settlement during World War I*, ed. and trans. Joachim Neugroschel (New York: Henry Holt and Co., 2002), originally written in Yiddish in 1920.

2. See Eric Lohr, *Nationalizing the Russian Empire: The Campaign against Enemy Aliens during World War I* (Cambridge, Mass.: Harvard University Press, 2003); Joshua Sanborn, *Drafting the Nation: Military Conscription, Total War, and Mass Politics, 1905–1925* (DeKalb: Northern Illinois University Press, 2003); Nicolas Werth, "Les déserteurs en Russie: Violence de guerre, violence révolutionnaire et violence paysanne (1916–1921)," in *La Violence de Guerre, 1914–1945,* ed. Stéphane Audoin-Rouzeau, Annette Becker, Christian Ingrao, and Henry Rousso (Paris: Histoire du temps présent, 2002); Peter Gatrell, *A Whole Empire Walking: Refugees in Russia during World War I* (Bloomington: Indiana University Press, 1999); Vladimir Buldakov, *Krasnaia smuta: Priroda i posledstviia revoliutsionnogo nasiliia* (Moscow: Rosspen, 1997); and Peter Holquist, "Violent Russia, Deadly Marxism? Russia in the Epoch of Violence," *Kritika: Explorations in Russian and Eurasian History* 4, no. 3 (Summer 2003): 627–652.

3. On Grabar', see William Butler's very fine biographical introduction in V. E. Grabar, *The History of International Law in Russia, 1647–1917: A Bio-Bibliographical Study,* trans. W. E. Butler (Oxford: Clarendon Press, 1990); the relevant portion of Lauri Mälksoo, "The Science of International Law and the Concept of Politics: The Arguments and Lives of the International Law Professors at the University of Dorpat/Iur'ev/Tartu 1855–1985," *British Year Book of International Law* 76 (2005): 383–502; and Vladimir Grabar', "Avtobiografiia" (15.I.1945), Manuscript Division, Tartu University Library, f. 38 [V. E. Grabar'], s. 1.

4. Vladimir Grabar's diary (Department of Rare Books and Manuscripts, Tartu University Library, Estonia), f. 38, s. 50, l. 6ob. (entry for 16/29 August 1914) [henceforth, "Grabar' diary"; dates given according to the Julian calendar (Old Style), which ran thirteen days behind the Gregorian calendar (New Style)].

5. Grabar' diary, 19 April 1915 (l. 85); Kudashev to Sazonov, 6 May 1915, *Krasnyi arkhiv* 2, no. 27 (1928): 15; Ministry of Foreign Affairs approving Grabar's resignation "on grounds of health" (Arkhiv vneshnei politiki Rossiiskoi imperii [Foreign Affairs Archive of the Russian Empire], Moscow [AVPRI], f. 323, op. 617, d. 105, l. 7).

6. Grabar' diary, entry for 20 November 1914 (l. 62ob.); for the account of the rape and murder of one girl by four Russian lancers on a train in Galicia, and their subsequent trial and execution, see Richard Boleslavski, with Helen Woodward, *The Way of the Lancer* (Garden City, N.Y.: Garden City Publishing, 1932), 37–47.

7. Grabar' diary, entries for 25 September and 20 November 1914 (ll. 37, 60ob.)

8. L. Voitolovskii, *Vskhodil krovavyi Mars: po sledam voiny* (Moscow: Voennoe izdatel'stvo, 1998), 124. Voitsekhovskii served in an army medical detachment dispatched to Galicia in December 1914.

9. Ansky, *Enemy,* 36; also pp. 6, 14. On the role of Cossack units in pillaging within the Russian Empire as well, see Eric Lohr, "The Russian Army and the Jews: Mass Deportations, Hostages, and Violence during World War I," *Russian Review* 60, no. 3 (July 2001): 404–419, here at 414–417.

10. "The Jews suffer more than anyone else" from the looting: Grabar' diary, entry for 20 November 1914 (l. 62ob.).

11. Ansky, *Enemy,* 8–9.

12. Ibid., 65–70; Grabar' diary, entry for 14 October 1914 (l. 44ob.); "Letters from Galicia" [anonymous report of Jewish military doctor in the Russian army, ca. mid-1915] (National Archives of the United Kingdom, London [NAUK] FO 371/1915/vol. 2445/file 155/doc. 124265/pp. 378–379).

13. "Letters from Galicia" (NAUK FO 371/1915/vol. 2445/file 155/doc. 124265/pp. 381–382); for a summary account of the Lwów pogrom, see Prusin, *Nationalizing*, 30–32.

14. Prusin, *Nationalizing*, 31.

15. Ansky, *Enemy*, 109, 278–283.

16. On German policy, see John Horne and Alan Kramer, *German Atrocities, 1914: A History of Denial* (New Haven, Conn.: Yale University Press, 2001), 161–74; and Isabel Hull, *Absolute Destruction: Military Culture and the Practices of War in Imperial Germany* (Ithaca, N.Y.: Cornell University Press, 2005).

17. Public proclamation, 25 August/7 September 1914 (Rossiiskii gosudarstvennyi voenno-istoricheskii arkhiv [Russian State Military Historical Archive], Moscow [RGVIA], f. 2005 [Grazhdanskoe upravlenie pri Stavke], op. 1, d. 12, l. 21).

18. Ansky, *Enemy*, 272–273. For the German conflation of the East with pestilence and contamination, see Paul Weindling, *Epidemics and Genocide in Eastern Europe, 1890–1945* (New York: Oxford University Press, 2000).

19. This typology found in the official 1912 General Staff study: General Staff Colonel Samoilo with General Staff Colonel Pototskii, *Avstro-Vengriia: Voenno-statisticheskoe opisanie. Chast' 1: Vostochno-Galitskii raion* (St. Petersburg: Military Typography, 1912), 149–172; similar predictions in General Major Khristiani (Professor of the General Staff Academy), *Voennyi obzor Galitsiiskogo teatra* (St. Petersburg: Tipografiia Skachkova, 1910), 87–106 and the General Staff Colonel Kulzhinskii, *Sopredel'naia s Podoliei polosa Galitsii* (Kiev: Tipografiia Okruzhnogo shtaba, 1914), 17–20, 45.

20. Mr. Jonathan Pollock to Ambassador George Buchanan, July 31/13 August 1915 (NAUK FO 371/1915/vol. 2445/file 155/doc. 121172/pp. 301–309). Pollock's report is the most sensitive to Jewish suffering among all those submitted to the Foreign Office. It stands in stark contrast to the reports of Professor Bernard Pares, Stanley Washburn (reporter for *The Times*), and the British military attaché, General Knox, who all accepted the Russian army's accusations of "Jewish espionage" at face value.

21. "Letters from Galicia" (NAUK FO 371/1915/vol. 2445/file 155/doc. 124265/pp. 378–379).

22. Holquist, "Forms of Violence in the First (1914–1915) and Second (1916–1917) Russian Occupations of Galicia and Bukovina," conference paper for "The Degeneration of War, 1914–1945," Yale University, April 24–25, 2004.

23. "Dokladnaia zapiska Kamergera Bazili," 16 Sept. 1914 (RGVIA, f. 2005 [Grazhdanskoe upravlenie pri Stavke], op. 1, d. 13, ll. 6–8ob); Ianushkevich to Goremykin, 19 Sept. 1914 (Rossiiskii gosudarstvennyi istoricheskii arkhiv [Russian State Historical Archive], St. Petersburg [RGIA], f. 1276 [Sovet ministrov], op. 10, d. 895, ll. 29–31ob.). Both documents can be found in *Mezhdunarodnye otnosheniia v epokhu imperializma: Dokumenty iz arkhivov tsarskogo i vremennogo pravitel'stva, 1878–1917*, ed. M. N. Pokrovskii (Moscow: Gosizdat, 1931–1939), series III, vol. 6, pt. 1, docs. 338, 349.

24. Ianushkevich to Goremykin, 19 September 1914 (RGIA, f. 1276, op. 10, d. 895, ll. 29–31ob.); reproduced in *Mezhdunarodnye otnosheniia v epokhu imperializma*, III, 6, 1, doc. 349.

25. Grabar' diary, 21 August 1914 (l. 10) and 28 October 1914 (l. 54). Other references to the prevailing antisemitism of virtually everyone connected with General Headquarters: 14 October 1914; 6, 20, 23 November 1914 (ll. 44ob., 57, 62ob., 63ob.); 14 March 1915 (l. 83). Throughout his diary, Grabar' employs scare quotes around the term *zhidy*.

26. Viktor Petrovich Obninksii to the Constitutional Democratic Party Congress in June 1915, *S"ezdy i konferentsii konstitutsionno-demokraticheskoi partii*, ed. V. V. Shelokhaev, Vol. 3, book 1: *1915–1917gg.*, comp. and ed. O. N. Lezhava (Moscow: ROSSPEN,

2000]), 82. (Constitutional Democrat politicians had excellent contacts with certain progressive segments of the army).

27. V. P. Obninskii to the Constituational-Democratic Party Congress in June 1915 (Ivanov) (*S"ezdy, 1915–1917*, p. 82); Pollock to Buchanan (Evert) (NAUK FO 371/1915/vol. 2445/file 155/doc. 121172/pp. 301–309).

28. Martin Martinovich Ichas to the Constitutional Democratic Party Congress in June 1915: *S"ezdy, 1915–1917gg*. p. 85.

29. Collection of antisemitic decrees in the military (Gosudarstvennyi arkhiv Rossiiskoi Federatsii, Moscow [GARF], f. 579 [P. N. Miliukov], op. 1, d. 2009, l. 5). Among the soldiers in this division there happened to be many Russian Jews.

30. "Letters from Galicia" (NAUK FO 371/1915/vol. 2445/file 155/doc. 124265/ pp. 378–379).

31. "Letters from Galicia" (NAUK FO 371/1915/vol. 2445/file 155/doc. 124265/ pp. 378–379).

32. Ansky, *Enemy*, pp. 5, 4; also pp. 24, 116; M. M. Vinaver to Constitutional Democratic Party Congress (*S"ezdy, 1915–1917*, pp. 66–67).

33. Grabar' diary, 14 October 1914 (l. 45).

34. Pollock to Buchanan, (NAUK FO 371/1915/vol. 2445/file 155/doc. 121172/ pp. 301–309).

35. Grabar' diary, entries for 28 October; also 20 and 23 November 1914 (ll. 54, 62ob., 63ob.)

36. "D. V." [Dmitrii Vergun], "Galitskie nachinaniia," *Novoe vremia*, 10 December 1914.

37. Zapiska Chikhacheva, December 1914 (AVPRI, f. 135, op. 474 [Osobyi politicheskii otdel], d. 159, ll. 75–95); see also the discussion in Prusin, *Nationalizing*, 40 and Bakhturina, *Politika*, 68.

38. Lohr, *Nationalizing the Russian Empire*, ch. 5; Bakhturina, *Politika*, 187–202.

39. Arkadii Iakhontov, "Pervyi god voiny (iiul' 1914–iiul' 1915): Zapisi, zametki, materialy i vospominaniia byvshego pomoshchnika upravliaiushchego delami Soveta ministrov," *Russkoe proshloe* kn. 7 (1996), 245–348, here at 292; *Prologue to Revolution: Notes of A. N. Iakhontov on the Secret Meetings of the Council of Ministers, 1915*, ed. Michael Cherniavksy (Englewood Cliffs, N.J.: Prentice Hall, 1967), 56.

40. Murav'ev to [Kudashev], 21 September 1914 (AVPRI, f. 323, op. 617 [Diplomaticheskaia kantseliariia], d. 92, ll. 2–5).

41. Grabar' diary, entry for 12 October 1914 (l. 43.)

42. Murav'ev to Kudashev, [ca. 8 October 1914] (AVPRI, f. 323, op. 617 [Dipkantseliariia], d. 92, ll. 128–133).

43. Kudashev to MID, forwarding Murav'ev's telegram, 11 October 1914 (AVPRI, f. 133, op. 470 [Kantseliariia ministra], 1914, d. 367, l. 74; excerpt published in *Mezhdunarodnye otnosheniia*, III.6.1, doc. 412, n. 2).

44. Kudashev to Murav'ev, 12 October 1914 (AVPRI, f. 133, op. 470 [Kantseliariia ministra], 1914, d. 367, l. 75; also found in *Mezhdunarodnye otnosheniia*, III.6.1, doc. 412, n. 2).

45. Murav'ev to Sazonov, 13/26 October 1914 (AVPRI, f. 133, op. 470 [Kantseliariia MID], 1914, d. 389, l. 37; reprinted in *Mezhdunarodnye otnosheniia*, III.6.1, doc. 412).

46. Grabar' diary, entry for 12 October 1914 (l. 43).

47. "Otchet o poezdke v Bukovinu," 30 November 1914 (AVPRI, f. 323, op. 617 [Dipkantseliariia], d. 92, ll. 19–32ob.); "Zaniatie iuzhnoi Bukoviny," 1 Jan. 1915 (AVPRI, f. 323, op. 617 [Dipkantseliariia], d. 92, ll. 50–62ob.)

48. Kudashev to Sazonov, 18 December 1914 (Hoover Institution Archives, Nikolai A. Bazili Papers, Box 3: File "General Headquarters, 1914–1917: Correspondence").

49. "Zaniatie iuzhnoi Bukoviny," 1 January 1915 (AVPRI, f. 323, op. 617 [Dipkantse-liariia], d. 92, l. 62ob.), with Ianushkevich's marginal notation at bottom. Ianushkevich's literal expression was "drive all the Jews to the Swabians" [k shvabam].

50. Grabar' diary, entry for 14 March 1915 (l. 83).

51. Kudashev to MID, 25 January 1915, no. 47 (AVPRI, f. 133, op. 470 [Kantseliariia Ministra], 1915, d. 177, l. 16); Kudashev to Sazonov, 26 January 1915 Krasnyi arkhiv 1 (26) (1928): 48–49. These endorsements of Murav'ev's telegrams and memoranda come, significantly, several days after Ianushkevich's directive of 22 January to expel the Jews.

52. I quote from the order to the Ternopil' and Czernowicz governors [n.d.] (appendix 38 to Otchet kantseliarii voennogo general-gubernatorstva Galitsii za period s 28-ogo avgusta 1914 po 1–e iiulia 1915 [Kiev: {n.p.}, 1916]; also, p. 33); the date is provided by S. G. Nelipovich, "Naselenie okkupirovannykh territorii rassmatrivalos' kak rezerv protivnika: Internirovanie chasti zhitelei Vostochnoi Prussii, Galitsii, i Bukoviny v 1914–1915," Voenno-istoricheskii zhurnal, no. 2 (2000): 60–69, here at 64–65. This order was ubiquitous and there are numerous references to it. (Two such orders are translated in the Jewish Conjoint report to the FO: NAUK FO 371/1915/vol. 2445/file 155/doc. 124265/pp. 350–351, 353). Almost all studies of the deportations overlook the "preemptive reprisal" rationale and focus solely on the charge of Jewish espionage.

53. "V Bukovine," Armeiskii vestnik, 15 February 1915 (no. 81); "V Stanislavov," Armeiskii vestnik, 29 March 1915 (no. 98); see also identical charges in S.K., "S duklian-skogo perevala," Prikarpatskaia Rus': Organ Russkoi narodnoi Organizatsii v Galichine (L'vov), no. 1526 (13/26 January 1915), p. 1. Professor Pares made similar allegations of Austrian atrocities in his report to the FO: Sir Bernard Pares, "A Memorandum on Polish Affairs," 9/22 June 1915 (NAUK FO 371/1915/vol. 2445/file 155/109226/pp. 229–239). I am unable to judge the reliability of Russian reports of Austrian atrocities, as I know of no study of the conduct of the Austro-Hungarian army in Galicia. Tens of thousands of Ruthenians did flee when the Austrians returned.

54. Vasilii Vasil'evich Olfer'ev to M. F. Shilling (MID), 24 February 1915, no. 47 (AVPRI, f. 135, op. 474 [Osobyi Politicheskii Otdel], d. 170, ll. 13–14).

55. Reproduced in Nelipovich, "Naselenie," 65.

56. Ansky, Enemy, 75–76. Several officials at Headquarters complained that Bobrinskii was not sufficiently harsh; Grabar' himself described Bobrinskii as "cautious": entries for 5, 6 November 1914; 14 March 1915 (ll. 57ob., 83).

57. Ianushkevich to Bobrinskii, 1 February 1915; Bobrinskii to Ianushkevich, 3 February 1915 (RGVIA, f. 2005 [Grazhdanskoe upravlenie pri Stavke], op. 1, dl. 12, ll. 89, 90). In March, Ianushkevich again tried to press Bobrinskii into applying these directives more energetically: Ianushkevich to Bobrinskii, 19 March 1915 (RGVIA, f. 2005 [Grazhdanskoe upravlenie pri Stavke], op. 1, d. 12, ll. 110–112). Again, Bobrinskii declined.

58. Rech', 5/18 April 1915, no. 3115, p. 2.

59. Otchet kantseliarii, pp. 31–33 and appendices 31–36; Otchet general-gubernatora Galitsii po upravleniiu kraem za vremia s 1-ogo sentiabria 1914 po 1–e iiulia 1915 goda (Kiev: Tipografiia kievskogo voennogo okruga, 1916), 16.

60. Otchet general-gubernatora Galitsii, pp. 15–16. Ansky had great difficulty entering Galicia at all (Enemy, 10–11). This policy bears comparison with the German Verkehrspolitik in Ober-Ost: see Vejas Liulevicius, War Land on the Eastern Front: Culture, National Identity, and German Occupation in World War I (New York: Cambridge University Press, 2000).

61. This exchange is found in the files of the police department, responsible for transporting and interning these individuals: GARF, f. 102, II-oe deloproizvodstvo

[Departament politsii MVD], op. 71, d. 123. The Council of Ministers discussed the issue on 10 March: *Sovet ministrov Rossiiskoi imperii*, pp. 147–148, 181. For the continuing reverberations of this debate, see [Council of Ministers], "Memorandum" [on relations with Stavka] [ca. June 1915] (RGIA, f. 1276, op. 10, d. 723, ll. 121–131, here at 127); *Prologue*, esp. pp. 38–40, 56–64; and Lohr, *Nationalizing the Russian Empire*.

62. General Marvin to General Bobrinskii, 14 March 1915 (*Otchet kantseliarii*, pp. 32–33 and appendix 37); "Spravka" for Chair of the Council of Ministers (ca. June 1915) (RGIA, f.1276 [Sovet ministrov], op. 10, d. 723, ll. 121–131).

63. General Viranovski to General Lomonovskii, 27 May 1915; Brusilov to Bobrinskii, 7 June 1915 (RGVIA, f. 2134 [8 armiia], op. 1, d. 85, ll. 47, 49); *Otchet kantseliarii*, p. 53; *Prologue*, 39–40.

64. Provisional Government Commissar Doroshenko to MID, 22 August 1917 (GARF, f. 1779 [Kantseliariia Vremennogo Pravitel'stva], op. 1, d. 1499, l. 10); "Spravka o deiatel'nosti Grazhdanskoi kantseliarii pri Glavnokomanduiushchem armiiami Iugo-Zapadnogo front" (late 1917) (RGVIA, f. 2005 [Grazhdanskoe upravlenie pri Stavke], op. 1, d. 75, ll. 1–1ob.); Bakhturina, *Politika*, 187–189.

Freedom, Shortages, Violence: The Origins of the "Revolutionary Anti-Jewish Pogrom" in Russia, 1917–1918

VLADIMIR P. BULDAKOV

Conventional wisdom holds that pogroms and antisemitism in general were provoked by criminals or bigots belonging to the Black Hundreds (*Chernaia sotnia*) and carried out by the "ignorant masses" during the period when Russia was governed by liberals and socialists. In contrast, the present article attempts to show that after the February Revolution there was a widespread upsurge in ethnic hatred and antisemitism. The destructive processes unleashed in revolutionary times encompassed ethnic conflicts, among which anti-Jewish pogroms steadily gained prominence. In this connection, the author believes that it is essential to determine the actual relationship between the objective factors determining the level of revolutionary violence (including the extent to which it targeted specific ethnic groups) and the subjective attitudes of various social strata to antisemitism and antisemitic agitation.

Preferring to concentrate on the political forces "responsible" for pogroms, researchers have not yet undertaken any serious attempts at assessing the scale of "revolutionary" antisemitism.[1] Historians frequently attribute the absence of a general picture of 1917–1918 antisemitism to the lack of relevant data. It is apparent, however, that no data of this kind can exist at all: the judicial system was completely paralyzed, while local authorities simply did not have time to record all cases of disturbances. The most important source concerning this problem remains the newspapers, notwithstanding all their evident limitations in this respect.

The Scale and the Effect of Antisemitic Agitation

The situation that emerged after the fall of the autocracy was characterized not so much by an outburst of antisemitic agitation as by the fear of it, especially in socialist circles, which included many Jews.

With regard to antisemitic agitation, one must distinguish between targeted actions and a spontaneous proliferation of antisemitic propaganda. The former were attributed to the "supporters of the old regime," the latter to the "ignorant masses." But, in fact, both the old regime's lower-level officials and the masses were equally disoriented and, therefore, subconsciously aspired to reduce any causal relationships to a search for enemies of all kinds. It is natural that, in the atmosphere of mounting chaos, even the most improbable rumors could become prevalent.

Spontaneous antisemitic agitation gained a foothold in the army. In June and July 1917 attempts to revolutionize the soldiers in Petrograd and Moscow were accompanied by agitation for pogroms;[2] in July, hostility was displayed toward cadets of Jewish origin at the Aleksandrovskoe Military School in Moscow. Some frontline regiments adopted resolutions to the effect that no lower-ranking officers of Jewish descent would be accepted.[3] Naturally, the anti-Jewish appeals found a most receptive audience among the "interested" persons: in July, it was reported from Odessa that the soldiers being sent to the front were subject to Bolshevik agitation tinged with antisemitism; in August, an organization of guard officers agitating for pogroms was discovered in Kiev.[4]

In rural areas, recorded cases of antisemitic agitation were rare: in May they took place in Olgopol *uezd* (district) in Podolia *guberniia* (province) and in July in Mogilev *guberniia*.[5] In July it was reported from Minsk *guberniia* that a nineteen-year-old assistant secretary of one of the *volost* (county) committees was inciting the peasants against "the bourgeoisie and the Jews," promising that both would soon have their throats slit.[6] It was also reported in July that 5,140 copies of pamphlets calling for pogroms had been found in the warehouse of the Trinity Monastery.[7] The latter case was exceptional: generally, the clergy favored passive forms of antisemitism.[8] Usually agitation was of a situational nature, and therefore it is difficult to specify the persons involved. Appeals to the peasantry rested on fantastic fabrications rather than political rhetoric, which they barely comprehended. For example, in August 1917, one of a number of leaflets distributed in the Mozhaisk *uezd* of Moscow *guberniia* spoke of the need to "overthrow the yoke of the socialist ministers, servants of Rothschild and Wilhelm," while another called for secret societies to fight against "German and Jewish dominance."[9] It is difficult to identify the circles that produced these texts. Nevertheless, it is worth mentioning that a "Slavic Group" engaging in antisemitic propaganda emerged among students in Yaroslavl in June and dispatched agitators to the villages.[10]

Large cities became centers of antisemitism. From March 1917 incitement of pogroms in Petrograd steadily increased,[11] and in July respectable people there were calling for a massacre of "Yids."[12] This activity took place in the city center and in squares adjacent to railway stations.[13] In August, several persons were arrested for inciting pogroms.[14] From early April 1917 similar incitements were reported in Moscow.[15] In August, people in breadlines were affirming that "the Yids have hidden the grain" in secret warehouses,[16] and antisemitic remarks were not uncommon even in discussions at the Moscow Soviet.[17]

In the provinces, antisemitism assumed undisguised forms. In July, leaflets calling for the eradication of the Jews were being distributed in Simferopol on behalf of a certain "Red Glove" organization.[18] The most diverse strata of the population, including local authorities, engaged in both deliberate and unpremeditated incitement. In July, the press reported on the existence of antisemitic sentiments among the local militia in Tiumen.[19] In September "anti-Ukrainian" and pro-monarchist antisemitic leaflets were distributed in Kiev,[20] while a "Society of the Brown Hand" posted leaflets on the walls in Orel calling for pogroms.[21]

In August, reports from Odessa noted some instances of priests addressing their parishioners with "counterrevolutionary preaching." Charges were made that the city food agency "as it is composed of Jews, is selling confiscated flour to speculators."[22] In autumn 1917, the cry that "the Yids are hiding foodstuffs and closing the shops" grew louder by the day.[23] There were attempts to organize pogroms in connection with Jewish or Christian holidays. Accounts noted that incitement had been carried out "in the assembly-house of the People's State Party [*Narodno-gosudarstvennaia partiia*]," and that an organization preparing a pogrom under the guise of a "struggle against the bourgeoisie" had been exposed.[24]

Various political forces actively promoted the antisemitic cause. In July, the Petrograd newspaper *Den'* cited a number of passages from the newspaper *Groza* calling for anti-Jewish pogroms and for the conclusion of a separate peace.[25] *Rassvet* reported that a Bolshevik speaker in Moscow asserted that the Mensheviks had sold themselves to the bourgeoisie and had united with the "Yid-socialists."[26] In November 1917, the writer Ilya Ehrenburg, while standing in a food queue with a number of ordinary Muscovites, witnessed an unconcealed form of agitation with respect to the election to the Constituent Assembly: "Those who are against the Yids—vote for list No. 5; those who are for the world revolution—vote for list No. 5" (Bolshevik).[27]

After the Bolsheviks seized power in Petrograd, antisemitic voices emerged not only from the ranks of the unemployed (who were saying "only Yids sit on the soviets") but also from the workers of the Putilov plant.[28] There were more than enough antisemites among the Bolsheviks. In Cherepovets, the Bolshevik leader Bashmakov constantly brandished a revolver and shouted: "Kill the Yids, save Russia!"[29] An investigation into the causes of the May 1918 pogrom in Smolensk revealed that some Red Army instructors had formed an organization preparing "a St. Bartholomew's Massacre" for the Jews.[30] The Soviet sources admitted that the cause of a peasant uprising that took place in Tambov *guberniia* in the autumn of 1918 had been rumors that confiscated foodstuffs were being transported to Germany in sealed freight cars, while the whole of Russia had become a colony lorded over by the Germans and Jews.[31]

The anti-Bolshevik forces seized upon the "Jewish-Bolshevik" theme in 1918. For example, in the south of Russia, a leaflet appeared that castigated "the wretched Yid-commissars" who desecrated icons.[32] Prior to the opening of the State Council at Ufa, Bishop Andrei Ukhtomskii rebuked the audience for having forgotten the Lord's commandments and replaced them with the commandments of "the German Jew Marx."[33] However, even without such sermons the common people were sure that the Jews had taken over all well-paid posts in Bolshevik Russia.[34]

In general, the antisemitic incitement of revolutionary times can hardly be characterized as planned and coherent. It derived more from an upsurge of prejudice than from the actions of certain political groups. On the other hand, "internationalist" counterpropaganda clearly failed to reach all the social spaces where spontaneous antisemitic notions were spreading.

Criminality and Ethnic Violence

A necessary precondition to pogrom situations is a high level of aggression within the social environment. The force of previous examples is also extremely important. The influence of criminals must not be underestimated in this context.

Ordinarily, criminal groups are either "international" or monoethnic: in the first, outcasts from many nationalities form groups that prey on all sectors of society. In the second, individuals of one nationality band together and tend to victimize their own co-nationals. In periods of instability, the ethnic patterns of criminality change in accordance with the vectors of social discontent: criminals have the option of disguising themselves as revolutionary "avengers," and the direction of their activity adjusts to society's concepts concerning hostility toward one or another ethnic group. A typical criminal/revolutionary case occurred during the February Revolution. Three sailors killed a lawyer named Shlozberg, possibly for being a member of the bourgeoisie. Later, in September 1917, when the case was being prepared for consideration at a court of justice, the accused rejected the services of Jewish lawyers and demanded instead that "true Orthodox defenders" be appointed.[35]

In 1917, the frequency of instances in which Jews were robbed by soldiers, deserters, or criminal elements posing as such was steadily on the rise. Most commonly, these robberies took place at railway stations.[36] Ekaterinoslav *guberniia* was notorious for assaults on Jews.[37] It should be noted, however, that Jews were not only the victims of robberies; they were also some of the perpetrators. For example, the well-known bandit Rabinovich-Goldstein was killed as he was being chased after committing a robbery.[38]

The scale of robberies was related to the view that Jews were getting richer through speculation, and in general, always had large sums of money in their pockets. In 1918, the Whites accused Jews of "speculating in government property bought for kopecks from the Germans." The Whites also maintained that Jews were falsely labeling them as antisemites.[39] Nevertheless, the press usually preferred to ignore such accusations for the sake of political correctness.

As the revolution progressed, Jews were increasingly the victims of robberies. The cruelty of the perpetrators simultaneously intensified.[40] In 1918, the geography of criminality widened (irrespective of the political affiliation of local authorities), and robberies became more targeted. In some places a certain symbiosis of pure criminality and "ideologically" motivated expropriation emerged.[41] Nevertheless, there is no direct correlation between the activities of criminals and the number of pogroms. The development of criminality had its own "professional" logic, usually quite remote from planned pogrom actions.

Soldiers and Antisemitism

In 1917–1918, soldiers and demobilized soldiers remained the most aggressive element of society. The organizing of pogroms and their participation in "ordinary" disturbances were equally significant. Soldiers typically rejected the idea that the principles of equal rights and liabilities should be extended to Jews. Jewish soldiers were frequently arrested on the pretext that Jews had no place inside the Russian army. Usually, army organizations passed resolutions condemning such actions.[42] In July 1917, one of the battalion committees in Odessa even passed an antisemitic resolution concerning the return of Jews to their former places of service.[43] The prospect of Jews as army officers evoked even stronger displeasure.[44]

The first anti-Jewish actions on the part of soldiers were the destruction of wine cellars. Such acts were especially widespread in the summer and autumn of 1917 in Bessarabia and Ekaterinoslav *guberniias*.[45] Soldiers engaged in equally intensive "revolutionary" antisemitic activity with respect to spontaneous, as well as authorized, searches for concealed foodstuffs. This activity was most pronounced at the end of the summer and in the autumn of 1917 in Podolia, Kharkov, and Ekaterinoslav *guberniias*, where Jewish merchants were blamed for raising prices, selling substandard goods, and even hiding merchandise at cemeteries.[46] In autumn 1917, authorized searches for hidden foodstuffs in Kishinev degenerated into the wrecking of Jewish wine cellars and were accompanied by antisemitic agitation. The soldiers beat up the mayor and the committee members who tried to stop the disturbances.[47]

It is believed that the first major anti-Jewish pogrom, which was perpetrated by soldiers in June 1917 in Kalush during the retreat from Galicia, was not directly connected to any food shortages. Widespread participation in the pogrom forced the army command to take drastic measures against the culprits, some of whom were executed by firing squads. Organizations of Jewish fighters, for their part, began to form self-defense units.[48] In autumn 1917 soldiers actively participated in bread riots and drunken riots that tended to turn into antisemitic actions. On 23 October, during a pogrom in the town of Skvir, several Jewish shops were wrecked, and windows in a number of houses were broken. It is worth noting that the *guberniia* commissar intended to dispatch detachments of Cossacks and cuirassiers to Skvir, but the local Soviet of Peasant Deputies vetoed his decision on the grounds that the soldiers would once again cause "anarchy and rioting."[49]

In general, despite the soldiers' noticeable presence in most of the pogroms, their participation is still best characterized as part of the extreme universal aggressiveness of the "man with a gun" rather than a uniquely antisemitic feature.

The Limits of Peasant Antisemitism

In 1917 and especially in 1918–1921, the peasantry demonstrated revolting and primitive patterns of social violence. Their social struggle was usually directed against a certain targeted enemy, although all sorts of "aliens" also fell under suspicion. The peasants' standard practice was to seize agricultural land and to cut down forests. Sometimes it was the Jewish tenants who suffered the most. There were attempts to organize pogroms at fairs,[50] and in July 1917, a number of villages in Ekaterinoslav *guberniia* passed resolutions that prohibited Jews from living in rural settlements.[51] In the autumn, village assemblies started to adopt resolutions that forbade the sale of essential commodities to Jews.[52] The peasant labor ethics had apparently clashed with a "different" way of life, and they perceived nonagrarian forms of vital activity as "parasitic." Under the influence of such perceptions, peasants (as well as ordinary residents of small towns) were unwilling to tolerate the "preponderance" of Jews in the *zemstvo* system of local administration.[53]

The peasants characteristically tried to gain support from third parties for their anti-Jewish activities. They frequently found this support in food committees, district commissars, and even local militia and police in addition to soldiers.[54] The "agrarian antisemitism" of the peasantry could easily turn against any authorities, and could manifest itself even in localities where there were no Jews. Thus, on 10 December 1917, peasants of Semenkovsk *volost* of Vologda *uezd* disrupted a community assembly after becoming enraged because instead of icons, a portrait featuring the "Jewish snout of Lenin" hung over the rostrum. The background for such behavior was Bolshevik requisitions.[55]

Peasant antisemitism remained part of their hostile conceptions concerning "aliens" who were the bearers of urban culture. But, at the same time, peasants' participation in anti-Jewish pogroms was opportunist rather than principled, because they treated all "aliens" with suspicion (especially when the latter were "incomprehensible"). Henceforth, their identification of Bolsheviks with "Yids" became a consistent feature.

The Townsman's Open and "Secret" Enemies

The townsmen were the clearest enemy of Jewry, with their antisemitic prejudices intertwined with economic interests. Urban antisemitism was reinforced by newcomers from the village and soldiers who were rooted in traditional culture. The conditions of social and political turmoil inevitably exacerbated the situation. The decisive role in the process was played by interruptions in supplies of essential commodities to the population.

Conflicts related to food and clothing shortages occurred as early as 1915, but their anti-Jewish bias became especially clear from the summer of 1917. In June there was a pogrom in a Petrograd suburb, provoked by rumors that merchants were sending footwear (which was in short supply) to Finland, and a number of Jewish-owned shops were looted.[56] As a rule, ordinary townsmen did not understand specific aspects of Jewish economic life. In July, in the town of Rezhitsa in Vitebsk *guberniia,* a cart of flour donated to a canteen for refugee children was commandeered by a mob shouting: "The Yids are removing flour, while the population starves."[57]

Bread riots began to degenerate into pogroms in August 1917. Thus, in Petrograd, after finding some hidden leather and butter, a mob started to menace all tradesmen. A deputy commissar who was trying to calm down the crowd was severely beaten up. The mob also beat up a Jew who attempted to protect this official.[58] On 22 August, the conflict caused by the sale of leather goods flared up again. Several Jews were manhandled despite many attempts by the militia to rescue them.[59] In Moscow, numerous conflicts took place on 22–23 August: a number of shops were looted, Jews were beaten, and there were clashes with the militia.[60]

A similar situation could be observed in Ukrainian cities and towns. On 2 August, in Chernigov, there was unrest among women assembled at the doors of the city food agency. The head of the local militia, Iankelevich, managed to placate the crowd, but was arrested for unknown reasons by soldiers who arrived there. Soldiers from a Ukrainian reserve regiment saved him from being lynched by the crowd.[61] In early August a food committee in Odessa received letters threatening an anti-Jewish pogrom if the price of bread was raised.[62] Under such conditions, even an insignificant conflict could provoke massive disturbances.

Antisemitism was linked to politics. In September in the town of Soroki in Bessarabia *guberniia,* people from the suburbs dispersed the city duma because it included representatives of the Jewish population.[63] On October 8, 1917, the commissariat in Odessa was besieged by Haidamaks (Ukrainian soldiers) shouting "Down with the Yid militia!" A representative of one Ukrainian organization barely managed to dissuade them from lynching the Jewish militiamen and starting a pogrom.[64]

In September, a local bread riot in Tambov was mistaken for an anti-Jewish pogrom because public anger spilled onto the streets on the night when Yom Kippur (the Day of Atonement) was being observed. The disturbances were sparked by the discovery of a barrel of rotten fish. As a result, all Jewish stores and refugees' shops in the city center were looted and wrecked. Jewish circles characterized the pogrom as anti-Jewish, whereas the local press, on the contrary, denied that it was of a specifically ethnic nature. Later, the Zionist newspaper *Rassvet* received a letter from its own correspondent that stated, with proper apologies, that the pogrom was not specifically anti-Jewish but general, and that in its course even large Russian shops had also suffered.[65]

In 1917, the urban dwellers believed that tradesmen and speculators were prominent among their major foes (alongside the "bourgeois" class). To be sure, the proportion of Jews in both categories was relatively high; in any case, the urban population was prone to shift the burden of social guilt onto the "aliens," that is, chiefly the Jews. Society generally tolerated the idea that any manifestation of dissatisfaction concerning an acute shortage of goods could "naturally" result in outrages against Jews. Thus, Russia entered the phase of "revolutionary" pogroms.

Bolshevik attacks on the Orthodox Church during 1918 stimulated pogromist attitudes. The adversaries of the Bolsheviks opportunistically used this factor for their own interests. But on the whole, at that time no authorities favored pogroms because they might further destabilize the situation and were totally uncontrollable.

The Development of Pogrom Actions

The number of major anti-Jewish pogroms in 1917 was relatively small; in any case, the so-called drunken pogroms were incomparably more numerous. The number of pogroms rose significantly in 1918 but apparently did not exceed the level of the years 1905–1907.

After the Kalush pogrom, other major pogroms took place in Ukraine. Most were directly connected to shortages of goods and food. On 12 September, seven freight cars with goods were looted in Kiev; then at Vladimir market, the crowd rushed into Eppelbaun's shop, looted it, and killed the female owner. Some workers, who were also members of a militia patrol, opened fire, but were disarmed and beaten up.[66] The Kharkov riots of 27 September were preceded by appeals spread in breadlines to topple the existing regime and to start an anti-Jewish pogrom. The mob subsequently attempted to loot a warehouse, in the course of which a person named Morein was lynched after being repeatedly thrown into the air and smashed against the pavement. He was finished off by a soldier who slit the victim's throat with a saber. From the city center, the looters proceeded to a wine cellar, where they were dispersed by machine-gun bursts.[67] A rumor that four hundred pairs of galoshes had been discovered at the Jewish trader Myshlaevskii's shop sparked a pogrom in Roslavl in Smolensk *guberniia* on 2 October. People started to search for the galoshes, other shops were looted, and the militia was beaten up. The outrage was accompanied by shouts: "Beat the Yids, traders, and the militia!" A Bolshevik named Nosov, who was a member of the local Soviet, was forced to shoot into the crowd, and then had to run for his life into Levenson's shop. Failing to catch him, the mob manhandled two Jews and tried to throw them from a bridge into the river. As a result of the disturbances, two people were killed and nearly twenty injured.[68] A press item stated that a pogrom took place in Starosiniavy in Podolia *guberniia* during October;[69] according to unconfirmed reports, a pogrom also occurred in Edintsy in Bessarabia *guberniia*.[70] A new wave of pogroms arose after the Bolshevik coup d'etat. Thus, in December 1917–January 1918, soldiers together with the local population reportedly carried out pogroms in Bograd in Bessarabia *guberniia* and in Mozyr *uezd* of Minsk *guberniia*.[71]

Sometimes the pogroms were thwarted by Jewish self-defense units. After the pogrom on 16 December 1917, which took place in Ovruch in Kiev *guberniia*, the local council of Jewish fighters formed a self-defense detachment, which then repulsed several assaults of local looters. Later this detachment helped to stop pogroms in Norinka, Slovechno, and other settlements.[72]

Gradually, pogroms began to acquire the "classical" features of violence against the defenseless. Especially prominent in this respect were the actions of Baltic sailors dispatched to Kilija in Bessarabia *guberniia* in late December. For three days in a row, the town was looted and burned, and local residents started to flee in order to save their lives. Some thugs proceeded to the neighboring Vilkovo, but encountered resistance there.[73] Apparently the sailors had intended to deliver a strike against local "counterrevolutionaries," but the brunt of it fell on local Jews.

In January 1918, some of the pogroms were related to the increased activity of Ukrainian nationalists[74] who also considered themselves revolutionaries. In mid-January, they initiated an anti-Jewish pogrom in Bratslav in Podolia *guberniia*, which was accompanied by lootings, arsons, and sporadic gunfire. There were a number of dead and wounded.[75] Even more bloodshed resulted from clashes between the Soviet and Ukrainian forces in Kiev. On 20 January, the "Ukrainians" arrested some members of the First All-Russian Congress of Jewish Fighters, and I. Ia. Gogol, one of the organizers of the Ukrainian Union of Jewish Fighters, was shot. In addition, both "Ukrainian" and Red Army soldiers broke into apartments in search of weapons and enemies, shooting all whom they deemed "guilty" in the process. On the night of 19–20 January, a number of Jewish shops were looted in various parts of the city. In total, more than one hundred

Jews were killed, apparently mostly by irregulars. Both the Central Rada and the victorious Bolsheviks proved unable to stop the atrocities.[76] In early March the events in Kiev followed the same scenario: when the city was being taken by the German-Ukrainian forces, the Haidamaks arrested and shot their victims under the slogan "Let us butcher all the Yids." Later, twenty-two bodies of Jews were collected from Vladimir Hill (Vladimirskaia Gorka) alone.[77]

It was not only armed bands identifying themselves as either Bolsheviks or Ukrainians that carried out pogrom violence in those months. For example, in early March in Dmitriev in Kursk *guberniia,* after a church service, a large crowd of churchgoers surrounded the building of the local commissariat and started to shout: "Beat the Yids and the commissars. Save Russia!" In the subsequent attack, Commissar Ageikin was killed.[78] This case was not unique—practically all anti-Bolshevik actions adopted antisemitic rhetoric.

The largest pogrom took place in Glukhov, Chernigov *guberniia*. It began at 5 PM on 7 March 1918; subsequently, for two-and-a-half days, the town was at the mercy of an enraged mob. Almost every schoolboy was killed and not even twelve-year-olds were spared. Men were taken from their homes, beaten with the butts of rifles, stabbed, or shot. Peasants from neighboring villages removed the loot in wagons. The pogrom was carried out under the slogan "Surrender all weapons! We are going to slaughter all the bourgeoisie and the Yids!" Afterwards, four hundred bodies of those shot and hacked to death were buried at the city cemetery. It was believed that retreating Soviet forces perpetrated the pogrom.[79]

Usually, the opposing parties either blamed each other for the pogroms or ascribed them to a third factor—"criminal elements." In reality, all three engaged in looting. In the first half of March 1918, "a band of hooligans" tried to start a pogrom in Fastov, but Red Guards stopped the disturbances.[80] In Kremenchug, after the Bolshevik retreat and the arrival of "Ukrainians," the city riffraff headed by local students attacked a synagogue and then proceeded to beat and kill Jews. After the Reds recaptured the city the outrages ended.[81] A pogrom with a number of fatalities reportedly took place in Gogolevo in Chernigov *guberniia* on 21 March. In Medvin, Kiev *guberniia,* local peasants "distinguished" themselves by burning shops and goods.[82]

In April 1918 the redeployment of large groups of armed men was accompanied by pogrom activity. Along the Kiev–Poltava railway line, there were incessant lootings, robberies, murders, and other acts of violence, perpetrated either by Haidamaks disembarking from the passing military trains or by local brigands.[83] In early April, in Novgorod-Severskii, "a band of Black Guards and sailors" numbering six hundred men, carried out an anti-Jewish pogrom. During three or four hours, the town was ransacked, and fifty-seven persons were killed (other sources cite sixty-two deaths). Neighboring small settlements experienced similar devastation: in Svirzh four persons were killed, in Grints there were fifteen murders, and in Sardinia Buda there were fourteen. Local peasants were among the participants in the pogroms.[84] In Radomysl, Kiev *guberniia*, peasants carried out a pogrom and fifteen persons perished.[85]

Bolshevik leaders repeatedly declared their intention to put an end to pogroms, but usually there was insufficient military force available to achieve this aim. On 29 April 1918, the eve of the Orthodox Easter, there were rumors in Vitebsk that all stocks of flour had already been consumed in the course of Passover. A mob started to loot and wreck Jewish shops and the militia did not interfere. The next day, a crowd of women went to wreck the food agency. Margolin, an employee of the food department, was beaten up. The militia again remained passive and the looters dispersed only when an armored car arrived on the scene.[86] On the night of 15 May, two companies of armed Red soldiers took to the streets of Smolensk, demanding the removal of Jews from their posts as "commissars and leaders." The menacing situation in the city continued for two days.[87]

In Mglin, Chernigov *guberniia*, an anti-Bolshevik action took place at a peasant assembly, and the chairman of the village executive committee, Shimanovskii, was killed. In order to suppress the disturbances, a punitive group was dispatched to the town. The soldiers started a pogrom, in the course of which fifteen Jews were massacred. The situation got so far out of control that one of the commanders shot two soldiers on the spot but then had to run for his life from his own troops.[88]

Many pogroms took place as the Red Army abandoned territories ceded to the Germans in accordance with the Brest-Litovsk peace treaty signed in March 1918. A report from Novgorod-Severskii stated, "For two months in a row, the local population has been terrorized by Bolshevik bands."[89] In May, in Surazh in Chernigov *guberniia*, Red Army soldiers turned their rifles against a Jewish self-defense force and embarked on "destroying Jewish houses and apartments" in order to punish "counterrevolutionaries."[90] At the railway station of Zernovo, Chernigov *guberniia*, during a retreat from Konotop to Briansk, the special Red Army unit under the command of Afanasy Remniev carried out a pogrom in which twenty Jews were killed and nineteen wounded.[91] Jews had to rely only on themselves. When abandoning Gomel, Red Army soldiers also tried to start a pogrom, but self-defense detachments killed several looters, and the rest of them fled.[92]

The withdrawal of German troops at the end of World War I contributed to a fresh wave of pogroms. In November, in Iampol, Ukraine, Austrian soldiers looted and damaged several Jewish shops and apartments. The Ukrainian *varta* (police) stopped the pogrom, opening fire on the Austrians.[93] Shortly afterwards, pro-Petliura rebels carried out pogroms in Belaia Tserkov' and Fastov.[94] Supporters of Makhno also became active. In Ekaterinoslav alone they looted nearly 500 shops and the number of deaths amounted to 1,200.[95] The situation inside Bolshevik-controlled Russia was equally grim. On 5 December 1918, a Red Army detachment was sent to quell an anti-Jewish pogrom in Dukhovshchina in Smolensk *guberniia* but instead joined the rioters. According to "White" sources, many people were killed or wounded.[96] Thus, by the end of 1918, revolutionary pogroms had acquired the qualitatively new character of actions that were carried out primarily by demoralized soldiers. Pogroms adopted the "classical form" of unrestrained massacres and looting of the defenseless.

The Specific Features of a "Revolutionary" Pogrom

In Russia, the "revolutionary" anti-Jewish pogroms during 1917–1918 constituted two major types: those that were a part of bread riots, and those carried out by masses of demoralized soldiers or retreating revolutionary detachments.

Antisemitic rumors played a significant role in inciting pogroms. Their importance was due to a number of factors. First, antisemitism was steadily gaining ground in educated society in 1917; even some university professors succumbed to it.[97] Second, the lower strata of society began to attribute their woes to the alleged perfidious activities of various "enemies." Third, the public appeal of "internationalist" pathos had not lasted long, and political parties started to resort to the "banned" weapon of ethnic hatred. Finally, having lost the former logical and moral guidelines, all strata of society became more or less infected with spontaneous nationalism.

The pogroms in Russia in 1917 differed from the earlier ones of the 1880s[98] and 1905–1907[99] and from the later wave of 1919–1920.[100] Pogroms, like all other types of disturbances, were mostly spontaneous and impulsive by nature. They usually occurred as a continuation of bread and "drunken" pogroms, and less frequently as a continuation of land seizures by the peasants. It is noteworthy that in 1918 pogroms were more systematically organized in Galician cities and towns than elsewhere. The pattern would always be the same: mobs made up of Polish women would assemble in front of Jewish shops to demand a discount, then some agitators would appear on the scene, blaming the speculators and, finally, a pogrom would start, with the active participation of hastily arriving soldiers and students.[101] In Russia, it was usually much more difficult to identify the actual instigators.

Pogroms were centered in both large cities and small towns, especially within the Pale of Settlement. As a rule, there were no apparent religious motives for them and only under the Bolshevik regime were antisemitic feelings noticeable in the course of some religious processions.

It is difficult to determine the total number of antisemitic excesses during 1917–1918. My database includes almost 1,350 ethnic conflicts. Anti-Jewish actions constitute approximately 25 percent of them, that is, more than 320 cases (antisemitic agitation, personal crimes, and collective violence). About 90 of these were full-scale pogroms. Most of them took place from August to October 1917 and from March to May 1918.

In general, pogroms of the years 1917–1918 were far less organized than anti-Jewish actions carried out in 1905–1907.[102] Frequently, these later pogroms were just ugly outbursts of social despair, "the aggression of impotence." There was nothing, of course, specifically revolutionary in the "revolutionary" pogrom, representing the "darkest" and most irrational aspect of Russian sociorevolutionary destructiveness.

Notes

In this chapter, the term *revolutionary anti-Jewish pogrom* will be applied to any violent action against Jews that took place at the time of the 1917 Revolution. The choice of this chronological framework has also been motivated by the fact that the antisemitic excesses in 1917–1918 represent the least analyzed subject in the existing literature on the problem.

1. Relying solely on "reliable" archival sources, the Ukrainian historian Volodymyr Serhiichuk sought to reveal those persons "really" responsible for the pogroms in his book, *Pohromi v Ukraïni, 1914–1920: Vid shtuchnykh stereotypiv do hirkoï pravdi, prikhovuvanoï v radians'kykh arkhivakh* (Kyiv: Vydavnitstvo imeni Oleny Telihy, 1998).

2. Mikhail Frenkin, *Russkaiia armiia i revoliutsiia. 1917–1918* (Munich: Logos, 1978), 54; Michael Beizer, *Evrei Leningrada, 1917–1959: Natsional'naia zhizn' i sovetizatsiia* (Jerusalem-Moscow: Mosty kul'tury, 1999), 43.

3. *Rassvet,* no. 1, 9 July 1917, 32; *Rassvet,* no. 2, 16 July 1917, 35.

4. *Rassvet,* no. 2, 16 July 1917, 35; no. 1, 9 July 1917, 33; no. 7, 20 August 1917, 32.

5. Gosudarstvennyi arkhiv rossiiskoi federatsii (State Archive of the Russian Federation) (GARF), f. 1791, op. 2, d. 219, l. 37; op. 6. d. 271, l. 4.

6. GARF, f. 1791, op. 6, d. 250, l. 137.

7. *Rassvet,* no. 3, 23 July 1917, 34; no. 7, 30 August 1917, 30; *Evreiskaia nedelia,* no. 30, 30 July 1917, 21.

8. Sviashchennik [Priest] Aleksandr P. Mramornov, *Sochineniia 1896–1919 gg.: zapiski, eparkhial'nye khroniki, publitsistika* (Saratov: Nauchnaia kniga, 2005), 288–289.

9. GARF, f. 1791, op. 6, d. 21, l. 88.

10. *Russkaia volia*, 29 July 1917; *Rassvet*. no. 1, 9 July 1917, 55, no. 3, 34.

11. See *Raionnye Sovety Petrograda v 1917 godu. Protokoly, rezoliutsii, postanovleniia obshchikh sobranii i zasedanii Ispolnitel'nykh komitetov*, vol. 35 (Moscow: Politizdat, 1966), 270; *Izvestiia*, 19 July 1917.

12. *Rassvet*, no. 2, 16 July 1917, 35.

13. Beizer, *Evrei Leningrada*, 43.

14. *Rassvet*, no. 7, 30 August 1917, 32.

15. *Russkie vedomosti*, 9 April 1917.

16. *Utro Rossii*, 23 August 1917; *Russkaia volia*, 25 August 1917.

17. GARF, f. 1791, op. 6, d. 272, l. 24; d. 22, l. 125; d. 272, l. 25.

18. *Russkoe slovo*, 17 July 1917.

19. *Rassvet*, no. 3, 23 July 1917, 34.

20. *Rassvet*, no. 9, 6 September 1917, 24; *Russkoe slovo*, 16 September 1917.

21. *Rassvet*, no. 13, 4 October 1917, 35; *Oktiabr'skii perevorot* (Petrograd: Novaia epokha, 1918), 74.

22. *Rassvet*, no. 2, 16 July 1917, 35; no. 4–5, 6 August 1917, 50; *Den'*, 30 August 1917.

23. *Iuzhnaia mysl'*, 14 September 1917.

24. *Narodnyi tribun*, 19 September 1917; *Rabochaia gazeta*, 4 October 1917; *Russkoe slovo*, 24 September 1917.

25. *Den'*, 7 June 1917.

26. *Rassvet*, no. 1, 9 July 1917, 31.

27. Il'ia Ehrenburg, *Dai oglianut'sia . . . Pis'ma, 1908–1950 gg.* (Moscow: Agraf, 2004), 85.

28. *Rassvet*, no. 14, 21 April 1918, 22–23; no. 18, 26 May 1918, 22; *Kazanskoe slovo*, 15 May 1918; *Rassvet*, no. 20, 9 June 1918, 30–31.

29. Vologskii oblastnoi arkhiv noveishei politicheiskoi istorii (Vologda Oblast Archive of Modern Political History) (VOANPI), f. 6350, op. 1, d. 21, ll. 5–6; d. 24, ll. 21–21ob.

30. *Svobodnaia Rossiia*, 22 May 1918; *Rassvet*, no. 20, 9 June 1918, 30–31.

31. GARF, f. 130, op. 2, d. 434, l. 2ob.

32. GARF, f. A-353, op. 2, d. 717, l, 1.

33. *Zavolzhskii letopisets*, 15 September 1918.

34. *A Russian Civil War Diary: Alexis Babine in Saratov, 1917–1922* (Durham, N.C.: Duke University Press, 1988), 125–128.

35. *Rassvet*, no. 10–11, 20 September 1917, 37.

36. GARF, f. 1791, op. 2, d. 219, l. 35, 43; op. 6, d. 250, l. 12.

37. GARF, f. 1791, op. 6, d. 240a, l. 15, 22, 71; d. 413, ll. 29ob, 87.

38. GARF, f. 1791, op. 6, d. 413, l. 87.

39. GARF, f. 446, op. 2, d. 46, ll. 18, 69.

40. GARF, f. 1791, op. 6, d. 272, l. 146; d. 396, l. 10; *Vydrodzhennia*, 9 June 1918; *Kievskaia mysl'*, 11 June 1918, 31 October 1918; *Russkie vedomosti*, 21 October 1917; Valerii V. Kanishchev, *Russkii bunt—bessmyslennyi i besposhchadnyi. Pogromnoe dvizhenie v gorodakh Rossii v 1917–1918 gg.* (Tambov: Tambovskii gosudarstvennyi universitet, 1995), 86.

41. *Kievskaia mysl'*, 16 July 1918; 24 August 1918; 1 November 1918; 30 November 1918.

42. Frenkin, *Russkaia armiia i revoliutsiia*, 251.

43. *Rassvet*, no. 7, 30 August 1917, 32.

44. *Evreiskaia zhizn'*, no. 18, 1917, 37; GARF, f. 2315, op. 1, d. 21, ll. 63–63ob.

45. GARF, f. 1791, op. 2, d. 171, l. 62, 64; *Oktiabr'skii perevorot* (Petrograd: Novaia Epokha, 1918), 75; *Russkie vedomosti*, 25 October 1917.

46. GARF, f. 1791, op. 6, d. 272, l. 2, 27; d. 460, l. 67; d. 381, ll. 18, 25; *Utro Rossii*, 23 August 1917; *Trud*, 16 September 1917; *Rassvet*, no. 7, 20 August 1917, 32; no. 10–11, 20 September 1917, 37; no. 14, 11 October 1917, 36; *Russkie vedomosti*, 23 October 1917.

47. GARF, f. 1791, op. 2, d. 171, l. 98; *Rassvet*, no. 15, 18 October 1917, 34.

48. Isaak Shteinberg. *Ot fevralia po oktiabr' 1917g.* (Berlin-Milan: Skify, [n. d.]), 60; *Den'*, 22 July 1917; *Rassvet*, no. 4–5, 6 August 1917, 50; *Zemlia*, 8 August 1917.

49. Serhiichuk, *Pohromi v Ukraïni*, 157–158.

50. *Rassvet*, no. 4–6, 6 August 1917, 49.

51. *Rassvet*, no. 3, 23 July 1917, 34.

52. *Svobodnaiia Bessarabiia*, 22 September 1917; *Rassvet*, no. 12, 1917, 27 September 1917, 36.

53. *Novoe vremia*, 4 October 1917.

54. Rossiiskii gosudarstvennyi voenno-istoricheskii arkhiv (Russian State Military Historical Archive) (RGVIA), f. 2067, op. 1, d. 22, l. 65; Serhiichuk, *Pohromi v Ukraïni*, 446; *Rassvet*, no. 15, 18 October 1917, 32.

55. VOANPI, f. 3837, op. 1, d. 39, l. 32.

56. *Evreiskaia zhizn'*, no. 23 (1917), 38.

57. *Rassvet*, no. 2, 16 July 1917, 30–31.

58. GARF, f. 1791, op. 6, d. 271, l. 37.

59. *Rassvet*, no. 7, 30 August 1917, 32.

60. *Rassvet*, no. 8, 30 August 1917, 33; no. 9, 6 September 1917, 24; no. 10–11, 20 September 1917, 37; *Russkie vedomosti*, 23 August 1917; GARF, f. 1791. op. 6, d. 271, l. 187–188; d. 386, l. 75.

61. GARF, f. 1791, op. 6, d. 459, ll. 69–70.

62. *Utro Rossii*, 4 August 1917.

63. *Den'*, 22 September 1917; *Novoe vremia*, 22 September 1917; *Russkaia volia*, 22 September 1917; *Rabochaia gazeta*, 27 September 1917; *Rassvet*, no. 13, 4 October 1917, 33; *Oktiabr'skii perevorot* (Petersburg, 1918), 75.

64. *Rassvet*, no. 15, 18 October 1917, 33.

65. GARF, f. 1791, op. 6, d. 26, l. 7; d. 592, l. 16; *Rassvet*, no. 10–11, 20 September 1917, 27; no. 13, 4 October 1917, 32; no. 16, 27 October 1917, 37; *Moskovskii listok*, 16 September 1917; *Evreiskaia nedelia*, no. 38–39, 29 September 1917, 20, 29; no. 42, 22 October 1917, 19.

66. *Utro Rossii*, 13–14 September 1917; *Kievlianin*, 13 September 1917; *Iuzhnyi krai*, 14 September 1917; *Rech'*, 15 September 1917; *Novoe vremia*, 14 September 1917; *Birzhevye vedomosti*, 13 and 15 September 1917; *Rassvet*, no. 10–11, 20 September 1917, 27; no. 12, 27 September 1917, 35–36; *Evreiskaia nedelia*, no. 41, 15 October 1917, 24–26.

67. *Russkoe slovo*, 28 September 1917; *Rassvet*, no. 13, 4 October 1917, 33; *Oktiabr'skii perevorot*, 73; Kanishchev, *Russkii bunt*, 84, 88.

68. *Russkoe slovo*, 4 October 1917; *Utro Rossii*, 17 October 1917; GARF, f. 1791, op. 6, d. 273, l. 79; *Rassvet*, no. 14, 11 October 1917, 35–36; *Evreiskaia nedelia*, no. 41, 15 October 1917, 20.

69. *Rech'*, 10 October 1917.

70. Serhiichuk, *Pohromi v Ukraïni*, 455.

71. Ibid.; *Rassvet*, no. 1, 15 January 1918, 33.

72. *Rassvet*, no. 3–4, 31 January 1918, 38.

73. *Russkie vedomosti*, 31 December 1917; *Rassvet*, no. 1, 1 January 1918, 33; Serhiichuk, *Pohromi v Ukraïni*, 455.

74. *Rassvet*, no. 8, 8 March 1918, 27–28.

75. Ibid., 28.

76. *Rassvet*, no. 5, 24 February 1918, 35; no. 8, 8 March 1918, 18–19, 20; no. 9, 17 March 1918, 18–20; *Visty Rady* (Poltava), 15 March (2), 1918; *Svobodnaia rech'* (Semipalatinsk), 24 February 1918.

77. *Rassvet*, no. 11–12, 7 April 1918, 32; no. 15, 28 April 1918, 18; Viktor A. Savchenko, *Simon Petliura* (Kharkov: Folio, 2004), 170–171.

78. Sergei N. Emelianov, *Spetsifika sotrudnichestva dukhovenstva tsentral'nykh zemledel'cheskikh gubernii s antibol'shevistskimi silami v gody grazhdanskoi voiny*, Sotsial'noe partnerstvo gosudarstva i tserkvi—ob'ektivnoe uslovie stabil'nosti politicheskoi sistemy grazhdanskogo obshchestva (Kursk: Kurskii gosudarstvennyi Universitet, 2004), 351.

79. *Rassvet*, no. 11–12, 7 April 1918, 29–30; no. 14, 21 April 1918, 1, 20, 21, 22; no. 16–17, 16 May 1918; *Nash vek*, 16 March 1918; Serhiichuk, *Pohromi v Ukraïni*, 448.

80. *Rassvet*, no. 9, 17 March 1918, 35.

81. Ibid.

82. *Nash vek*, 21 March 1918; Serhiichuk, *Pohromi v Ukraïni*, 447, 448.

83. *Rassvet*, no. 16–17, 16 May 1918, 25, 26.

84. *Kievskaia mysl'*, 24 May 1918; *Rassvet*, no. 16–17, 16 May 1918, 26–27; Serhiichuk, *Pohromi v Ukraïni*, 448.

85. Serhiichuk, *Pohromi v Ukraïni*, 446.

86. *Rassvet*, no. 16–17, 16 May 1918, 27–28; *Golos Samarkanda*, 15 May 1918.

87. *Svobodnaia Rossiia*, 22 May 1918; *Rassvet*, no. 20, 9 June 1918, 30–31.

88. *Rassvet*, no. 18, 26 May 1918, 10; Serhiichuk, *Pohromi v Ukraïni*, 448.

89. *Kievskaia mysl'*, 24 May 1918.

90. *Rassvet*, no. 18, 26 May 1918, 10–11.

91. *Kievskaia mysl'*, 11 August 1918.

92. *Rassvet*, no. 18, 26 May 1918, 9–10.

93. Serhiichuk, *Pohromi v Ukraïni*, 174–175.

94. GARF, f. 446, op. 2, d. 123, l. 115.

95. Serhiichuk, *Pohromi v Ukraïni*, 451, 448.

96. *Novoe utro iuga* (Ekaterinodar), 19 December 1918.

97. Mikhail P. Chubinskii, *God revoliutsii (1917). (Iz dnevnika)*, Oktiabr'skaia revoliutsiia: ot novykh istochnikov k novomu osmysleniiu (Moscow: IRI RAN, 1998), 324; *Rassvet*, no. 16, 27 October 1917, 37.

98. See Irwin Michael Aronson, *Troubled Waters: The Origins of the 1881 Anti-Jewish Pogroms in Russia* (Pittsburgh, 1990); John D. Klier, *Imperial Russia's Jewish Question, 1855–1881* (Cambridge University Press, 1995).

99. See Shlomo Lambroza, "The Pogroms of 1903–1906," in *Pogroms: Anti-Jewish Violence in Modern Russian History*, ed. John Klier and Shlomo Lambroza (Cambridge University Press, 1992), 195–247; Abraham Ascher, "Anti-Jewish Pogroms in the First Russian Revolution, 1905–1907," in Yaacov Ro'i, ed., *Jews and Jewish Life in Russia and the Soviet Union* (Ilford, U.K.: Frank Cass, 1995), 127–145.

100. See Elias Heifetz, *The Slaughter of the Jews in the Ukraine in 1919* (New York: Seltzer, 1921); Nahum I. Shtif, *Pogromy na Ukraine* (Berlin: Vostok, 1922); V. A. Polyakov, "Zhutkie dni na Ukraine," in *Evreiskaia letopis'*, no. 2 (1923); Joseph Schechtman,

Pogromy dobrovol'cheskoi armii na Ukraine (Berlin: Ostjüdisches Historisches Archiv, 1932); Henry Abramson, *A Prayer for the Government: Ukrainians and Jews in Revolutionary Times, 1917–1920* (Cambridge, Mass.: Harvard University Press, 1999).

101. *Rassvet,* no. 25–26, 21 July 1918, 40.

102. Vladimir P. Buldakov, *Oktiabr' 1905 g.: Tsarskii manifest i evreiskie pogromy,* Revoliutsiia 1905–1907 godov: vzgliad cherez stoletie (Moscow: MGOU, 2005), 158–168.

PART 2

Responses to Pogroms

~*~ 5 ~*~

Preventing Pogroms: Patterns in Jewish Politics in Early Twentieth-Century Russia

VLADIMIR LEVIN

The word *pogrom* was very popular in Russia at the beginning of the twentieth century. Starting on 6 April 1903, when a sudden and cruel pogrom broke out in Kishinev (Chişinău), this word did not cease to be an important and frequent element in Jewish political discourse. And indeed, the first years of the century witnessed a terrible wave of pogroms: from Kishinev and Gomel in 1903, through 43 pogroms during the conscription campaigns for the Russo-Japanese War in 1904, and the 50-odd pogroms between January and mid-October 1905. This rising tide of violence culminated in the "October Days" of 1905, during which almost 3,000 Jews were reported to have perished in a total of 660 pogroms. A return to quiet was punctuated by disorders in Białystok (June 1906) and Siedlce (September 1906)—both characterized by massive participation of army troops.[1] Between autumn 1906 and 1914, there were no pogroms in tsarist Russia, but the threat and fear of them remained present until the fall of the empire in 1917.

This persistent reality, together with the politicization of the Jewish street, forced Jewish political movements to devise strategies for response to the threat of pogroms. This article will analyze and establish a structural framework for the instruments and tools that a number of Jewish political groups used in their attempts to prevent pogroms. It will not deal with fundamental responses to antisemitism such as the Zionist and territorialist movements, Jewish liberalism and integrationism, or Jewish socialism. These ideological and political movements proposed solutions that were to be achieved in the future for the Jewish people as a whole. It will also not deal with the attempts—mostly unsuccessful—of prominent Jews from abroad to reverse the anti-Jewish policies of the Russian government. Instead, I will concentrate on measures proposed and applied in the period under review in Russia; these were meant to prevent the next pogrom, which was expected tomorrow or in the near future. Three patterns that emerged in the early twentieth century will be considered: intercession, self-defense, and systematic struggle against antisemitism. The article will also discuss the levels on which the anti-pogrom measures were applied (local, provincial, national), their timing and chances for success, as well as their connections to different political forces among Russia's Jews.

Modern Jewish historiography has reached the conclusion that the tsarist government had no part in organizing pogroms.[2] But the majority of contemporary Jewish observers and participants in the events were more than sure that the pogroms were not spontaneous. Rather, it was thought that the ruling central and local bureaucracy had prepared and supported anti-Jewish violence.[3] Therefore, anyone conducting research on the responses to pogroms should keep in mind that all measures taken to prevent them were, ultimately, directed toward the Russian authorities.

Intercession

The first pattern—intercession—was the most traditional one. For 2,000 years, the attempt of a privileged Jew or a Jewish leader to intercede with non-Jewish authorities was the accepted means for preventing disasters.[4] This approach was commonly used in late imperial Russia. On the eve of the Kishinev pogrom in 1903, a delegation of Jews visited the governor, the vice-governor, and the chief of the police and asked for protection.[5] Before the pogrom in Białystok in 1906, Jewish representatives also interceded with local officials.[6]

Intercession could be accomplished in two ways: on the one hand, Jewish representatives could appeal to the feelings of duty, law, and justice of an administrator; on the other hand, they could offer a bribe. Intercession could be made on three levels: local police, provincial governors, and the higher administration in St. Petersburg. On the local level, it seems that the most successful way was bribery. In many places, a "tax" for paying off the police officials was imposed by community leaders. If the *ispravnik*—a local police officer—was not an ideological antisemite and acted effectively, a pogrom could be prevented, especially in a small shtetl.[7]

Strategies of intercession directed toward provincial governors focused on their duty to keep order. Such intercessions were in many cases very disappointing because local officials often responded with accusations that Jews were, in fact, guilty of organizing and supporting the revolution.[8] Again, the ability of a governor to prevent mass disorders, including pogroms, depended on many factors. Among these were his willingness to protect Jews, his competence, the number of troops at his disposal, and the general situation.[9] Generally speaking, after the reestablishment of public order following the Russian Revolution of 1905, many governors succeeded in preventing pogroms. The best-known cases of preventing pogroms by the authorities were connected with Kiev (Kyiv). In September 1911, when rumors of a pogrom spread after the assassination of Prime Minister Piotr Stolypin, his successor Vladimir Kokovtsov, who also was in Kiev, acted very decisively. While General-Governor Fedor Trepov "literally did not know what to do," Kokovtsov summoned three Cossack regiments to the city and thus calmed spirits. When a delegation of Jews "from the market" visited him with a plea to prevent the approaching pogrom, all orders had already been given.[10] A second case of preventing a seemingly almost unavoidable pogrom also occurred in Kiev in October 1913, on the day the jury's verdict in the Beilis trial was announced. Again, troops were brought in and the crowds calmed down and dispersed.[11]

On the national level the intercession had, of course, a political nature. Beginning in 1905, Jewish political leaders took up the task. For example, Genrikh (Heinrich) Sliozberg—one of the leading lawyers protecting Jewish interests—reported in his memoirs that on the third day of the October pogroms, he and another member of the Union for the Achievement of Full Rights for the Jewish People in Russia visited the newly appointed prime minister, Count Sergei Witte, and warned him of a pogrom being planned in Kiev.[12] Although Witte was as worried as his visitors, this intercession yielded no results. In contrast, several days later Sliozberg and Baron Horace Gintsburg—considered the chief spokesman for Russia's Jews in the second half of the nineteenth century—visited the new minister of internal affairs, Petr Durnovo. According to Sliozberg, the wave of pogroms ceased after this visit.[13] Two months later, the relief committee for pogrom victims sent another delegation to Witte, presenting him with a declaration claiming that "the initiative and support for pogroms came from the government" and demanding a decisive statement against the anti-Jewish violence. Again, according to Sliozberg, this declaration pushed the Council of Ministers to issue orders and circulars against the pogroms.[14] (A Hebrew newspaper even reported that Witte "will not allow pogroms to break out any more; in all towns in the Pale resources were gathered, which made it possible to suppress any pogrom within half an hour").[15] Sliozberg was on the right wing of contemporary Jewish politics and always opted for relations with the government;[16] therefore, he ascribed the cessation of pogroms to the visits of both delegations, although this cannot be confirmed from the available evidence.

In this regard, it should be mentioned that anti-pogrom intercession was a part of a much bigger issue in Jewish politics—the question of *shtadlanut* (the traditional Hebrew term for intercession). The new "modern" Jewish political forces rejected *shtadlanut* as a system based on discreet personal relations whereby the Jewish side could get results only through self-humiliation. The new politics was "meant to take place at the national level, subject to public discussion and led by representatives of the people."[17] This thesis was accepted by all modern political organizations; only the Orthodox Jewish politicians consciously opted for the traditional, discreet way of dealing with non-Jews.[18] However, during extraordinary and dangerous events like pogroms, these principles were in many cases sacrificed for the sake of preserving lives and property. Except for socialists such as Bundists and Labor Zionists, members of all other Jewish political groups undertook one kind or another of intercession when a pogrom seemed imminent.

The last anti-pogrom delegation to intercede on the national level, to Prime Minister Stolypin, was organized in April 1907 by the members of the Second Duma. Eight Duma deputies from the Pale of Settlement, comprising Jews and non-Jewish leftists, met with him to direct his attention to rumors about Easter pogroms and to the pogrom-mongering of the "Black Hundreds," a far-right monarchist and antisemitic organization. As a result, Stolypin sent a circular to governors, demanding the prevention of pogroms and threatening officials who failed to take their responsibility for maintaining order seriously.[19] After this, there were no further delegations to the highest authorities because there were no immediate threats of pogroms on a large scale. On the local and provincial levels, however, intercession was practiced in subsequent years when rumors reappeared. For instance, the situation in Kiev during the above-mentioned Beilis blood libel trial was so tense that in advance of Easter in 1912 the rabbis of Kiev visited the local governor and asked him to prevent a pogrom that seemed to be looming.[20]

Indeed, an intercession could be made only when there was a direct threat of a pogrom. Even if an intercession could successfully prevent a pogrom, there was no assurance that after a while a new intercession would be not needed. It is impossible to estimate the degree to which intercessions succeeded because there are no clear indicators of their influence on specific officials. Existing sources suggest that intercessions achieved the desired results only rarely. The authorities acted according to their understanding of the situation and certainly did not need a reminder that their duty was to protect order. When there was a firm and clear desire not to allow pogroms, the local administration also did its best.

Self-Defense

The second pattern of preventing pogroms involved Jewish self-defense. While Jewish communities organized themselves informally for defense during the 1881–82 pogroms, the Kishinev pogrom in 1903 prompted much more organized efforts; these were linked to political movements and enjoyed wide public support.[21] Less than half a year after Kishinev, in August 1903, a mob of looters in Gomel met trained and armed Jewish self-defense squads numbering two hundred men. The account of one Jewish newspaper declared the encounter in Gomel to have been "more a fight than a pogrom."[22] Similar claims were made about events in Zhitomir in April 1905[23] and Białystok in June 1906.[24] Such encounters allowed the authorities and the spokesmen for the Russian Right to speak of "pogroms by Jews against Christians."[25]

As in the case of intercession, the effectiveness of self-defense in preventing pogroms (as opposed to resistance during an actual outbreak) can be questioned. Organizers believed that the knowledge that Jews were armed and prepared to fight back could deter potential *pogromshchiki*. For example, in Vilna (Vilnius), during the October 1905 wave of pogroms, twelve democratic organizations, Jewish as well as general, published a joint appeal with an explicit threat: "We warn that even smallest attempt of pogrom will meet the most energetic repulsion from all our united forces and that the malicious intent will be strangled at its birth."[26] As Simon Dubnov put it later in his memoirs, the appeal

> made an appropriate impression. The organizers of the pogrom could not know that we had established the committee for self-defense, which collected weapons and money to buy weapons. The Bund and Poalei-Zion organized separate self-defense units and prepared for energetic activities. This circumstance could have a cooling effect on the *pogromshchiki*.[27]

While willing to stress the importance of the warning, Dubnov still felt obliged to express doubt about its result. Indeed, there were only a few pogroms in the northwestern region in 1905 (similar to the situation during the waves of 1881–1882 and 1918–1920).[28] Evidently, it was impossible to prove that the threat of armed resistance prevented violence. Conversely, the spread of publicity about the very existence of self-defense units could potentially increase hostility toward Jews among Christians.[29]

Jewish self-defense was organized by Jewish political movements. At first these were by Zionists and Bundists; the new Jewish Socialist organizations—the Zionist Socialist Workers Party, the Jewish Social Democratic Workers Party (Poalei-Zion) and the Jewish Socialist Workers Party—began their own self-defense efforts somewhat later.[30] It seems that the initial Zionist drive toward self-defense was dependent mostly on the young members of Poalei-Zion (Labor Zionist) groups. When these groups separated from the Zionist Organization in 1905–1906 and established three separate socialist parties, the participation of the "general" Zionists in self-defense diminished significantly and their attitude toward self-defense became ambivalent: they did not reject it in principle but showed no initiative.

Self-defense played an important role in the activities of the Jewish socialist parties. On the one hand, self-defense was powered by the revolutionary idealism of socialist youth, imbued by feelings of human and Jewish honor. A good expression of these emotions appeared in a 1903 brochure written by Nahum Shtif and Ben-Zion Fridland, which proclaimed: "The evil in Kishinev was not that a few dozen Jews fell . . . but that only two in the enemy camp were killed, killed accidentally! . . . That is shameful, terrible!"[31] On the other hand, each party organized fighting units as a means of struggle against the Russian authorities.[32] In most cases, the party squads simultaneously served as the nucleus of self-defense and as a vehicle for accomplishing the party's other tasks. Before 1905, these tasks usually involved protection for political demonstrations, but during the revolution the new tasks became more important: fighting the police, expropriating money from the "bourgeoisie," and pressuring employers to improve working conditions. Nonetheless, after the shock of Kishinev, the Jewish elite as a whole supported the idea of self-defense. For instance, Maksim Vinaver, a prominent Jewish liberal and a leading member of the Constitutional Democratic Party, gave virtual carte blanche to a Bund representative in 1904 to purchase weapons, reportedly declaring, "What do you want? We are all, in fact, Bundists."[33]

During the revolution, the confrontation between the socialists, on the one hand, and the liberals and Zionists, on the other, became extremely sharp. Nonetheless, Zionists and liberals both continued to support self-defense. As evidence of this, it was included in the program of action proposed by Sliozberg to the second Congress of the Union for the Achievement of Full Rights in November 1905.[34] Even the complete failure of the socialists' self-defense efforts during the October pogroms, when those efforts were easily overcome by the army, only slightly affected the positive attitude of the Jewish elites toward self-defense. However, this support was expressed mostly on the declarative (and probably financial) level. Thus, Vladimir Jabotinsky—a Zionist leader and bitter enemy of the Bund—wrote in early 1906, "Self-defense and the revolutionary struggle could at least raise the spirit of the Jewish people."[35] A liberal weekly stated a year later that "self-defense was a fragile but precious hedge, which Jews built as counterbalance to organized violence."[36]

At first glance, Jewish self-defense was very fragmented—each political group and party worked separately when organizing their members and sympathizers, collecting money, and purchasing weapons. Only in rare cases did all groups coordinate their preparations. During the pogroms, cooperation was usually ad hoc. Secondly, self-defense was a distinctively local enterprise: local people were engaged in protecting their towns from pogroms. At most, a self-defense unit from a larger town could be sent to a shtetl in its vicinity when rumors about a pending pogrom were spreading.[37]

Given that the fighting squads belonged to specific parties, their central party institutions did try to coordinate activities on the national level. Operations began with centralized fundraising in Russia and abroad and continued with centralized purchases of weapons, which were then distributed through local organizations. The Bund even formed a commission of its Central Committee, which directed all military activities of the Bund, including self-defense brigades. (The commission was called *Mayim*—literally "water" in Hebrew—an antonym of its actual engagement with firearms and explosives.) The centrality of cooperative effort in preventing pogroms came to the fore in the debate of the Bund's Central Committee in June 1906, following the pogrom in Białystok. A leading Bund publicist, A. Litvak (Khaim-Yankev Helfand), proposed that the party should publicize a proclamation warning that it would "blast with dynamite a [whole] town" wherever a new "military" pogrom (a pogrom in which large numbers of regular troops participated) occurred. Other members pointed out that such a threat was not only unrealistic but would also embitter the whole Russian population toward Jews. Litvak modified his proposal and suggested blowing up only administrative buildings. In the end, the Central Committee did not reach a decision. Litvak wrote in his memoirs that similar ideas about responding to pogroms with explosives circulated in the Bund as early as 1903, following the pogrom in Kishinev.[38]

Not only revolutionary parties and Zionists organized self-defense. Repeating tactics first encountered in 1881, local Jews often took measures to prevent pogroms. A good example may be found in the experience of a certain Yurchenko, an agent of the secret police Okhrannoe otdeleniie, in Kiev. Yurchenko was sent to the shtetl of Tal'noe in Kiev *guberniia* to organize the surveillance of a group of Zionist-Socialists. Upon arrival, he took up residence at an inn and began his work. He soon realized, however, that local Jews, aware of his identity, were following him closely, and he decided to return to Kiev. When he asked the innkeeper to return his identification documents so that he could depart, the latter answered that the documents had been given to the police and that the local commander had ordered that Yurchenko be brought to him. When Yurchenko offered to go alone, the innkeeper refused and personally took him in a cab to the police station. The officer on duty searched Yurchenko, and finding that he was carrying a firearm, wanted to arrest him. Yurchenko had to reveal his identity, and with his cover blown, he returned immediately to Kiev. The local police officer warned him that he could not ensure his personal security, since Jews saw in every newcomer a possible pogrom organizer and were capable of physically harming such suspects.[39] This course of action—surveillance of a newcomer and turning him in to the police—demonstrates that in such cases the initiative could be taken by the politically unengaged local population rather than by revolutionary groups.

If the first precondition of Jewish self-defense was a threat of a pogrom, immediate or imminent, the second precondition was the ineffectiveness of the police. In other words, "self-defense" in the form of organized groups of armed people could exist—illegally, of course—when state authorities did not have total control over the internal security situation. As revolutionary energy petered out in 1907 and the authorities were able to reestablish order, it became harder to maintain self-defense squads and this pattern completely disappeared. Although the threat of pogroms was in the air in subsequent years and the idea of self-defense had not disappeared, no party tried to revive it. The Bund even liquidated its central storage of weapons in 1909, which had been collected in previous years both to fight with the government and to take action against pogroms.[40] In 1911, when a great pogrom was expected in Kiev following the assassination of Prime Minister Stolypin, a letter opened and inspected by the secret police stated that students at Kiev University spoke about self-defense, but this idea was abandoned because there were "no money, no people, no weapons."[41] Similar talk was heard, again without any result, when rumors spread in Kiev about a planned pogrom in anticipation of the conviction of Mendel Beilis in 1913.[42] Self-defense revived only after the revolution of 1917, when authority and order dissipated.

Systematic Struggle against Antisemitism

The third pattern was developed by Jewish liberals. Instead of undertaking ad hoc measures, they proposed, as a part of their political program, a systematic and organized struggle against antisemitism. This approach, it was believed, would not only help to prevent anti-Jewish violence in the immediate sense, but would also advance the more general goal of full emancipation. As early as the pogroms of 1881–1882, Jewish liberals believed that the inequality of Jews and the numerous restrictions on them were the main reason for the pogroms: non-Jews, seeing how the state itself humiliated Jews, felt secure and legitimate about insulting them. Therefore, full emancipation was in their eyes the most important precondition for preventing anti-Jewish violence.

The first part of the liberal scheme involved public politics. First, they participated in court trials after pogroms. Their goal was not so much to bring the actual *pogromshchiki* to justice; rather, they wanted to unmask the "real" organizers of pogroms—the local and central authorities.[43] A similar mission was pursued in 1906 by Jewish members of the First Duma, who pointed to the alleged role of the government in the pogroms and demanded its resignation.[44] No less important was the effort to place responsibility for the pogroms on the Russian government in the eyes of European public opinion. The leaders of Jewish liberalism stood behind special newsletters issued in Berlin, Paris, and London in order to disseminate information about Russia to the European press.[45] In these actions, Zionists acted similarly to liberals: the most detailed book about pogroms aimed at the foreign reader—*Die Judenpogrome in Russland*—was published by Zionists in 1910 in Germany.[46]

The second part of the liberals' program was a day-to-day effort to diminish antisemitism. Here, the liberals acted alone, since other forces inside Jewish politics were quite far from such an approach. The Zionist and Territorialist movements basically saw the future of Jews overseas, while the socialist Bund hoped that "in the long run, the problem would solve itself, socialism would make the masses friends."[47] Although the Bund demanded that the non-Jewish socialist parties conduct a struggle against antisemitism among their nations, the Bund itself did not undertake any serious work among non-Jews.[48] Only the liberals, who believed that Russian Jewry would stay forever in Russia and that the tsarist regime would be replaced by a democratic, but not socialist, state, were interested in the systematic campaign against antisemitism.

The most important Jewish liberal organization in early twentieth-century Russia was the Jewish People's Group, headed by Maksim Vinaver and Genrikh Sliozberg and founded in December 1906 in St. Petersburg. During the first half of 1907, it tried to establish local branches in the Pale of Settlement.[49] The founding convention of the group formulated as one of its four tasks an "organized struggle against antisemitism."[50] The convention did not explain what was meant by this "struggle," but a detailed program was formulated by a provincial conference in Vilna two months later. In contrast to other decisions of the conference, this program was not published but only sent to local leaders of the group. The program consisted of the following points: insuring the cooperation of Belorussian, Lithuanian and Polish newspapers (since this decision targeted the north-western region of the Pale); publication of brochures and calendars in Lithuanian and Belorussian; the establishment of bookstores for the dissemination of progressive literature; distribution of literature by "democratic elements of the non-Jewish population"; organizing public lectures; and fundraising for these goals among the group members. Two points in the program are worth citing. The first declared that, "All members of the Jewish People's Group are obliged to observe the activities of antisemitic organizations and the participation of the local authorities in them, and to inform the Central Committee about all facts in these areas." The second point stated, "In the case of any indication of preparation for antisemitic actions threatening the people, the members of the group should immediately inform the Central Committee and undertake local measures for its prevention."[51] In other words, liberal activists were to monitor the preparations for pogroms and at an opportune moment turn for protection to the local authorities. At the same time, they were to give the leadership in St. Petersburg an opportunity to involve the central authorities. These tactics were, in fact, rooted in the tradition of intercession with local and St. Petersburg authorities to prevent pogroms, albeit now organized on a national level.

The long-term mission against antisemitism continued even after the Jewish People's Group was outlawed by the authorities in June 1908. By necessity, this work was undertaken behind the scenes. The main tool of St. Petersburg Jewish liberals was the publishing house Razum ("Reason"), which operated without any obvious signs of being a Jewish enterprise. Its goal was, in the words of its manager, Solomon Pozner, "with the help of books, brochures, popular calendars, and leaflets to introduce to the broad masses of people the situation of Jews, to shatter prejudices about them, to expose the evil fabrications of the Black Hundreds' press, [and] in general, to preach the idea of peaceful coexistence of the nationalities in Russia."[52] The publishing house indeed printed dozens of books and brochures dealing with the "Jewish question" in Russia. In order to make these publications more credible to the average Russian reader, the names of Jewish authors were replaced with pseudonyms or initials. This practice differed from the widespread custom at the time of signing with a pseudonym. In the Jewish case, it aimed at concealing not the identity of the author but his or her Jewish origin. In order to avoid police persecutions, the sharpest works were printed anonymously without mentioning either author or publisher. Many books and brochures of this publishing house were devoted to the pogroms and in "simple Russian language" explained "who in reality organizes the pogroms and who needs them."[53] At the same time, Jewish liberals tried to influence some Russian newspapers in the time-honored fashion of providing "subsidies." It is understandable that such agreements remained secret, but the few mentions in the archival documents show that subsidies were paid to several progressive newspapers whose readership included the lower strata of Russian society.[54]

Liberal activities were not limited to St. Petersburg. In Moscow, the Society for Disseminating Correct Information about Jews and Jewry was established in 1907 as a rival organization to the Petersburg People's Group. The Moscow society launched a similar publishing program, printing brochures about the "Jewish question."[55] A similar association opened in Kiev two years later,[56] although it specialized in publishing brochures of historical content, written mostly by the historian Ilia Galant. He tried in his works to refute myths about Jews leasing churches in Ukraine in the early seventeenth century and the blood libels there in the eighteenth century.[57] The Independent Society for Disseminating Correct Information about Jews and Jewry was established in Odessa in late 1912; a similar organization appeared in Warsaw in the following year.[58]

Among the Jewish political movement, only the liberals conducted "an organized struggle against antisemitism." One can argue that every political movement valuing the future of Jews in Russia should have promoted a similar program. And indeed, the proponent for the formation of a political organization for Orthodox Jewry, Faivel Meir Getz, also advocated for a regular and organized struggle against antisemitism and pogroms.[59] In his brochure, written in 1903 but published only in 1907, he proposed that a new party of observant Jews should spread "apologetic and polemic" books debunking antisemitic propaganda.[60] He rejected, however, any

overtly political struggle against pogroms and antisemitism. He even went
so far as to blame the St. Petersburg Jewish liberal leadership, members of
the First Duma, for the pogroms in Białystok and Siedlce. Getz claimed that
these pogroms were a response to speeches against the government.[61] In
his view, there was no justification for confronting the government. On the
contrary, Jews should stress their loyalty to the existing authorities. In
this way they would prevent violence as well as improve their overall civil
and political situation.

Getz's program was never implemented. On one hand, Orthodox Jewish leaders were unable to reach a consensus about the organization of a
political party in those years. On the other hand, all of the proposals calling for Orthodox political organization from 1907 to 1914 failed to include
any statements on the struggle against antisemitism. The latter fact shows
that the rabbis who led the Orthodox political movement did not consider
systematic work against the pogroms important. They retained their approach of stressing the political loyalty of Orthodox Jewry in general and
of intercessions with the authorities in specific cases.[62]

*   *   *

None of the three patterns for preventing pogroms discussed in this
essay achieved its goal. Intercession helped only when the authorities were
willing, and able, to help. Self-defense squads could not always frighten
the potential *pogromshchiki* or withstand the might of regular troops. No
less important, self-defense activities could often be seen as (and, in reality, were) an expression of revolutionary opposition. The long-term program of struggle through education and propaganda simply did not have
enough time to reduce the intensity of antisemitism among non-Jews before the fall of tsarism. In the end, there was little that Jews could do by
themselves to prevent anti-Jewish violence. Because the factors that encouraged this violence had slight connection with the actual behavior of
Jews, their practical activity could do little to prevent it.

Notes

1. Shlomo Lambroza, "The Pogroms of 1903–1906," in *Pogroms: Anti-Jewish
Violence in Modern Jewish History,* ed. John D. Klier and Shlomo Lambroza (Cambridge:
Cambridge University Press, 1992), 197–228.

2. On the pogroms of 1881–82, see I. Michael Aronson, *Troubled Waters: The Origins
of the 1881 Anti-Jewish Pogroms in Russia* (Pittsburgh: University of Pittsburgh Press,
1990), 217–235; I. Michael Aronson, "The Anti-Jewish Pogroms in Russia in 1881," in
Klier and Lambroza, *Pogroms,* 44–61. On the pogroms of 1903 and 1905–1906, see
Lambroza, "The Pogroms of 1903–1906," in Klier and Lambroza, *Pogroms,* 195–247.

3. The most comprehensive example of this view is the chapter "Bureaukratie und Pogromorganisation," in *Die Judenpogrome in Russland,* ed. Leo Motzkin (Cologne: Jüdischer Verlag, 1910), 1:224–327.

4. On intercession in European Jewish history see, for example, François Guesnet, "Politik der Vormoderne: 'Shtadlanuth' am Vorabend der polnischen Teilungen," *Jahrbuch des Simon-Dubnow-Instituts* 1 (2002): 235–255.

5. Lambroza, "The Pogroms of 1903–1906," 197–198; Edward H. Judge, *Easter in Kishinev: Anatomy of a Pogrom* (New York: New York University Press, 1992), 52; Haim Shorer, ed., *Ha-pogrom be-kishinov bi-mlot 60 shana* (Tel Aviv: World Federation of Bessarabian Jews, 1963): 87; Motzkin, *Die Judenpogrome,* 2:10.

6. Yulii Gessen, "Belostokskii pogrom," *Evreiskaia entsiklopediia,* vol. 5 (St. Petersburg: Obshchestvo dlia nauchnykh evreiskikh izdanii, 1910), 172.

7. As a paradigmatic example, see the story by Sholem Aleikhem, "A khasene on kleyzmer," in "Ayzenban geshikhtes," *Ale verk fun sholem-aleykhem* (New York: Forverts, 1944), 7:129–137 (second pagination). See also Motzkin, *Die Judenpogrome,* 1:255–256.

8. See Motzkin, *Die Judenpogrome,* 1:250–253.

9. On the Russian governors, see Richard G. Robbins, *The Tsar's Viceroys: Russian Provincial Governors in the Last Years of the Empire* (Ithaca, N.Y.: Cornell University Press, 1987), 148–199.

10. Vladimir Kokovtsov, *Iz moego proshlogo: vospomonaniia 1903–1919gg.* (Paris, 1933, reprint The Hague: Mounton, 1969), 1:478, 487.

11. Sergei Stepanov, "Delo Beilisa," in *Delo Beilisa* (Moscow and Jerusalem: Gesharim-Mosty Kul'tury, 1995), 400–401.

12. Genrikh Sliozberg, *Dela minuvshikh dnei* (Paris: Izd. Komiteta po chestvovaniiu 70-ti letniago iubileia G. B. Sliozberga, 1934), 3:177–178.

13. Sliozberg, *Dela minuvshikh dnei,* 3:180.

14. Ibid., 3:188.

15. *Ha-tsefira,* no. 268 (30 December 1905): 2.

16. On Sliozberg, see Brian Horowitz, "Genrikh Sliozberg: shtrikhi k politicheskomu portretu," *Vestnik Evreiskogo universiteta v Moskve* 2, no. 15 (1997): 186–205.

17. Eli Lederhendler, *The Road to Modern Jewish Politics: Political Tradition and Political Reconstruction in the Jewish Community of Tsarist Russia* (Oxford: Oxford University Press, 1989), 156.

18. On the profiles of different Jewish political trends in relations with non-Jews, see Ezra Mendelsohn, *On Modern Jewish Politics* (Oxford: Oxford University Press, 1993), 15, 21, 26.

19. *Rassvet,* no. 14 (13 April 1907): 23; *Ha-zeman,* no. 80 (12 [25] April 1907): 1; no. 81 (13 [26] April 1907): 1.

20. *Ha-modia,* no. 26 (30 March 1912): 389.

21. See Simon Dubnov, *Kniga zhizni* (Riga: Jaunātnes Grāmata, 1934), 1: 408; Henry J. Tobias, *The Jewish Bund in Russia: From Its Origin to 1905* (Stanford, Calif.: Stanford University Press, 1972), 222–223.

22. *Der Fraynd* (20 September 1903): 1, cited in Lambroza, "The Pogroms of 1903–1906," 209; and, Tobias, *The Jewish Bund,* 227.

23. Jonathan Frankel, *Prophecy and Politics: Socialism, Nationalism and the Russian Jews, 1862–1917* (Cambridge: Cambridge University Press, 1981), 147; Lambroza, "The Pogroms of 1903–1906," 223.

24. Abraham Ascher, "Anti-Jewish Pogroms in the First Russian Revolution, 1905–1907," in Yaacov Ro'i, ed., *Jews and Jewish Life in Russia and the Soviet Union* (Ilford, England: Frank Cass, 1995), 137.

25. As an example see the book of a prominent antisemite, Aleksei Shmakov, *Svoboda i evrei* (Moscow: Moskovskaia gorodskaia tipografiia, 1906). It contains a large selection of news items from far-right newspapers (pp. LV, CCLXIX–CCCXVII, DXXVII–DXXVIII, DXLI–DXLIII).

26. "K grazhdanam g. Vil'no," 22 October 1905, Central Archives of the History of Jewish People in Jerusalem (CAHJP), P1/3.

27. Dubnov, *Kniga zhizni*, 2:34. The General Jewish Workers Union in Russia and Lithuanian, more commonly known as the Bund, was established in 1897. Poalei-Zion was the name for the proletarian Zionist and Territorialist organizations, which split into three distinct socialist parties: the Zionist-Socialist Workers Party, the Jewish Socialist Workers Party, and the Jewish Social-Democratic Workers Party (Poalei-Zion).

28. See the article in this volume by Vladas Sirutavičius and Darius Staliūnas.

29. See, for instance, a news report on the discussion in the Akkerman (Kherson *guberniia*) municipal council in December 1905, where it was said: "this fact [that Jews are buying weapons] will arouse anger among the Russian inhabitants." It appeared in *Ha-tsefira*, no. 263 (25 December 1905): 3.

30. See Frankel, *Prophecy and Politics*, 154.

31. [Nahum Shtif and Ben-Zion Fridland], *Chemu nas uchit' pokushenie Pinkhusa Dashevskogo?* (London: Molodoi Izrail, [1903]), 7–8, cited in Frankel, *Prophecy and Politics*, 599, n. 105.

32. See Shlomo Lambroza, "Jewish Self-Defence during the Russian Pogroms of 1903–1906," *The Jewish Journal of Sociology* 23 (1981): 123–134 (reprinted in Herbert A. Strauss, ed., *Hostages of Modernization: Studies on Modern Antisemitism, 1870–1933/39*, vol. 3/2 [Berlin: W. de Gruyter, 1993], 1244–1256); Tobias, *The Jewish Bund*, 226–227.

33. Rafael Abramovich, *In tsvey revolutsiyes* (New York: Arbeter-ring, 1944), 1:189–190, cited also in Tobias, *The Jewish Bund*, 242.

34. *Voskhod*, no. 47–48 (1 December 1905): 24.

35. Cited in Frankel, *Prophecy and Politics*, 154.

36. *Svoboda i ravenstvo*, no. 40 (16 August 1907): 3.

37. As, for example, the self-defense unit from Gomel, which went to protect the Jews in nearby Rechitsa on 24 October 1905, and fell into an ambush prepared by the *pogrom-shchiki*. See Motzkin, *Die Judenpogrome*, 2:466–467; Albert Kaganovich, *Rechitsa: Istoriia evreiskogo mestechka Iugo-Vostochnoi Belorussii* (Jerusalem: Kaganovich, 2007), 85–87.

38. A. Litvak, *Vos geven: etyudn un zikhroynes* (Wilno: Kletzkin, 1925), 244–246. See also Shlomo Lambroza, "Jewish Responses to Pogroms in Late Imperial Russia," in, *Living with Antisemitism: Modern Jewish Responses*, ed. Jehuda Reinharz (Hanover, N.H. and London: Brandeis University Press, 1987), 272.

39. Gosudarstvennyi arkhiv Rossiiskoi Federatsii (Gosudarstvennyi arkhiv Rossiiskoi Federatsii) (GARF), f. 102, op. 1906, d. 20, ch. 25b, ll. 25–26 (microfilm in CAHJP, HMF 1034.1).

40. Leib Berman, *In loyf fun yorn* (New York: Unzer Tsayt, 1945), 315.

41. Vladimir Liubchenko, " 'Pogrom visit v vozdukhe': obshchestvennye nastroeniia v Kieve posle pokusheniia na P. A. Stolypina (po materialam perliustratsii)," *Vestnik evreiskogo universiteta* 1(19) (1999): 277.

42. Genrikh Ioffe, "Delo Beilisa," in *Delo Beilisa*, 345.

43. Such policies were initiated already after the 1871 pogrom in Odessa by several Jewish lawyers; see Benjamin Nathans, *Beyond the Pale: The Jewish Encounter with Late Imperial Russia* (Berkeley: University of California Press, 2002), 321. With the outbreak of the pogroms in November 1905, the Central Committee of the Union for the Achievement of Full Rights and a group of Jewish liberals in Moscow sent lawyers to

the provinces in order to investigate the anti-Jewish violence. *Voskhod,* no. 47–48 (1 December 1905): 23.

44. On the Jewish deputies in the First Duma, see Sidney Samuel Harcave, "The Jewish Question in the First Duma," *Jewish Social Studies* 6 (1944): 155–176; Yitzhak Maor, "Yehudei rusiyah bi-yemei ha-dumot," *He-avar* 7 (1960): 49–51; Rafail Ganelin, "Pervaia Gosudarstvennaia Duma v bor'be s chernosotenstvom i pogromami," *Osvoboditel'noe dvizhenie v Rossii* (Saratov, 1992), issue 15, 113–140; Christoph Gassen-schmidt, *Jewish Liberal Politics in Tsarist Russia, 1900–1914: The Modernization of Russian Jewry* (New York: New York University Press, 1995), 37–44; Vladimir Levin, "Yehudei rusiyah ve-shalosh ha-dumot ha-rishonot: ha-behirot ve-hashe'ela ha-yehudit ba-dumot (1906–1912)" (M.A. thesis, Hebrew University of Jerusalem, 1997), 21–28; Shmuel Galai, "Evreiskie pogromy i rospusk i Gosudarstvennoi dumy v 1906 godu," *Voprosy istorii,* 2004/9, 23–42 (I thank Dr. Arkadii Zeltser for bringing this latter publication to my attention).

45. Victor Kel'ner, "Aleksandr Braudo i bor'ba s antisemitizmom v Rossii v kontse 19-nachale 20 v.," *Vestnik Evreiskogo universiteta v Moskve* 2 (1993), 107–108.

46. Motzkin, *Die Judenpogrome.*

47. Tobias, *The Jewish Bund,* 221.

48. See, for example, Tobias, *The Jewish Bund,* 221.

49. On Jewish People's Group see Alexander Orbach, "The Jewish People's Group and the Jewish Politics, 1906–1914," *Modern Judaism* 10 (1990): 1–15; Gassenschmidt, *Jewish Liberal Politics,* 157–59; Vladimir Levin, "Ha-politika ha-yehudit ba-imperiya ha-rusit be-idan ha-reaktsiya, 1907–1914" (Ph.D. thesis, Hebrew University of Jerusalem, 2007), 132–147.

50. *Pervyi uchreditel'nyi s"ezd Evreiskoi Narodnoi Gruppy* (St. Petersburg: Svoboda i ravenstvo, 1907), 4. The other three tasks were the struggle for the civil, political, and national equality; the development of economical forces of Jewry; and the development of spiritual forces of Jewry.

51. GARF, f. 4, op. 1907, d. 142, l. 2 (microfilm in CAHJP, HMF 80).

52. Solomon Pozner, "Stranitsy proshlogo (iz vospominanii o A.I. Braudo)," in *Aleksandr Isaevich Braudo, 1864–1924: Ocherki i vospominaniia* (Paris: Kruzhok russko-evreiskoi intelligentsii, 1937), 84.

53. Pozner, "Stranitsy proshlogo," 85. On the publishing house "Razum," see Victor Kel'ner, "Izdatel'skaia deiatel'nost' S. V. Poznera i nekotorye voprosy obshchestvennoi zhizni v Rossii v nachale XX v.," in idem, *Ocherki po istorii russko-evreiskogo knizhnogo dela vo vtoroi polovine XIX–nachale XX v.* (St. Petersburg: Rossiiskaia natsional'naia biblioteka, 2003), 97–114; idem, "Aleksandr Braudo," 109–110.

54. Tsentral'nyi gosudarstvennyi istoricheskii arkhiv Sankta-Peterburga (Central State Historical Archive of St. Petersburg) (TsGIA SPb), f. 2049, op. 1, d. 51, l. 5; d. 63, ll. 4, 6.

55. A. S. Katsenel'son, "K istorii vozniknoveniia obshchestva rasprostraneniia pravil'nykh svedenii o evreiakh," Rossiiskii gosudarstvennyi istoricheskii arkhiv (Russian State Historical Archive) (RGIA), f. 1693, op. 1, d. 23, ll. 12–16, 32. For the report of the Society for 1907, see ibid, d. 2.

56. *Evreiskii mir,* no. 3 (21 January 1910): 30.

57. Ilia Galant, *Arendovali li evrei tserkvi na Ukraine?* (Kiev: Rabotnik, 1909; 2nd ed.: 1914); idem, *Ritual'nyi protsess v Dunaigorode v 1748 godu* (Kiev: Rabotnik, 1911); idem, *Zhertvy ritual'nogo obvineniia v Zaslavle v 1747 godu* (Kiev: Rabotnik, 1912).

58. *Vestnik OPE,* no. 17 (November 1912): 151; no. 20 (February 1913): 138; no. 26 (December 1913): 122; *Rassvet,* no. 8 (22 February 1913): 25; *Novyi Voskhod,* no. 24 (19 June 1914): 14.

59. On Getz, see I. Ch. [Ilia Cherikover], "Getz Faivel Meir Bentselovich," *Evreiskaia entsiklopediia*, 6:467; Sliozberg, *Dela minuvshikh dnei*, 3:256–257; Dubnov, *Kniga zhizni*, 1:160, 2:13, 25; *Yahadut Lita*, vol. 2 (Tel Aviv: Am ha-sefer, 1972): 142.

60. Faivel-Meir Getz, *V svete pravdy* (Moscow: I. N. Kushnerev, 1908), 74; idem, *Ad matai tahrishu! kol kore le-shlumei emunei israel* (Vilna: Dfus Garber, 1907), 14.

61. Faivel-Meir Getz, *Kuma israel* (Poltava: E. A. Rabinovich, 1913), 10.

62. On Orthodox politics in this period, see Vladimir Levin, "Orthodox Jewry and the Russian Government: An Attempt at Rapprochement, 1907–1914," *East European Jewish Affairs* 39, no. 2 (August 2009): 187–204.

~~ 6 ~~

"The Sword Hanging over Their Heads": The Significance of Pogrom for Russian Jewish Everyday Life and Self-Understanding (The Case of Kiev)

NATAN M. MEIR

This paper seeks to understand the role that the pogrom as idea played in the self-understanding of the urban Jewish community of the late Russian Empire (looking specifically at the case of Kiev) and in its relations with non-Jewish residents of the city. Great attention has been paid to the mechanics of the waves of pogroms that engulfed Ukraine and other areas of the Russian Pale of Settlement, and especially the role of official policy and institutions, but we still do not fully understand to what extent the specter of anti-Jewish violence played a determining role in the everyday lives of urban Jews as part of the larger fabric of relations between Jews and non-Jews in the urban environment of the Russian Empire. The heavy emphasis on pogroms and Judeophobia in the classical historiographical literature and in collective memory makes necessary a reevaluation of the role that sporadic—even rare—outbreaks of anti-Jewish violence played in the identities and interactions that characterized quotidian existence.

Interethnic relations in Kiev, as in many cities and large towns in the Pale of Settlement, were extremely complex. In a city defined as officially "Russian" by the state, Ukrainians and Jews made up significant proportions of Kiev's population, and experienced similar, simultaneous trends of acculturation to Russian cultural norms and growing nationalist self-differentiation. In turn, the ethnic Russians of Kiev often felt compelled to reinforce their own national identity in various ways. Though often segregated by language and residential patterns, the three groups did interact and even influence each other in a number of significant ways, and these interactions were by no means all characterized by animosity or hostility. On the other hand, antisemitism played an increasingly important role in the multiethnic environment as nationalist tensions grew and as government policies made clear its official antagonism toward Jews in imperial society.

On the whole, the threat of pogrom seems to have played strikingly little role in the lives of Kiev Jewry before 1905, despite the considerable blow that the 1881 pogrom had dealt the community. Scholars have already challenged the assumption that pogroms were the primary factor in Russian Jewish emigration, noting, inter alia, that most emigrants came from the relatively pogrom-free Russian northwest, while another reservoir of emigration was Austrian Galicia, where there were no pogroms at all.[1] While there is no doubt that the threat—or memory—of violence played a role for some Jews who decided to leave Russia, a perusal of reports in the Jewish press makes clear that economic factors, and for some, the very real possibility of expulsion from their home, were much more important for most emigrants. Moreover, there were many Jews who remained in Russia, determined to forge a place for themselves within imperial society; as Benjamin Nathans's recent study notes, "while there is little doubt that the pogroms helped transform the landscape of Jewish politics in Russia, the notion that they permanently crippled . . . the broader hopes for integration and emancipation cannot withstand scrutiny."[2]

By contrast, in the decade between the 1905 pogrom and the outbreak of World War I, Kiev's Jews experienced a loss of nerve. The community now lived in fear of the next outbreak of violence, and even experienced mass flight on several occasions when rumors of an impending pogrom were particularly strong. As was true for much of Russian Jewry, the last years of the tsarist regime saw Kiev's Jews in a sort of suspended animation, waiting for the other shoe to drop. As we shall see, the key to understanding the impact of each pogrom on subsequent periods was the political and ideational context in which each took place, and the nature of the accusations that were made against the Jews—*all* of the empire's Jews—in each case. Thus, though the circumstances of Kiev's Jews were in some ways unique, the conclusions drawn from this paper can tentatively be extended to that of Russian Jewry as a whole.

Before continuing, two preliminary notes: First, this paper consciously distinguishes between pogroms, which are violent riots that emerge from below (i.e., not organized by the state, at least in the tsarist period), and government measures against Jews, which could sometimes be described as "violent" when carried out in a brutal and cruel fashion (as in the case of some expulsions) but that did not usually pose a threat of personal injury to Jews. And second, although for the sake of clarity the following remarks utilize a periodization scheme centered around pogroms, as my argument makes clear I would not choose 1881–1882 as a decisive turning point for Kiev Jewry; by contrast, the pogrom and the many other historic events of 1905 make that year a clear turning point for the Jews of Kiev and the empire as a whole.

Before 1881

Jews had lived in Kiev on and off since the Middle Ages, but for much of the early modern period Jews were only permitted to enter the city for brief periods to trade. New Jewish settlement began in 1781 after the first partition of Poland and intensified after the second in 1793, when Right-Bank Ukraine—with its hundreds of thousands of Jews—was annexed to the Russian Empire. The establishment of the Pale of Settlement, with the inclusion of Kiev province, legalized Jewish residence in Kiev.[3] However, in 1827 Tsar Nicholas I approved an expulsion order of Jews from the city, which was not rescinded until the early years of the reign of Alexander II, when certain categories of Jews—merchants, artisans, graduates of institutions of higher education, and veterans—were permitted to settle outside the Pale of Settlement and in previously closed cities such as Kiev. Thus Kiev, in the heart of the Pale, was open only to certain groups of Jews, who had to obtain special residence permits in order to settle there.

Kiev grew rapidly in the 1860s and 1870s, becoming the dominant center of the developing agricultural and industrial sectors of the Russian southwest, as well as an important hub for finance, administration, and education. Its population nearly doubled in the decade between 1864 and 1874, when it reached 124,000, and doubled yet again between 1874 and 1897. Its Jewish population also grew swiftly, multiplying fivefold from 3,000 in 1863 to 14,000 in 1874 (totaling 11 percent of the total population) and reaching 32,000 in 1897.[4] In that year Jews made up 12 percent of the total population.

As Jews became more visible in Kiev, the debate over their place in the city became more heated. By the 1870s they were the largest religious minority in Kiev, and some observers began to complain about the increasingly Jewish character of the city: the influence and conspicuous consumption of the Jewish merchants, the perception of Jewish traders "taking over" commerce, the visibility of Jewish brokers in front of the commodities exchange. Traditional accusations against the Jews of Kiev were heard repeatedly: they were bent on corrupting the Orthodox population and "corrupting the working population" of the city by selling them liquor; they traded mostly in contraband and stolen goods; they wanted to take

control of the meat trade; they engaged in unwholesome speculation, bro-
kering, and usury.[5] Anti-Jewish writers, whether journalists, churchmen,
or municipal politicians, always hearkened back to Kiev's pre-1859 golden
age, when Jews had not been permitted to settle there. There were often
intimations that the government would do well to revert to that earlier
policy, which would obviously necessitate expelling those Jews currently
residing in Kiev. If Jews had to be let in, they wrote, the government
should—at the very least—strictly enforce the existing regulations regarding Jewish entry, and expel those individuals without proper residence
permits.[6] Thus, almost from the very beginning of the modern Jewish
presence in Kiev, the threat of expulsion, whether on an individual or a
mass scale, loomed large in the imagination of both Jews and non-Jews. In
the words of journalist A. E. Kaufman, writing in 1880, "Kiev Jews live in
constant fear: the gates of the city are now open to them, now closed. As
soon as they start to settle in and feel at home, there comes another threat
of expulsion."[7] It was this threat—and not that of mass violence—that
continued to serve as the paradigm for "action" against Jews until the early
twentieth century, and even beyond.

After 1881

As throughout the Pale of Settlement, Jews—and many non-Jews—
were shocked by the scale and intensity of the wave of pogroms that over-
ran many of the empire's western provinces in 1881 and 1882. The investigation carried out after the pogrom by Count P. I. Kutaisov claimed that
there were two opinions in Kiev about the causes of the pogroms. Some
were convinced that they emerged out of centuries of hatred for Jews. But
local Jews were certain that the pogroms had been stirred up by revolutionaries, because however strong Christian hate, it could not have materi-
alized in so powerful a fashion—and in so many places simultaneously—
without an organization to coordinate it.[8] Whatever the validity of this
assumption, it reveals that Jews in Kiev did not underestimate the extent
of Christian animosity but rather doubted its ability to manifest itself in
the form of physical violence. This, despite the fact that pogroms had occurred in recent memory (in Odessa in 1821, 1849, 1859, and 1871), while
the horrific massacres that took place in the context of the seventeenth-
century Chmielnicki and eighteenth-century Haidamak uprisings also
continued to live in Jewish collective memory. The fact remained, however, that most Russian Jews alive in 1881 had not themselves experienced
mass violence on the scale of a pogrom. Indeed, neither Jews nor most any-

one else could envision the wave of violence that would engulf the Pale, even given the considerable provocation that preceded it. After the pogrom, the Hebrew writer Yitzhak Yaakov Weissman wrote to the Hebrew newspaper *Ha-melits* that

> the rumors had been spreading in our city for quite some time that there were people planning ill for our people, but who believed that in our time and in a city as respected as ours, with thousands of soldiers as well as government officials, something like this would happen, something out of the Middle Ages?[9]

Jews in other parts of the empire were apparently just as unprepared. A report in another Hebrew newspaper written before the pogroms had started but published afterward told of the rumors that had been spread throughout Poland that "the peasants were getting ready to attack the Jews during the coming holiday [Passover]," which, although they "cast fear into the hearts of Jews living in villages. . . . [were] in and of themselves they unworthy of attention. . . ."[10] As I. Michael Aronson has shown in his study of the 1881 pogroms, even those who wished ill to the Jews "did not expect rioting to occur as a result of the anti-Jewish newspaper campaign" or in the wake of the assassination of Alexander II.[11] The state of panic that Kiev Jews experienced seems to have begun only after the very first pogrom in Elizavetgrad, when a pogrom in Kiev became a very real possibility.[12]

It is interesting to note that the rioting mobs in Kiev were heard to cry not only the familiar "Beat the Yids" (*bei zhidov*) but also to utter calls to expel Jews from the city where they had taken over all the trade and pushed prices up (the reality was just the opposite).[13] The call for expulsion was thus very much part of anti-Jewish discourse in Kiev, whether in the mouths of officials, disgruntled peasants, and townspeople, or even among Jews considering the hazards faced by illegals in Kiev. *Pogromshchiki* must have been aware of the terrible consequences that expulsion meant for Jews, and this threat may have been meant to terrorize in addition to being a genuine expression of animosity.[14]

That Jews did not feel threatened by pogrom violence before 1881 is not particularly surprising. What is more unexpected, especially given that the Kiev pogrom was by some accounts the most serious in scope of all those that occurred in 1881–1882,[15] is that there is little evidence that the 1881 pogrom did anything substantially to change that perception in subsequent decades. Letters such as that composed by the Kiev's "Jewish aristocracy" (*atsilei b'nei Kiyov*), published in December of 1882, reproaching prosperous Jews of the city for flaunting their wealth in the eyes of Kiev's Christian population, did not reappear in ensuing years.[16] Indeed, Jewish visibility in the city continued to grow, as did the Jewish population. One of the most visible elements of Kiev Jewry was its philanthropy; the Brodsky family and others, among the wealthiest entrepreneurs in the empire, donated generously to both Jewish and non-Jewish charities. The passion of Kiev's Jewish benefactors was undoubtedly capital projects, especially those in the field of health and medicine: over the course of the 1880s and 1890s, they added one magnificent building after another to Kiev's skyline, housing hospitals, clinics, sanatoria, and medical institutes. Physically as well as metaphorically, these edifices, often named after one or another deceased member of the Brodsky, Zaitsev, or other illustrious Jewish family, did not do much to reflect a lower Jewish profile in Kiev. However, at public occasions such as grand openings and gala banquets, their patrons and directors often stressed that the facilities were open to both Jews and non-Jews, in language couched to emphasize that Jews, far from being clannish and backward, were broadminded and forward-looking; Jewish welfare institutions, illustrating the universal value of charity, promoted acceptance of Jews by the larger society.[17] What Christian peasant or townsperson who had been treated at a Jewish hospital would take part in a pogrom? We can only guess at the extent to which this was a real consideration in the minds of Jewish philanthropists and medical professionals; certainly, sources from the period do not reveal such direct syllogisms—or perhaps leaps of faith would be a better term.

In the everyday life of Kiev's workplaces, social clubs, and voluntary organizations, a mixture of segregation and integration between Christians and Jews meant that toleration and even camaraderie were practiced in some circles, while interethnic tension and hostility remained a fact of life. Government policies mandating or encouraging segregation, which multiplied in the 1880s and 1890s, bolstered the latter trend. On the other hand, the Kiev Literacy Society counted both Christians and Jews among its board members and operated programs open to individuals of both religions, in addition to courses geared specifically to the needs of Jewish students.[18] The percentage of Jews in some public school districts was as high as 29 percent, but universities and gymnasia imposed quotas on Jewish students, while some private schools barred Jews altogether.[19] What all this meant for the security of Kiev's Jews is difficult to determine. Residential patterns are similarly ambiguous in meaning for the researcher. Does the fact that Jewish residential concentration decreased in a few neighborhoods mean that Jews felt more comfortable living among Christians, or that they feared that the continued existence of Jewish "ghettos" in the city could serve as provocation for animosity and even violence?

One piece of evidence that seems to demonstrate that interethnic tensions were—at least to some extent—always brewing beneath the surface is an 1884 report from Kiev to a St. Petersburg newspaper recounting the tale of a dispute between two market-women at the Zhitnyi bazaar, one Jewish, the other Russian Orthodox, which escalated to a brawl that threatened to explode into a full-scale pogrom. According to the report, the Jewish trader's husband, "a hefty Jew," gave his wife's antagonist a whack, whereupon a crowd of artisans and laborers moved in to defend the Russian woman and began to rain blows upon the Jewish man, who managed to escape their grasp. Part of the throng scattered the Jewish woman's dried fish all over the market, while others went after the women's husband, crying "Beat the Jews!" A passing trader managed to calm the crowd, averting large-scale violence.[20] Was this a common occurrence? It is difficult to say: on the one hand, opportunities for tensions to erupt were myriad; on the other hand, the fact that this fracas was worthy of being printed in one of the capital's newspapers suggests that incidents of this kind might have been rather more rare. Either way, the many details, sometimes rather peculiar, included in the report seem to vouch for its authenticity, though certain aspects—"the Jew started it by provoking a Christian"; "the mob shouts, 'Beat the Jews!' "—are reminiscent of common tropes from pogrom (or near-pogrom) narratives. (The 1883 pogrom in Ekaterinoslav was touched off by "the cries of a peasant woman at the market" after her unruly son was cuffed by a Jewish salesman.)[21] Perhaps the figure of "the passing trader" is somehow representative of the pacifying effect of the small but growing sphere of civil society in urban Russia; individuals who had meaningful interactions (i.e., outside the realm of commerce) with members of other religious or ethnic groups were less likely to engage in violence against others from the same group.[22]

Even more strangely, none of the Jewish newspapers of the empire I have surveyed mentioned this episode, or any similar "near-pogrom" occurrences in Kiev in the interval between 1881 and 1905—despite the abundance of incidents that could be considered provocations. In 1894, an incident of insider trading at the Kiev Exchange ended with the investor who had lost 8,000 rubles attacking the Jews who had sold him the worthless shares. The Hebrew newspaper *Ha-melits* proclaimed that the sad story would give Jew-haters reason to abuse and slander Jews as a group—in its words, "to call all Jews bloodsuckers and cheaters"—but remarkably did not refer to the possibility of physical violence.[23]

In some rare cases, not only did a provocation not spark a violent incident, but Jews got the authorities to condemn the antisemitic episode itself. In 1897, one Goldfarb, a Jewish student at Kiev University, brought a
suit against the Christian Boltushevich for calling him a *"zhid."* Goldfarb
won the suit and the man was fined twenty rubles—not a huge sum, but
significant nonetheless.[24] The fact that a Jew (albeit a student, who might
be a bit more daring than an ordinary Jew) was willing to bring such a
suit at all reveals a surprising level of self-confidence, both in the profile of
Jews in Kiev and in the Russian legal system as a whole (where, by this
point, Jews were not even permitted to serve as full attorneys).

There is no doubt that many of Kiev's Jews experienced insecurity on
a daily basis, but not because of the threat of physical violence. Rather,
they lived in "constant anxiety and fear" of the roundup (*oblava*), a phenomenon unique to Kiev and its labyrinth of legislation on Jewish settlement in the city. In a pattern that became increasingly frequent over the
last two decades of the nineteenth century, the Kiev police would raid
Jewish homes in the middle of the night to uncover individuals or families
staying in the city without the requisite permission; they were then de-
tained, fined, and expelled (sometimes in chains along with common criminals).[25] Both advocates and opponents of this tactic acknowledged that
many of the deportees soon returned to Kiev, so plentiful were the economic opportunities there. However, in some cases entire groups, such as
porters and cabmen, were expelled en masse; this happened in 1881, 1886,
and again in 1891. Another, more mundane but no less menacing, danger
was economic downturn leading to a dearth in employment opportunities.
It seems to have been a combination of these two factors that led to the
departure of large numbers of Jews from Kiev in the early 1890s.[26]

While the situation of Kiev's Jews was in some ways unique, the inse-
curities they faced—particularly the threats of expulsion and economic
failure—were not very different from those faced by Russian Jewry as a
whole.[27] The May Laws of 1882 included a clause forbidding "new settlement" by Jews in a rural area or village, which was often interpreted
broadly and used to expel families from areas they had inhabited for generations, forcing them into the ever more crowded towns and cities of the
Pale. (Here we must also note the brutal expulsion in 1891 of thousands of
Jews from Moscow.) And of course millions of the empire's Jews, hemmed
in by residential, occupational, and educational restrictions, lived in poverty, many seemingly surviving on the very air. These, indeed, were the
chief threats to Russian Jewry and the primary incentive for emigration.
Whether it is wise to refer to government restrictions as a "legislative po-

grom," "cold pogrom," or "silent pogrom" is open to debate, but perhaps these terms obscure unnecessarily the very important (to my mind) distinction between physical violence and administrative measures, however cruel.[28] More significantly, they elide the largely socioeconomic factors that contributed to the 1881–1882 pogroms (which were *not* organized by the government) and the political and ideational characteristics of the official restrictions that followed.

That the real threat to Kiev's Jews lay not in the mob but in the authorities seemed to be bolstered by a suggestion made by right-wing city councilor F. N. Iasnogurskii in 1902 that the city petition the government for permission to expel all of its Jews. The mayor moved that as the proposal did not fall under the purview of the municipal administration, that it not even be accepted for consideration. While this was clearly not an idea that most people considered desirable or even realistic, the fact that such a suggestion could be made in the city council at all must have been unsettling, to say the least.[29]

We must also address the question of proto-Zionism, or Palestinophilism, to which much attention has been paid in the literature, particularly thanks to Jonathan Frankel's magisterial *Prophecy and Politics*, which examines the role of 1881 in the emergence of Jewish nationalism and socialism. While the importance of the pogroms for the development of ideas of Jewish "self-emancipation" cannot be discounted, the history of intellectuals and movements that has dominated the study of Russian Jewry tends to produce a somewhat lopsided portrait that sometimes gives the impression that the pogroms which ostensibly fueled the proto-Zionist movement continued to be a constant reminder of why this new idea was so important. In fact, there was no mass adoption of nationalist ideals in the wake of 1881; indeed, though the Palestinophile movement gained a few followers in the immediate aftermath of the pogroms (David Vital estimates it at 14,000 in 1885, with peripheral supporters adding perhaps double or triple that number), its popularity soon waned and its membership declined in the 1890s.[30] A report in one Hebrew newspaper notes that wealthy Jews in Kiev gave money to the Hovevei Zion (Lovers of Zion) group immediately after the pogrom, but as soon as the new minister of interior Tolstoi had been appointed—signifying, they thought, a new direction in state policy—they stopped their contributions.[31] This is not to discount the significance of these years for the development of the *ideas* of Jewish nationalism, and the role of 1881 in that process, but rather to present a more realistic analysis of the growth of mass support for Zionism. The new Jewish ideology that did gain large-scale support at the turn of the century—Bundism—was

motivated much more by the proletarianization of Russian Jewry and the
need for a new expression of Jewish identity, though of course also by opposition to the tsarist regime, which was understood to have sponsored
the pogroms. Frankel has shown that 1881 was crucial for the ideational
development of the movement, but support for Jewish social democracy
gained mass dimensions only in the 1890s.[32] (The geographical evidence
also points away from a central role for pogroms in the emergence of the
Jewish labor movement, as the movement's birthplace is generally acknowledged as Vilna, a city that did not experience pogroms.)[33]

Also too, the memories that immigrants passed on to their children
and grandchildren decades after they had left the Russian Empire likely
had a role in magnifying the place of the pogrom in Russian Jewish life
and the decision to leave. When such stories are told years after the fact,
economic factors are often forgotten or brushed over while the more dramatic tales of pogroms and violence are highlighted. In the post-Holocaust
era, they also fit better into the widely accepted narrative of Jewish
persecution.[34]

The extent to which Kiev's Jews felt at home—or at least aspired to
feel at home—in their city in the pre-1905 era is illustrated by a history of
Kiev Jewry published in 1902 by communal activist Israel Darewski. Darewski argued that the Khazars (a Turkic people who had converted to Judaism) settled Kiev in the eighth century, before the city was settled by Russians (or the Rus') in the ninth century.[35] Remarkably, Darewski also
argued that the Khazars had called the place "Zion," perhaps because of the
connection between the hills of Kiev and the mountain called Zion. Later,
the Russians corrupted "Zion" into "Kiev" in a complex linguistic transition that Darewski described in detail.

Darewski thus audaciously turned received history on its head: Kiev
was not the Russian Orthodox "Jerusalem of Russia" and the mother of
Russian cities, but rather a second Jewish Jerusalem, having been originally named after the holy city itself. Indeed, Jews had been there even
before Russians and, as Darewski went on to show, had maintained a presence for much of subsequent history. Darewski's stance is even more daring when we call to mind the continuing charges on the part of contemporary antisemites that Jews were bent on conquering Kiev (which had *never*
been theirs) and using it as a base from which to enslave all of Russia.
Keeping in mind that the book was written in Hebrew, we may interpret
his project in a number of ways. Perhaps it was his way of expressing that
Kiev's Jews felt at home in the city, and rightfully so, since they had been
there for a millennium. The message to his home community was one of

reassurance, providing them with a local Jewish myth that would help to bind them to the place despite charges (written into law) that Jews did not belong there. It may also have been an attempt to create a shared sense of community among Jews who were divided among themselves, sometimes seemingly irrevocably. The book might also be seen as historical foundation for a confident Jewish existence on Russian soil: that even the city reputed to be most hostile to Jews was in reality a Jewish city. While some Kiev Jews who were secure in their place in the city and in imperial society as a whole would probably have chosen to read Darewski's interpretation as confirming their own self-confidence, most would likely have seen it as a call for Jews to fight for their right to call Russia their rightful home, and for equal rights as equal citizens. Whatever the interpretation, the history does reveal a certain optimism among Kiev's Jews at the turn of the century. But only a few years after the book's publication, that optimism was to be shattered by 1905 and subsequent events.

After 1905

According to contemporary reports, Kiev was caught as unawares by the 1905 pogrom as by the pogrom of 1881. On 24 October, just days after the days-long riot, a local Jew wrote that

> all are stunned by the recent events. . . . Who could have imagined that a wonderful celebration of freedom by tens of thousands of people from all classes of the population would turn into such a tragedy?[36]

It is indeed unclear why the community was caught by surprise, since rumors of an impending pogrom had been circulating for some time— perhaps even since the Kishinev pogrom two years earlier.[37] After that event, in a speech about the Jews of the city, one antisemitic Kiev councilor had referred cryptically to "the expected occurrences in Kiev."[38] Apparently, the possibility that a pogrom would actually take place in Kiev was inconceivable to most of the city's Jews. As Kiev historian Michael Hamm notes, "some [Jews] had apparently concluded that pogroms were relics of the past; ethnic peace, after all, had reigned for decades. . . ."[39]

It soon became clear that the aftereffects of the 1905 pogrom would be much longer-lasting than those of 1881. Perhaps the first sign of this was the very real possibility that there would be another pogrom to follow the first: in March 1906, there were rumors of an impending pogrom, and trains bound for Austria-Hungary were reported to be full of Jews fleeing the city.[40] The fact that laborers at one of Kiev's shipbuilding yards passed a resolution in May voicing their opposition to the possibility of another pogrom and calling on all workers to defend citizens from attacks on their freedom, life, and property was not necessarily reassuring to Jews; the incident seems to reveal that the menace of pogrom still hung in the air.[41] A month later, there were reports that a leaflet was being distributed around the city calling on Russians to beat their enemies, in the name of the Central Russian Patriotic Committee.[42]

Life was affected in more ordinary ways as well. The records of the library of the Kiev Literacy Society record a precipitous drop in Jewish attendance in the year after the pogrom, from 55 percent to 32 percent; this, after the proportion of Jewish readers had climbed from one-fifth in 1897 to one-third in 1899 to 55 percent just before the violence broke out. Clearly, the pogrom severely damaged Jewish willingness to mingle with their Christian neighbors, even in such a benign environment as a lending library. Several years later, after a terrible flood of the Dnepr (Dnipro) River, only seven of the thousands of Jewish families in the low-lying neighborhood of Podol took refuge at the district's solidly built Contract House; an observer claimed that most Jewish flood victims, remembering their experience of the pogrom, were too afraid to come to the Contract House and chose instead to take shelter in damp garrets where, presumably, they would not have to mingle closely with Christians or be an easy target for anti-Jewish violence.[43] Their fears do not seem out of place when we read that in that same year, bands of *soiuzniki* (members of the right-wing Union of Russian People) wandered the streets of Kiev, asking, "Jew or Russian?" and beating up those Jews foolish enough to tell the truth.[44] The increasing violence was accompanied by roundups more vicious than those experienced before 1905 (including humiliating daytime razzias), not surprising given the threat that all Jews were now said to pose to the very existence of the Russian Empire itself.[45]

The last few years of the tsarist regime can without doubt be called the most insecure of all those preceding them. The assassination of Prime Minister Petr Stolypin by Dmitrii Bogrov in 1911 led to a frenzy of right-wing antisemitic rhetoric, and a pogrom in Kiev was only averted when the governor-general issued a decree specifically banning such an occurrence.[46] For all their talk of defending Jewish national pride, self-defense groups such as those organized by the Bund had little chance of success in the face of official repression and internal division. Moreover, Kiev Jews were at the epicenter of the Beilis affair which, while in essence a national event, had direct implications for the Jews who lived in the city where the trial was taking place. Far-right organizations were very active in Kiev, often distributing publications such as "The Doubleheaded Eagle" in public places (sometimes in the heart of the Jewish neighborhood of Podol) calling for revenge for the killing of the boy Andrei Iushchinskii, allegedly a victim of Jewish ritual murder. The authorities seemed to be doing little or nothing to suppress their provocation—in some case even attending a local gathering of right-wing forces—and Jewish newspapers reported that Kiev Jews feared the outbreak of a fresh pogrom.[47] Indeed, an observer remarked that Kiev's Jews, always haunted by the specter of pogrom, "lived with a sword hanging over their heads."[48] Whether it was Easter, the anniversary of Stolypin's assassination, or even Election Day, their enemies were sure to find a propitious time to attack. The numerous near-pogroms that occurred during these years were fictionalized poignantly by Sholom Aleichem in his novel *The Bloody Hoax* (*Der blutiger shpas*), who described wealthy Jews taking out foreign passports to ensure a quick escape, prosperous middle-class Jews hocking furs and jewels at the city's pawn shops, and poor Jews rushing to the train station only to sit there waiting with thousands of others like them until, finally, the governor issued a declaration banning a pogrom.[49]

One aspect of Jewish life that did not seem—at least at first glance—to be affected by the growing insecurity of Jewish life was large-scale philanthropy. From 1898 to 1912, the millionaire sugar baron Lazar' Brodsky (and after his death in 1904, his heirs) made five significant grants to the Jewish Hospital for, among other facilities, an infectious diseases ward, a new children's ward, and a generating station to provide electrical power to the entire hospital complex. Close behind the Brodskys was Maks Rafailovich Zaks, who financed an ophthalmology ward, a chapel, a bakery, and a seltzer water production facility. The Gal'perin family, for their part, facilitated the construction and outfitting of a ward-sanatorium for first-stage tuberculosis patients and a urological ward.[50] A nervous diseases ward donated by the Frenkel' family brought the total number of hospital divisions to fourteen. In this fifteen-year flurry of expansion, a new facility was added approximately every two years. Another Jewish communal institution that benefited from capital funding was the local burial commission; in 1913, new structures at the Jewish cemetery included a beautiful undertaker's house, a new stable and garage, and an impressive stone fence.[51]

If nothing else, the ongoing building was an acknowledgment of the inevitability of continued Jewish existence in Russia, since even if millions emigrated, there would still be millions left behind—who would continue

to need medical care and, eventually, burial. For Kiev's Jewish million-
aires, it may also have been an attempt to restate their faith in a stable and
prosperous Jewish future in the Russian Empire. As such large-scale philanthropic projects were often an attempt by prominent Jews to gain favor
in the eyes of the government and the public, perhaps after 1905 they took
on additional significance in the eyes of the donors as a much-needed prophylactic against anti-Jewish attitudes. After all, the Jewish Hospital treated
hundreds of Christian patients every year.[52] But, of course, lavish Jewish
welfare institutions could also provoke envy on the part of other Kievans.
There is also the possibility, though less likely, that the constant construction at a time of crisis for Kiev and Russian Jewry indicated a more asser-
tive state of mind. Perhaps these hospital buildings were political statements expressed in stone, not words, by individuals who did not usually
engage in oppositional politics: they proclaimed to the tsarist regime, and
possibly to right-wingers, antisemites, and would-be *pogromshchiki* as
well, that Jews were in Kiev to stay.

*   *   *

Benjamin Nathans has argued that historians must look beyond the
seemingly ever-present "crisis" in Russian Jewish history, to focus on
changes that occurred between the moments of calamity—changes that
were subtle but that nonetheless had just as great an impact in the *longe
durée*.[53] This paper has sought to do just that, but the task is a great deal
more challenging when one reaches the post-1905 period, and especially
1911. During the last years of tsarism, Russian Jewry seemed to lurch from
one crisis to the next with little respite. To retroject this experience onto
the previous quarter-century (or more), however, is incorrect. So why is the
temptation so strong to do just that?

Part of the problem in understanding the place of pogroms in Russian
Jewish history is the perception that they occurred in "waves," which suggests that each surge of violence was fundamentally similar to the other
just as one wave in the ocean is indistinguishable from the next. For example, in his seminal work on the Zionist movement, David Vital wrote that
"pogroms were rare after 1884 [but] were *renewed* in 1903," suggesting
that the two occurrences were actually part of a larger, overarching phenomenon.[54] But though some of the circumstances and factors giving rise
to each set of pogroms may be similar, the reality is that 1881 and 1905 saw
two very different phenomena. First of all, the historical context in the
two cases varied greatly; much had changed from the end of the reign of
Alexander II to the outbreak of the revolution of 1905. Jews had continued

to find their place within Russian society, even occupying prominent positions in industry, the professions, and intellectual life, even as official restrictions pushed more and more young Jews into the revolutionary movement.[55] The growing specter of acculturated and converted Jews slipping unnoticed into the heart of Russian life (literature, government service, and—through intermarriage—the Church) was discussed openly.[56] Thus, by 1905 Jews were both a more integral element of imperial society and, as a result, even more feared and hated in some circles than before.

Moreover, the pogroms of 1881–1882 were basically a one-time occurrence, with only a few more anti-Jewish riots taking place in 1883, most notably in Ekaterinoslav. The structural framework of the 1905 pogroms was completely different, as the violence directed against Jews was part of a much larger phenomenon of societal unrest. There is also evidence that the content of the two pogrom outbreaks was substantially different, as has been pointed out by Hans Rogger: whereas accusations against Jews in 1881 centered around the charge of exploitation, in 1905 the charge that was being hurled at them by the government and various groups within society was much more serious by far: sedition.[57] If in 1881 the mobs rioted to exact revenge on the Jews and take back what was rightfully theirs, in 1905 they rioted to protect the fatherland.[58] Once the specific instabilities in the social fabric that had given rise to the pogroms of 1881–1882 had passed, the threat of violence really was over; the peasants and townspeople had settled the score, albeit in a frenzy of drunkenness, and thus all, it seemed, were prepared to call it quits. (This impression seems to be borne out by Kutaisov's tendentious but intriguing observation that after the pogrom, peasants exhibited "an outstanding goodnaturedness, diametrically opposed to the frenzy of their actions during the disorders. They had, as it were, given vent to all their accumulated bile, all their anger against the Jews . . . and [considered] their task completed. . . .)[59] Expulsion or economic ruin was the worst that an unpredictable, but basically sane, government could threaten. But after the earthquake of 1905, the ground settled into a much more unsteady position. If Jews posed a mortal threat to an empire that seemed already to be heading toward collapse, anything was possible. And this was especially true now that the fate of Russia's Jews seemed to lie in the hands of mobs that were both unpredictable and irrational, mobs to which even government officials were joining up or at least showing sympathy. In the final analysis, no one—neither Jew nor Christian—knew who was holding the sword that hung over the heads of Kiev's Jews, or when it would fall.

Acknowledgments

This chapter has been possible in part by a grant from the British Academy. I am grateful to David Rechter, Leah Hochman, David Engel, Abigail Green, and John Klier for their helpful comments. All errors remain my own.

Notes

1. Simon Kuznets, "Immigration of Russian Jews to the United States: Background and Structure," *Perspectives in American History* 9 (1975): 86–93.

2. Benjamin Nathans, *Beyond the Pale: The Jewish Encounter with Late Imperial Russia* (Berkeley and Los Angeles: University of California Press, 2002), 187.

3. *Evreiskaia entsiklopediia*, s.v. "Kiev"; *Jewish Encyclopedia*, s.v. "Kiev"; *Encyclopedia Judaica*, 1st ed., s.v. "Kiev"; Michael Hamm, *Kiev: A Portrait, 1800–1917* (Princeton, N.J.: Princeton University Press, 1993), 3–17, 117–121; M. I. Kulisher, "Evrei v Kieve: Istoricheskii ocherk," *Evreiskaia starina* 5 (1913): 351–366, 417–438; Iulii Gessen, "Getto v Rossii," *Evreiskii mir* no. 13 (1 April 1910); idem, "Mnogostradal'naia obshchina," *Evreiskii mir* 22 (25 September 1910).

4. Yakov Lestschinsky, "Di idishe bafelkerung in Kiev fun 1897 biz 1923," *Bleter far idishe demografye, statistik un ekonomik* 5 (1925): 50.

5. *Kievlianin* no. 146, 10 December 1866; 582–583; no. 138, 18 November 1872: 1–2.

6. See, for example, *Kievlianin* no. 93, 25 April 1880.

7. A. E. Kaufman, "Cherta osedlosti v miniatiure," *Russkii evrei* (1880), no. 16: 613.

8. P. I. Kutaisov, "Pogromy v Kieve i Kievskoi gubernii" in *Materialy dlia istorii antievreiskikh pogromov v Rossii,* ed. G. Ia. Krasnyi-Admoni (Petrograd-Moscow: Gosudarstvennoe izdatel'stvo, 1923), 428.

9. *Ha-melits* 5 May 1881: 346.

10. *Ha-magid* 4 May 1881 (22 April 1881 o.s.).

11. Irwin Michael Aronson, *Troubled Waters: The Origins of the 1881 Anti-Jewish Pogroms in Russia* (Pittsburgh: University of Pittsburgh Press, 1990), 75–93.

12. *Materialy dlia istorii antievreiskikh pogromov,* 413; Aronson, *Troubled Waters,* 97.

13. *Materialy dlia istorii antievreiskikh pogromov,* 396.

14. Aronson, *Troubled Waters,* 87.

15. *Evreiskaia entsiklopediia,* s.v. "Kiev."

16. *Ha-melits* no. 50, 9 January 1883. Compare Yehuda Leib Levin (Yehalel), "Yakiru ve-yed'u," *Ha-melits* no. 10, 9 March 1882: 173, cited in Jonathan Frankel, *Prophecy and Politics: Socialism, Nationalism, and the Russian Jews, 1862–1917* (Cambridge: Cambridge University Press, 1981), 77.

17. See, for example, *Ha-melits* no. 81, 1 November 1885: 1311–1317 on the inauguration of Kiev's new Jewish Hospital building.

18. Kievskoe Obshchestvo Gramotnosti, *Otchet za . . . god* (Kiev, 1896–1906).

19. *Nedel'naia khronika Voskhoda,* no. 24, 13 June 1899: 732; *Izvestiia Kievskoi gorodskoi dumy* no. 6 (June) 1906; Kievskaia gorodskaia uchilishchnaia komissiia, *Otchet . . . za 1909g.* (Kiev, 1911).

20. *Sankt-Peterburgskie vedemosti* no. 175, 27 June 1884: 3.

21. Charters Wynn, *Workers, Strikes, and Pogroms: The Donbass-Dnepr Bend in Late Imperial Russia, 1870–1905* (Princeton, N.J.: Princeton University Press, 1992), 111.

22. For an intriguing analysis of the role of civil society in interethnic conflict, see Ashutosh Varshney, "Ethnic Conflict and Civil Society: India and Beyond," *World Politics* 53, no. 3 (April 2001): 362–398. I am grateful to David Engel for this reference.

23. *Ha-melits* no. 121, 27 May 1894.

24. *Nedel'naia khronika Voskhoda* no. 38, 21 September 1897: 1040–41.

25. See, for example, *Nedel'naia khronika Voskhoda* no. 23, 5 June 1894 and no. 60, 21 October 1901.

26. *Ha-melits* no. 85, 15 April 1891 and no. 107, 15 May 1891.

27. Note, for example, that large-scale expulsions took place in the autumn of 1881 not only in Kiev but also in Orel, Tambov, and Dubno. Frankel, *Prophecy and Politics*, 68.

28. For "legislative pogrom," see S. M. Dubnow, *History of the Jews in Russian and Poland* (Philadelphia: Jewish Publication Society, 1916), II, 309; for "cold pogrom," see S. M. Berk, *Year of Crisis, Year of Hope: Russian Jewry and the Pogroms of 1881–1882* (Westport, Conn., and London, 1985), 180; for "silent pogrom," see Nathans, *Beyond the Pale*, 257.

29. *Voskhod* no. 35, 29 August 1902, p. 13.

30. David Vital, *The Origins of Zionism* (Oxford: Clarendon Press, 1975), 157; Frankel, *Prophecy and Politics*, 116.

31. *Ha-melits* no. 101, 24 December 1884: 1657.

32. Ezra Mendelsohn, *Class Struggle in the Pale* (Cambridge: Cambridge University Press, 1970); Wynn, *Workers, Strikes, and Pogroms*, 144ff.; Henry Tobias, *The Jewish Bund in Russia: From Its Origins to 1905* (Stanford, Calif.: Stanford University Press, 1972). On the other hand, 1881 also did not mark the absolute *terminus a quo* of revolutionary activism, as Erich Haberer makes clear in *Jews and Revolution in Nineteenth-Century Russia* (New York: Cambridge University Press, 1995).

33. Moshe Mishkinsky, *Reshit tenu'at ha-po'alim ha-yehudit be-rusyah* (Tel-Aviv: Tel-Aviv University, 1981), 32–33.

34. See Steven J. Zipperstein, *Imagining Russian Jewry: Memory, History, Identity* (Seattle: University of Washington Press, 1999).

35. Israel Darewski, *Le-korot ha-yehudim be-Kiyov* (Berditshov: Hayim Ya'akov Sheftel, 1902), 8.

36. *Voskhod* no. 42–43, 27 October 1905: 51–52.

37. Hamm, *Kiev*, 192.

38. *Voskhod* no. 18, 1 May 1903: 14

39. Hamm, *Kiev*, 193. Sam Johnson has shown that a similar kind of shock was displayed by British Jews: in the coverage of the *Jewish Chronicle* to the Kishinev pogrom of 1903, "no connection was, for instance, made to the pogroms of 1881–1882." Sam Johnson, "Responses to Tragedy: Kishinev and the Jewish Press," presented at "The History and Culture of Russian and East European Jewry: New Sources, New Approaches: The Jewish Press in Russia," Moscow, 9–11 December 2007.

40. *Khronika evreiskoi zhizni* no. 11, 22 March 1906: 27.

41. Ibid., no. 20, 25 May 1906: 37.

42. Ibid., no. 22, 8 June 1906: 31.

43. *Razsvet* no. 17, 3 May 1908: 24–25.

44. Ibid, no. 25, 29 June 1908: 28 and no. 30, 3 August 1908: 23. For a similar incident several years later, see Tsentral'nyi derzhavnyi istorychnyi arkhiv Ukraïny, Kyïv (Central State Historical Archive of Ukraine, Kyiv) f. 1010, op. 1, spr. 159.

45. See, for example, *Razsvet* no. 20–21, 24 May 1909: 28; *Evreiskii mir* no. 35, 23 December 1910: 32; *Novyi voskhod* no. 27, 5 July 1912.

46. Vladimir Liubchenko, " 'Pogrom visit v vozdukhe': obshchestvennye nastroeniia v Kieve posle pokusheniia na P. A. Stolypina (po materiialam perliustratsii)," *Vestnik Evreiskogo universiteta v Moskve* 1 (1999), 19: 272–286.

47. *Novyi voskhod* no. 11, 15 March 1912: 11–12; no. 12–13, 22 March 1912: 23–24; no. 14, 5 April 1912: 21.

48. Ibid., no. 37, 13 September 1912.

49. Sholom Aleichem, *The Bloody Hoax*, trans. *Alliza Shevrin* (Bloomington: Indiana University Press, 1992), 97. Eliezer Friedmann recalled a similar scene in his memoirs, *Sefer ha-zikhronot* (Tel-Aviv, 1926), II: 369–371.

50. P. T. Neishtube, *Istoricheskaia zapiska v pamiat' 50-ti letiia sushchestvovaniia Kievskoi Evreiskoi Bol'nitsy, 1862–1912g.* (Kiev, 1913), 166–167.

51. Ger. Bad—s [G. E. Gurevich], "Kievskaia evreiskaia obshchina v 1913 g.," *Vestnik evreiskoi obshchiny* no. 3 (March 1914): 34; Gershon Badanes [G. E. Gurevich], "Kievskaia evreiskaia obshchina na Vserossiiskoi Vystavke 1913 g. v Kieve," *Vestnik evreiskoi obshchiny* no. 2 (September 1913): 31.

52. See, for example, *Nedel'naia khronika Voskhoda* no. 45, 6 November 1894: 1194 and Gershon Badanes [G. E. Gurevich], "Kievskaia evreiskaia obshchina na Vserossiiskoi Vystavke 1913 g. v Kieve," *Vestnik evreiskoi obshchiny* no. 4 (October 1913): 20–21.

53. Nathans, *Beyond the Pale*, 9.

54. Vital, *Origins*, 179 (emphasis added).

55. Nathans, *Beyond the Pale;* Chae-Ran Y. Freeze, *Jewish Marriage and Divorce in Imperial Russia* (Hanover, N.H.: Brandeis University Press and University Press of New England, 2002); Mendelsohn, *Class Struggle in the Pale*.

56. See Harriet Murav, *Identity Theft: The Jew in Imperial Russia and the Case of Avraam Uri Kovner* (Stanford, Calif.: Stanford University Press, 2003); Gabriella Safran, *Rewriting the Jew: Assimilation Narratives in the Russian Empire* (Stanford, Calif.: Stanford University Press, 2000); Eugene M. Avrutin, "A Legible People: Identification Politics and Jewish Accommodation in Tsarist Russia" (Ph.D. diss., University of Michigan, 2004), esp. Chapter 6.

57. Hans Rogger, "Conclusion and Overview," in *Pogroms: Anti-Jewish Violence in Modern Russian History*, ed. John D. Klier and Shlomo Lambrozo (Cambridge: Cambridge University Press, 1992), 342. True, Jews had been charged with "international conspiracy" in 1881, but that reference to the fantastical idea of a world Jewish *kahal* was a relatively minor theme at the time and did not extend to visions of revolutionary Jews seeking to overthrow the tsarist government.

58. For other differences between these "waves" and the views of Simon Dubnow and Ahad Ha-am on the matter, see Frankel, *Prophecy and Politics*, 136ff.

59. *Materialy dlia istorii antievreiskikh pogromov*, 403; Aronson, *Troubled Waters*, 121.

PART 3

Regional Perspectives

❧ 7 ❧

The Possibility of the Impossible: Pogroms in Eastern Siberia

LILIA KALMINA

Siberia as a whole, and even more specifically, eastern Siberia, the vast colonial borderlands of the Russian Empire, would seem the least likely area for anti-Jewish pogroms.[1] Virtually none of the factors advanced to explain pogroms in the Pale of Settlement was present. Jews were few, constituting no more than 1 percent of the population of Siberia, and were widely dispersed. Moreover, none of the typical complaints leveled against the Jews of the Pale—economic exploitation, religious fanaticism, the secret machinations of the *kahal,* ancient traditions of religious or ethnic rivalry—was applicable in Siberia. Far from being seen as "exploiters"—despite occasional ritualistic claims on this score—Jews were generally welcomed for their contribution to the economic development of the region. There was no danger, for example, of an "overconcentration" of Jewish tradesmen or artisans. Siberian Jews fully exemplified the "assimilation narratives" identified by Gabriella Safran: they quickly adapted to an alien culture and displayed their ability to think and look just like representatives of the dominant nationality.[2]

Background

As a rule, Jews arrived in Siberia unwillingly, as convicted criminals who came as exiles starting in the eighteenth century. During the reigns of Tsars Nicholas I and Alexander II, other categories of Jews were also allowed there. Even with the temporary migrations of these nonconvicts, exiles remained the first, most numerous, and most stable group of Siberian Jews. Opposition arose to this trend among Siberian governors-general, who consistently were against the exile of Jews because it increased the Jewish population. The "problem" was aggravated by the fact that exiled Jews were followed by members of their families, whose numbers equaled or surpassed those of the exiles themselves. By 1898, there were 7,946 Jews in the territory of the Irkutsk governorship (encompassing virtually the whole of eastern Siberia), including 4,197 people who had come there of their own free will.[3]

By the end of the nineteenth century, the profile of Jewish exiles had changed drastically. At this time, those exiled for antigovernment activities joined the existing motley combination of thieves, robbers, and vagrants. The numbers of the more "political" newcomers soon exceeded those of previously exiled Jews who had been sent to the east because of petty crime. As a result of the Jews' active role in all the revolutionary parties, the proportion of Jews among all exiles increased from 13.8 to 18.6 percent between 1908 and 1914, while the percentage of other ethnic categories steadily diminished.[4] In some regions, the percentage was even higher: between 1878 and 1905, a total of 455 Jews were exiled to Yakutiia on political grounds—more than half of all political exiles during that period.[5]

A second group of Siberian Jews was composed of cantonists (child soldiers) and soldiers who had completed their active service and wished to remain in the area. They possessed the strongest claims to civil rights among Siberia's Jews because they were permitted to leave the Pale of Settlement after their service was completed. Having preserved their religious identity during their military service, they were the most committed members of the Siberian Jewish religious communities. Other Jewish groups were not numerous. These included a few agricultural settlers who had come to develop Siberian lands on the basis of a law dated 20 November 1835 stating that Jews willing to be engaged in agriculture were to be given plots in Tobolsk *guberniia* (a province ruled by a civilian governor) and Omsk *oblast* (an area ruled by a military governor) in Siberia. They numbered only 1,317 persons and their descendants later dispersed all over Siberia. In addition, a scattering of craftsmen and traders had "arrived accidentally" in Siberia under various circumstances.[6]

A law dated 15 May 1837 sought to limit the Jewish population of Siberia, prohibiting access to the region for all categories of Jews except criminal exiles and soldiers on active duty. The provisos of the law stipulated that exiled Jews be settled separately to the east of Lake Baikal and Yakutsk province, far from "native" Siberian peoples. But from the very beginning it was evident that it was impossible to apply the law in Yakutiia. All uninhabited lands were unfit for human habitation, and to the east of Lake Baikal, Jewish settlers, mainly elderly people, were doomed to starvation, as they were unable to pursue farming in the harsh Siberian climate. They were forced to earn their living with seasonal work, domestic service or begging. Jews were formally allowed to settle among

Russian "old-timers" in Siberia only after passage of a law on 12 June 1860.

Organized Jewish life in Siberia faced great challenges. At best, a small community of settlers might establish a prayer house, but it was impossible to recreate the full panoply of Jewish religious life, especially given the absence of trained religious leadership. In addition, as noted above, Russian law governing Jewish settlement in Siberia specifically forbade them to settle in compact communities.

Paradoxically, antisemitism also faced challenges in Russia's eastern borderlands. Russian officials posted to the east might bring Judeophobic rhetoric with them, but they did not find an appropriate target for their prejudices. Stressing that Siberia was, after all, part of the Russian Empire, Vladimir Rabinovich has suggested that exiles and immigrants brought and preserved antisemitic attitudes to the area as a means of defining their own identity.[7] Even taking these factors into consideration, this explanation is an oversimplification: it does not clarify why antisemitic rhetoric or public attitudes were *not* translated into action. It seems more likely that the general population displayed the typical characteristics of a frontier society in the form of a rough-and-ready toleration for all. Moreover, it was widely accepted that the average "Siberian" showed little deference or respect for higher authority.

The example of one imperial institution—the Russian Orthodox Church—often seen as hostile to the Jews, is illustrative. The Siberian Orthodox leadership was, in fact, more concerned with encouraging the moral probity of its scattered flocks than in stirring up religious antagonism. In Irkutsk, for example, Orthodox Church leaders in the 1880s rejected the wave of xenophobia that swept over Russia and stressed to the faithful the sinfulness of pogrom-mongering.[8] If, as Benjamin Nathans argues, discrimination against Jews in Imperial Russia was the result of the clash between an *ancien régime* and the devotion of Jews to a traditional way of life,[9] the second factor was totally absent in Siberia. The Orthodox Church tolerated Siberian Jews mainly because of their nontraditionalism; their way of life did not differ greatly from that of other Siberians.

Yet, there were events in eastern Siberia that have been described as pogroms. Most of the nineteenth century was free of anything that could be accurately described as such, although a few outbreaks of violence on the eve of the twentieth century will be noted here. The wave of pogroms of 1881–1882 in the Pale did not extend to Siberia. When pogroms occurred in 1905 in Irkutsk and Tomsk, and in 1916–1917 in Krasnoiarsk, Bogotol, Biysk, Novonikolaevsk, Barnaul, and some villages in Tomsk and

Yenisei provinces, they were part of wider sociopolitical dramas associated with revolution and war. Indeed, it is questionable whether they should be considered "anti-Jewish pogroms" at all. In any event, the very unlikelihood of eastern Siberia as a venue for pogroms makes their occurrence worthy of the scholar's attention.

Certain features characterize the pogrom-style violence that finally arrived in Siberia. Violence spread from west to east, and never advanced east of the Lake Baikal region. "Pogroms" in 1905 (Irkutsk and Tomsk) and in 1916 (Krasnoiarsk) never began as purely anti-Jewish events. Even when they expanded to include attacks on Jews, they never focused solely on a Jewish target. In both cases, the violence began as riots against the authorities, as a form of public discontent in the context of social instability. The setting in Irkutsk and Tomsk was the all-Russian railroad strike that was a feature of the Revolution of 1905; in Krasnoiarsk, it was a protest against the shortage of goods, including foodstuffs, high prices, and the decline in living standards caused by World War I. Let us examine the three outbreaks in some detail.

Irkutsk

The events in Irkutsk that have been described by some researchers as an anti-Jewish pogrom began on 13 October 1905. On that day, railroad workers declared a strike, which was followed the next day by a citywide wave of meetings. Two days later, leaflets of both an economic and political nature were distributed throughout the city. In response, on 16 October, Black Hundreds–style antirevolutionary forces began to organize, leading to violent clashes between them and the striking workers. At no point did this agitation or violence affect the Jews of Irkutsk. The first "anti-Jewish" events occurred only on 17 October, when an antirevolutionary mob attempted to storm the offices of the Trans-Baikal Railroad, which was serving as the headquarters for the striking workers. The mob savagely beat anyone attempting to flee the building. In the course of the disorders, ten people were killed and twenty wounded, including Russians and Jews.[10] In the melee, the Jewish brothers Ilya and Jacob Winer were killed when they rushed to protect one of the strikers and were set upon by the violent mob. Despite the later characterization of the event, I regard the Winers as accidental victims whose ethnoreligious identity was irrelevant to their status as victims. Meanwhile, however, other events did indeed take on a truly anti-Jewish orientation. Though democratic forces had succeeded in blocking previous attempts by the Black Hundreds to provoke mass disorders, agitators successfully induced a mob to rob Jewish shops, and began to beat Jews and other opponents alike. Even after suppression of the strike and the restoration of public order, Jews had reason to fear pogroms for another few days.

It is useful to contrast the October 1905 events in Irkutsk with the "October Days" in the Pale of Settlement. The latter featured wide-scale attacks on the Jews in the aftermath of Tsar Nicholas II's political concessions contained in the October Manifesto. Those pogroms, which usually broke out while people were celebrating the promulgation of the manifesto, were overtly political. The reported defacing of imperial portraits and regalia during these celebrations outraged loyalists. The riots were often connected to alleged shots fired at loyalist demonstrations. Jews were the most prominent but not the only victims of *pogromshchiki* during the counterrevolution. Their concentration in certain neighborhoods and districts, as, for example in Kiev and Odessa, provided a specific "Jewish" geographical target for Black Hundred-style bands in 1905.

In Irkutsk, by contrast, Jews were not singled out as revolutionaries or "trouble-makers." The mob never followed advice to "beat the Yids." The Jewish identity of the Winer brothers became apparent only at their funeral. Nevertheless, despite its Jewish overtones, at the time the Winer funeral was seen primarily as a demonstration by the "progressive and democratic public." One brother, Ilya, had been active in the local Zionist movement,[11] and fellow members took the floor to deliver a eulogy at the funeral. Thus, many Irkutsk residents (and later researchers as well) attributed a "Jewish" aspect to the events in October 1905.

Tomsk

Compared to Irkutsk, the counterrevolutionary nature of the disorders and the element of premeditation in Tomsk were much more in evidence. The riots occurred on 21–23 October 1905, after news of the October Manifesto reached the city. The *pogromshchiki* did not disguise their intentions. Reportedly, they assembled a list of their intended victims and asked the local archbishop to give his blessing to their proposed actions. Although the riots took place against the background of the all-Russian strike, the Jews were identified at the very start as the enemy of stability, law, and order. There were no such disastrous and clearly anti-Jewish pogroms in other parts of Siberia, confirming our contention that the wave of pogroms declined in intensity from the west to the east. Due to lack of space, the discussion here of the events in Tomsk will not go into further detail because the city is situated in western Siberia and, therefore, somewhat outside the geographical framework of this paper. It is included here for the purposes of comparison to more easterly parts of the region.[12]

Krasnoiarsk

The Krasnoiarsk riots of 7 May 1916 more closely resembled pogroms in the Pale, particularly in their elements of premeditation and instigation. The pogrom grew out of a stereotypical clash between Jews and non-Jews: specifically, a quarrel between a Jewish shop girl and a Russian woman. A crowd gathered and began to attack the shop owner. Significantly, it was reported that "by chance" the rioting women had stones hidden in their shopping bags, which strongly implies that plans had been made in advance. The riot escalated and more than sixty shops, mainly Jewish, were destroyed. Archival evidence suggests that Colonel Martynov, the commander of the Krasnoiarsk garrison, successfully deployed his troops to suppress the riots, although some soldiers sympathized with the *pogromshchiki* and exploited the opportunity to steal goods. Nevertheless, the colonel did his best to disperse the mob. In any case, a Jewish delegation later met with General Karneev, who came to Krasnoiarsk to investigate the incident, and expressed their gratitude to Martynov. According to some rumors, the Jews were merely being supported by one of their own because Martynov was of Jewish origin. At any rate, the riot was suppressed by regular troops because the police were unable to cope with the situation. At least one police officer, Ignatov, was beaten by the rioters.[13]

The fact that Jewish shops bore the brunt of the looting gives this incident its particular "Jewish" coloration. Ironically, Jewish losses would probably have been greater had there been a concentrated Jewish district. I have already mentioned the 1860 law that banned compact Jewish settlement in Siberia, ordering Jews to settle among the Russian population. The reports of high-ranking Siberian authorities indicated that this stipulation helped Jews to acculturate into the majority population and to assume the "settled way of life" that was a desideratum of tsarist policy regarding the Jews.[14] It is thus no surprise that *pogromshchiki* had trouble targeting Jews when Jewish and Russian families lived in one and the same house.

Participants

On the basis of contemporary accounts it is possible to determine the social status of participants in the Siberia disorders with some precision.

They tended to be petty shopkeepers, peasants, and craftsmen, usually not very successful ones. Clearly an element of business-related jealousy and a desire to eliminate rivals played a role. Workers and Cossacks did not figure in the pogroms as they did in the Pale, where Cossacks in particular were prominent during World War I and the Civil War. The sole clash between Cossacks and Jews recorded in the archives occurred in 1896. In that year, Cossacks demanded the eviction of some Jews from the settlement (*stanitsa*) of Sretenskaia, where the governor-general had permitted them to settle on the supposition that they would assist in the economic development of the region.[15] Jews had resided there for decades, but Cossacks felt slighted in the competition for markets.[16] A word about Jewish economic activity in Siberia is in order here. Small net profit or trading at a loss (initially, at least, in order to attract more customers) were characteristic of economic activity among Jews in the region, and they often offered contracts for lower prices and took leases on more profitable conditions. Contemporary researchers observed that Russian Jews did not demand high prices but relied on a rapid turnover at lower prices.[17] In Siberia, this characteristic was particularly striking: for former exiles their status as irreplaceable middlemen in trade, with a reliable customer base, was more important than immediate profit. The purely economic motives of the Cossack petition are evident from the fact that it targeted only the richest Jews, their most successful rivals. In any event, Cossacks sought to deal with Jews by means of peaceful petitions, without resorting to violence.

Even during the Civil War there were no confrontations between Cossacks and Jews in the region. Moreover, in November 1919, *Sibirskii kazak* (The Siberian Cossack), the official organ of the Siberian Cossack Army, published an article titled "Siberian Cossacks and Antisemitism." The author rejected rumors that Cossacks were planning pogroms, declaring that Cossacks would never fight against civilians. The article asserted that Jews living in towns under the protection of the Russian government and its laws should not bear any responsibility for the actions of Jewish commissars and Bolsheviks. In case of riots, the Cossacks offered the Jews protection and promised to repress the *pogromshchiki*.[18]

In times of relative economic stability in Siberia, representatives of different ethnic communities developed a form of social compact that mitigated against intercommunal violence. When commercial rivalry was expressed in demands for the eviction of Jews (and other non-Russians), as in Verkhneudinsk and Barguzin, or in calls for an economic boycott of "others," as in Irkutsk and Krasnoiarsk, such initiatives invariably failed. Most citizens strongly opposed the eviction of Jews and condemned anti-Jewish boycotts.

Large-scale merchants interested in the economic development of the region refused to part with their Jewish agents and frequently demanded that discriminatory action directed against Jews be curtailed. Twenty-seven of the largest firms in Irkutsk sent a letter to the Irkutsk Stock Exchange Committee in 1914 in which they insisted on the right of Jewish residents from other cities to operate in Irkutsk. From their point of view, a ban on Jewish merchants visiting the town threatened to harm regional trade.[19] Three years earlier, Irkutsk merchants had threatened to stop all donations to the Irkutsk Commercial College if the authorities did not reduce the restrictions on Jewish enrollment imposed by the *numerus clausus*.[20] Under such pressure, even the local police ignored orders to remove Jews, as they were seen to contribute to the development of the towns where they resided.[21] Local authorities in general dismissed petitions that Jews be expelled from specific towns and villages, attributing the petitions to the desire to eliminate commercial rivals.[22]

In times of crisis, however, this compact could break down; World War I provides an apt example. The obsession with Jewish "treason" that marked the Russian army in the field infiltrated Siberia and poisoned interethnic relations there. Soldiers returning from the front condemned the disgraceful activities of Russian Jews, their complicity with the enemy, their espionage and treason, and their profiteering and other harmful economic activities. As one soldier wrote, "Everybody realized that among the black marketeers who raised prices on consumer goods, Jews and their banks played the main role."[23] In Siberia, as well as in the heart of the empire, Jews could serve as the scapegoats for all the regime's military and supply failures. Nevertheless, as the disorders of 1905 indicate, Jews in Siberia (with the obvious exception of those exiled for political crimes) were not widely regarded as revolutionaries.[24] Indeed, Siberia, with its dispersed Jewish population, was hardly receptive to the politics of the various Jewish revolutionary parties such as the Bund.

Instigators?

Contemporary scholarship has largely rejected the claim that the Russian government instigated, tolerated, or welcomed pogroms at any level. At most, scholars have tended to contrast the energetic actions taken by provincial authorities in 1881–1882 with the indecision and paralysis that marked their response in 1905 in the face of the turmoil of revolution and counterrevolution. The Siberian authorities' response during the events described above most often conformed to the pattern of apathy and passivity. Even if they were not guilty of direct involvement in pogroms, they seem guilty of passivity, as the following examples reveal.

In 1905, the governor-general of Irkutsk (*Irkutskoe General-Gubernatorstvo*, one of two eastern Siberian general-governorships, in contradistinction to the city of Irkutsk), Pavel Innokentievich Kutaisov, took no action to prevent pogroms, but at the same time did not oppose the organization of public self-defense units, which included non-Jews as well as Jews.[25] Although local Jews expressed gratitude that he did not authorize "patriotic" (i.e., hooliganistic) demonstrations, his failure to take preventive measures emboldened these elements.[26]

Local politics could also play a role. The Krasnoiarsk disorders in 1916 took place when secular forces, led by Yenisei's governor Jacob Georgievich Gololobov, and the religious authorities headed by Archbishop Nikon were locked in a power struggle. Rather than strongly condemning the rioters themselves, Nikon sought to place the blame for the disorders on the inaction and connivance of the governor. In turn, in his reports to his superior, the governor-general of Irkutsk (Aleksandr Ivanovich Pilts), Gololobov attempted to conceal the social and political elements in the disorders. He tried to dismiss the riot as nothing more than interethnic conflict between Russians and Jews, seeing its roots in "a lack of public sympathy toward Jews." A complex political and socioeconomic situation in the midst of wartime was thus dismissed as "a Jewish pogrom."

Four sets of actors characterize the "Siberian pogroms" that took place during the first decades of the twentieth century in Irkutsk and Tomsk. The first were high-ranking Siberian officials whose duty was to put an end to riots but who in reality were unwilling to take any decisive measures; in a sense, they were "passive *pogromshchiki*." The second group was comprised of low-ranking policemen, who as a rule appeared to approve of pogroms and even occasionally participated in them. Significantly, when describing police activities during pogroms in Krasnoiarsk, the two enemies—Yenisei Governor Gololobov and Archbishop Nikon—concurred that "low-ranking policemen were standing idly by or acting very passively, displaying indulgence and even sympathy for the robbers," as the governor wrote to Pilts. As Nikon stated, Russian shops suffered less damage than Jewish ones because police officials took greater care to protect them.[27] Nevertheless, Archbishop Nikon conceded that Russian merchants and their expensive goods irritated the population just as much as the Jewish ones. Governor Gololobov claimed that the reason why four times as many Jewish as Russian shops were destroyed was that there were so many more of them.[28] This contention is dubious because the Jews of Krasnoiarsk amounted to slightly more than 2 percent of the population. The third group—the active *pogromshchiki*—was composed of owners of small shops, peasants, and criminal elements. As a center of exile and hard labor, Siberia attracted many marginal criminal elements who, after serving their sentence, remained in the area without any occupation. Having arrived from western regions, they were often considered to harbor antisemitic attitudes and were regular participants in ethnically oriented disturbances. The fourth group consisted of the democratically minded public, including the intelligentsia, the clergy, substantial merchants, and some workers who actively resisted the *pogromshchiki*.

The inclusion of members of the clergy in the category of resistance requires some explanation. Although the Russian Orthodox clergy cannot be described as uniformly active opponents of antisemitism, some of them did actively oppose pogroms as a part of their obligation to defend the public order. In his *Letopis'* (Annals), Nil Romanov, a regional historian and chronicler, wrote about the funeral service for Archbishop Veniamin, claiming that it was due to his moral authority with believers that he was able to prevent the disorders that threatened in 1891.[29] We should also mention Nikon, Archbishop of Krasnoiarsk, who so openly expressed his appreciation of the role of Jews in the town's social life that the Black Hundred sympathizers gave him the sobriquet of the "King of the Yids."[30] His sharp criticism of the 1916 disorders is noteworthy but, indeed, it was also linked to his desire to discredit his rival Gololobov. Understandably, town leaders opposed mob violence. In a special session of the Krasnoiarsk Town Duma, city councilors condemned the pogrom and expressed confidence that their fellow townspeople "would not lose control and would refrain from further riots."[31] Evidently, thus, there were pragmatic people in Siberia who understood the true role and diverse functions of Siberian Jews in the region's economy and in public life. Such people realized that those qualities were more important than any hypothetical evils borne by Jews or any prejudices connected with them.

* * *

Anti-Jewish pogroms in Siberia were rare events, engendered by socioeconomic crises. During periods of political stability and relative economic well-being, Siberians were tolerant of strangers of all types, affording them ample scope to find their economic niche. This generally applied to the Jews, who were few in number and widely dispersed throughout the territory. Siberian society for the most part avoided the Judeophobia that was increasingly evident in the heartland of Russia and in the provinces of the Pale of Settlement.[32] Siberia had no need for Jewish scapegoats, and Judeophobic sentiments espoused by tsarist officials appointed to the region found no wide resonance in Siberian society. At most, there was an element of envy and rivalry with the small number of Jews who had "made it" in the east. This was balanced by the grudging recognition among local figures that Jews played a useful role in the economic life of the region.

The revolutionary year of 1905 proved to be a watershed. Although the disorders in Irkutsk and Tomsk were not political pogroms in the sense that characterized the "October Days" in the Pale, they alerted Jews to the reality that periods of instability threatened their property and even their physical safety. This feeling of insecurity was confirmed by the Krasnoiarsk riot of 1916, which also showed the extent to which wartime xenophobia and antisemitism could spread in the wake of military defeat and demoralization. Nonetheless, the spread of the anti-Jewish movement was gradual, and it weakened perceptibly as it moved from west to east. Unlike the situation in the more western parts of Russia and its neighbors during World War I and the Civil War, groups in Siberia, such as the Cossacks, proved to be defenders rather than enemies of the Jews. Consequently, even passive Siberian Jews began to reconsider their political apathy. It was telling that Ilya Winer, one of the victims of the Irkutsk pogrom, died as a defender of striking workers but was eulogized at his funeral as a Zionist. Cultural and political changes came slowly to Siberia, but they did arrive, and Jews could not but acknowledge this.[33]

Acknowledgments

This study was carried out with the support of the International Center for Russian and East European Jewish Studies in Moscow.

Notes

1. The term *eastern Siberia* refers to Yenisei, Irkutsk *guberniias* (provinces), Transbaikal and Yakutsk *oblasts* (regions), in accordance with the administrative division of the region at that time.

2. Gabriella Safran, *Rewriting the Jew: Assimilation Narratives in the Russian Empire* (Stanford, Calif.: Stanford University Press, 2000), 193.

3. Gosudarstvennyi arkhiv Irkutskoi oblasti (State Archive of Irkutsk Oblast') (GAIO), f. 25, op. 6, k. 449, d. 196, ll. 28–29.

4. Nikolai Shcherbakov, "Chislennost' i sostav politicheskikh ssyl'nykh Sibiri (1907–1917 gg.),"*Ssyl'nye revolutsionery Sibiri (XIX—Fevr. 1917g.)*, issue 1 (Irkutsk: izd-vo IGU, 1973), 225.

5. Pavel Kazarian, "Chislennost' i sostav politicheskikh ssyl'nykh evreev v Yakutskoy oblasti 1878–1905 gg.," *Evrei v Sibiri i na Dal'nem Vostoke: istoriia i sovremennost': Materialy IV regional'noi nauchno-prakticheskoi konferentsii 25–26 avgusta 2003g.* (Krasnoiarsk; Birobidzhan: Klaretianum, 2003), 29.

6. For details, see Lilia Kalmina, *Evreiskie obshchiny Vostochnoi Sibiri (seredina XIX v.-fevral' 1917 goda)* (Ulan-Ude: IPK VSGAKI, 2003), 86–90.

7. Vladimir Rabinovich, "Evrei ili sibiriak?," *Ab imperio* 4 (2003): 132–133.

8. Nil Romanov, *Letopis' goroda Irkutska za 1881–1901 gg.* (Irkutsk: Vostochno-Sibirskoe Knizhnoe izdatel'stvo, 1993), 258.

9. Benjamin Nathans, "Russko-Evreiskaia vstrecha," *Ab imperio* 4 (2003): 29.

10. Natalia Orekhova, "Evreiskii pogrom v Krasnoiarske v 1916 g.," *Istoriia evreiskikh obshchin Sibiri i Dal'nego Vostoka: Materialy II regional'noi nauchno-prakticheskoi konferentsii 25–27 avgusta 2001g.* (Krasnoiarsk; Irkutsk: Klaretianum, 2001), 53.

11. The Zionist movement that sprang up in Siberia at the beginning of the twentieth century was not initially a mass phenomenon. Its adherents regarded the Zionist idea as a commercial project or as a symbol of adherence to what they perceived as European ethical and spiritual values. There were only a few Zionist ideologues, mainly in Irkutsk and Tomsk—the acknowledged centers of the Zionist movement in Siberia. The strong economic position of Jews in Siberia, and their desire to secure it more firmly, may explain their lack of interest in the Zionist idea at that time. After the wave of pogroms of 1905 reached Siberia, the local Jewish intelligentsia realized the value of the struggle for national self-determination. Interest in Zionism grew steadily after 1917, and it became the most influential trend among Siberian Jews. In the first general elections for local leadership in Siberia, Zionists won the majority in all the Jewish communities of Siberia and the Far East. In 1919, there were fifty-six Zionist organizations at the district and town levels. Three congresses were held in Siberia: Tomsk (1903), Irkutsk (1912), and again in Tomsk (1918).

12. For details, see Victor Yushkovskii, *Tomskie evrei: litsa na polotne* (Krasnoiarsk: Klaretianum, 2005), 81–93.

13. Gosudarstvennyi arkhiv Krasnoiarskogo kraia (State Archive of Krasnoiarsk Region) (GAKK), f. 595, op. 48, d. 1074, ll. 2, 5.

14. Rossiiskii gosudarstvennyi istoricheskii arkhiv (Russian State Historical Archive), f. 383, op. 15, 1852, d. 18271, l. 174.

15. Lilia Kalmina and Leonid Kuras, *Evreiskaia obshchina v Zapadnom Zabaikal'e (60-e gody XIX veka—Fevral' 1917 goda)* (Ulan-Ude: Izdatel'stvo BNC, 1999), 82.

16. GAIO, f. 29, op. 1, department 3, d. 216. ll. 273, 276–277, 309, 336.

17. Ilya Orshanskii, *Evrei v Rossii* 1 (St. Petersburg: Tipografiia M.Chana, 1872), 112, 140; V. Zombart, *Evrei i khoziaistvennaia zhizn'*, 1 (St. Petersburg: "Razum," 1912), 175.

18. Viktoriia Romanova, *Vlast' i evrei na Dal'nem Vostoke Rossii: istoriia vzaimootnoshenii (vtoraia polovina XIX v.–20-e gody XX v.)* (Krasnoiarsk: Klaretianum, 2001), 141.

19. GAIO, f. 25, op. 9, k. 975, d. 3084, l. 13.

20. Vladimir Voitinskii and Aleksandr Gornshtein, *Evrei v Irkutske* (Irkutsk: Izdatel'stvo Khoz. Pravleniia Irkutskogo Otdela Obshchestva Rasprostraneniia Prosveshcheniia mezhdu Evreiami v Rossii, 1915), 161–163.

21. Kalmina, *Evreiskie obshchiny Vostochnoi Sibiri*, 166, 168.

22. Gosudarstvennyi arkhiv Zabaikal'skogo kraia (State Archive of Transbaikal Region), f. 1(o), op. 1, d. 17139, ll. 214–215; d. 13937, ll. 6, 9; Natsional'nyi arkhiv Respubliki Buriatiia (National Archive of the Republic of Buriatiia), f. 123, op. 1, d. 305, l. 10.

23. GAKK, f. 595, op, 48, d. 1074, l. 3.

24. Andreas Kappeler, *Rossiia—mnogonatsional'naia imperiia: vozniknovenie, istoriia, raspad* (Moscow: Traditsiia-Progress-Traditsiia, 2000), 247.

25. "Governor-General of Irkutsk Governorship" was the title of the Governor of eastern Siberia from 1887.

26. Voitinskii and Gornshtein, *Evrei v Irkutske,* 141–142.

27. GAKK, f. 595, op. 48, d. 1074, l. 3.

28. Ibid., ll. 3–4.

29. Romanov, *Letopis',* 258–259.

30. Orekhova, "Evreiskii pogrom," 54.

31. Ibid.

32. Kappeler, *Rossiia,* 201.

33. Voitinskii and Gornshtein, *Evrei v Irkutske,* 327–329.

Was Lithuania a Pogrom-Free Zone? (1881–1940)

VLADAS SIRUTAVIČIUS AND DARIUS STALIŪNAS

U ntil very recently, evaluations of the relations between Lithuanians and Jews generally reflected the ethnic identity of individual authors. Thus, Lithuanian and general historiography asserted
that—prior to the events of 1941—life in Lithuania was not characterized
by everyday violence against Jews, to say nothing of eruptions of mass
violence described as anti-Jewish pogroms.[1] In contrast, some Jewish authors considered that conflict and a level of violence that foreshadowed the
Holocaust prevailed in Lithuanian–Jewish relations prior to 1941.[2] Postu-
lating a tradition of nonviolence, Lithuanians sought to explain some local
inhabitants' participation in the mass killing of Jews by emphasizing the
influence of the policies of Nazi Germany. Jewish historians interpreted
the events of 1941 and those following as a manifestation of a deep Lithuanian hostility toward Jews that could be triggered by certain political
conditions. Recent research suggests that both sets of explanations are far
too simplistic.

In order to better understand the post-1941 situation, it is vital to examine anti-Jewish violence as well as other aspects of interethnic relations
in the preceding period. A useful starting point is a consideration of the
first modern mass violence against Jews in Eastern Europe, the pogroms
of 1881–1882. The assumption of contemporaries and of modern historiography was that the so-called northwest region of the Russian Empire
(present-day Lithuania and Belarus) managed to avoid pogroms, unlike the
empire's southern, Ukrainian region.[3] Recently, Russian historians have
challenged this assumption.[4] To resolve this dispute, it would be useful to
offer a specific definition of what phenomena fall into the category of a
"pogrom."

Usually, the term *pogrom* is defined as a collective act of violence committed by one segment of the population against another. The term is usually applied to anti-Jewish acts aimed at the destruction of property or
violence against individuals, in some instances even leading to fatalities.[5]

Collective acts of violence are analyzed in academic literature on the basis of several criteria: their mass character, intensity, and duration. While there is a basic scholarly consensus regarding these indicators, there is less agreement about their qualitative aspects. For example, what are the benchmarks for the degree of intensity, the number of participants, or the duration? Are the three indicators of equal importance?

The authors of this article seek to answer these questions in the course of an examination of anti-Jewish violence in the northwest region of the tsarist empire, and interwar Lithuania. A pogrom is defined simply as acts of violence committed by a group of people against Jews, who are targeted specifically because of their identity as Jews. The violence must have a mass character, occurring either in areas of concentration, such as marketplaces, or dispersed over a specific inhabited area. Special attention is directed to the mass nature of the violence, particularly to its intensity, the involvement of groups, as well as to whether the aggression was directed against property and/or persons. We do not consider duration to be of equal significance, since it was shaped by such factors as the number of people involved, the intensity of the acts of violence, and the actions of the authorities. On the other hand, we argue that the *reaction of the responsible authorities* (primarily local) should be an important indicator that shapes collective acts of violence. It is precisely the reaction of public authorities— indicated by their assessment of the situation and their practical actions— that best demonstrates the social importance and significance of eruptions of coercion and violence.

The *causes* of pogroms are a topic of continued scholarly debate. Some researchers argue for the impossibility of ever establishing precise causality.[6] Those who do, fall into two broad categories: those who find psychological explanations, seeking the sources of violence in the individual's mentality and behavior, and those who favor structural factors, considering that various social, economic, and political changes in society prompt ethnic tension, aggression, and eruptions of violence. These are not hardand-fast categories, and some scholars have attempted to combine them.[7] Utilizing existing scholarship, we seek to ascertain what factors prompted ethnic tensions to intensify and develop into pogroms in the lands of Lithuania.

The most recent research has demonstrated that, contrary to past assumptions, pogroms in Lithuania occurred and were not just isolated phenomena. True, growing tensions between Christians and Jews in the early 1880s in many cases failed to develop into "classic" pogroms. The conflicts, which generally erupted in or near taverns as a consequence of drunkenness, in marketplaces, or during the induction period of new army recruits, tended to be brief and involve a small number of people. Even larger-scale incidents were usually stopped at their outset. Only the events in Prienai (Suvałki *guberniia*), on 3 August 1882, can be classified as a full-scale pogrom. The conflict, which lasted around three hours, began in the market when a female peasant refused to pay a Jewish woman for apples she had tasted. During the incident, according to various sources, between fifteen and twenty Jews were wounded and Jewish property also suffered. Between fifty-five and seventy Jewish houses, and between eleven and seventeen shops and eight inns were damaged. The Jews estimated the total damage at around 20,000 rubles, although official reports claimed that the sum was half that number.[8]

A new upsurge in ethnic tension was recorded in 1900 in both official tsarist Russian documents and in the illegal press. More than twenty clashes, which generally occurred on Sundays, church holidays, market days, or during fairs when people gathered from neighboring and more distant villages and towns, were recorded in northern Lithuania districts (Panevėžys and Šiauliai).[9] During the 1905 revolution, a number of small conflicts turned into mass clashes between Jews and Lithuanians in Dusetos and subsequently in Buivydiškės.[10]

World War I, and the struggle for the creation and preservation of independent nation-states, created propitious conditions for unbridled acts of violence. A number of well-known incidents took place in the former Grand Duchy of Lithuania—in Lida (Belarus) and Vilnius—where Polish legionnaires conducted pogroms against the Jews.[11] A similar but smaller conflict erupted during the summer of 1919 in Ukmergė. As far as can be judged from the documentary record, Lithuanian authorities immediately attempted to stop any violence against Jews and to punish the culprits. An outbreak in Panevėžys in 1919 remains controversial. A shot was allegedly fired at Lithuanian forces from a Jew's house during the battle between Lithuanian and Bolshevik forces for Panevėžys. This incident spurred soldiers to attack the building's inhabitants and to loot nearby Jewish shops.

During the 1920s there was no lack of minor conflicts, the defacing of non-Lithuanian signs being especially frequent at the beginning of the decade. One of the more serious conflicts in the 1920s occurred on 1 August 1929 in Kaunas when leftist workers, mostly Jews, marked the Day of Struggle against Imperialist Wars with a demonstration. A clash with Lithuanian workers ensued and there was unrest that night in Vilijampolė when members of some radical organizations such as the right-wing Geležinis vilkas (Iron Wolf) began to patrol the streets and beat up any Jews they met. According to reports, some officials also participated in the action.

Instances of the distribution of anti-Jewish flyers, the defacing of signs, window breaking, and collective violence increased in the second half of the 1930s. One of the more serious anti-Jewish pogroms in the Second Republic of Lithuania took place in Leipalingis on the afternoon of Sunday, 18 June 1939, after the celebration of the feast of the Assumption of the Virgin Mary had ended. When several peasants took shelter from the rain in a Jewish shop, an argument followed that led to the breaking of windows in Jewish houses. Only police intervention saved the Jews from physical harm. It is noteworthy that according to the available data, there were no instances of any deaths in interwar Lithuania as a result of anti-Jewish riots, even those that grew into pogrom-scale incidents.

Although Lithuanian–Jewish relations became more troubled during the year of the first Soviet occupation (1940–1941), there still were almost no instances of collective violence. The most serious recorded conflict occurred on 19 June 1940, when a domestic conflict between a Lithuanian soldier and a Jew in Marijampolė devolved into two days of violence against Jews, including breaking the windows of their houses. Although not yet entirely clarified through documentary evidence, the context of this violent outburst suggests that it was perpetrated by local civilians.[12] All the other conflicts were minor and the question can be raised as to whether it is more appropriate to treat them as "ordinary domestic hooliganism" rather than outbreaks of xenophobia or antisemitism.

The confrontations described above suggest that, despite the existence of anti-Jewish violence in Lithuania, it never attained the same scale as in Ukraine or other neighboring regions. This still leaves the question of what factors caused even the small-scale collective violence in Lithuania that did nonetheless occur prior to 1941.

Research devoted to manifestations of collective violence against Jews in Lithuania has identified an "external factor" that contributed to the intensification of ethnic tension. One of the more important causes of more frequent physical clashes between Christians and Jews during the early 1880s was undoubtedly knowledge about pogroms in the south of the Russian Empire, which was disseminated by the press, rumors, and refugees.[13] In the 1930s, elements of Lithuanian society were enamored of Nazi and fascist ideas, including antisemitism. A Lithuanian State Security Department bulletin explaining the strengthening of antisemitism stated that

> a wave of antisemitism arriving from the West is also encountering ever greater reverberations in Lithuania. The excesses of Tauragė and Telšiai against the Jews and ultimately the hatred of the Jews that has increased among Kaunas workers . . . clearly show that the soil in Lithuania is favorable for antisemitism.[14]

Foreign diplomats also noted Germany's influence on the spread of antisemitic sentiment.[15] Nevertheless, the interwar phenomenon of "external influence" should not be overestimated, for two reasons. First, no external factors can influence a society or part of it if there are no "local" preconditions. Second, it is a logical assumption that the conflict with Germany, the most antisemitic state of that time, over the Klaipėda region should have reduced hostility toward Jews. If it did not decline at that time, especially in 1939, it means there were probably other causes.

It is also theoretically possible to regard as factors of "external influence" the diverging geopolitical orientations of Lithuanians and Jews that developed at the end of the 1930s. Whereas Lithuanians looked to an independent Lithuania and Nazi Germany, Jews were more oriented toward the Soviet Union. In the opinion of some researchers, precisely this circumstance further complicated Lithuanian–Jewish relations and exerted considerable influence on the Lithuanians' notable participation in the implementation of the Holocaust.[16] Analogies from recent research on the Holocaust in Poland suggest that the Soviet occupation was a very important catalyst for antisemitic sentiments.[17] But here the question arises whether Lithuanian society was actually "politically set" against Moscow at the beginning of the Soviet occupation. If this was indeed the case, how does one explain the participation of many people in the first meetings in support of Soviet power and the numerous requests to the new authorities to improve economic life, and other requests?

In speaking about Lithuanian society from the second half of the nineteenth to the start of the twentieth century, it is possible to distinguish between three different levels of antisemitism: elite (noble), "popular" (peasant), and governmental (bureaucratic). Aristocratic society's view of the Jews is accurately described as "repulsive, yet indispensable."[18] Although the nobility considered Jews to be *alien*, nevertheless in many cases, especially in economic activities, it was unable to manage without them.

In view of the Russian imperial authorities' discriminatory policies toward Jews, their toleration of antisemitic articles in the press, and the widespread belief among high-ranking officials in the existence of a worldwide, anti-Christian secret *kahal* (Jewish communal governing board), they can legitimately be reproached for their Judeophobic views. Both traditional and some contemporary scholarly literature speculates whether the authorities had a direct interest in pogroms, in promoting them or not hurrying to stop them.[19] Nevertheless, the historical literature is dominated by the view that the authorities did not promote anti-Jewish violence and attempted to stop it once it erupted. The fact that individual officials of lower rank, as well as police officers, occasionally joined the rioters and that they were reluctant or unable to stop pogroms does not reflect the general attitude of the authorities, who feared pogroms. This general statement holds true for the situation in the early 1880s in Lithuania and Belarus. The local authorities, especially the governor-general and governors, made every effort to prevent pogroms and to suppress them if they started. The officials proposed making the punishment for rioters more severe, assembling as large a police and military force as possible at those places where unrest might occur, laying telegraph lines between military encampments and the cities, calming the inhabitants with various announcements, and so on. The authorities' role is well-illustrated by the aforementioned Prienai pogrom. It broke out because no advance precautions had been taken for possible clashes, there was no military unit in the city, and the city was not connected by a telegraph line to those places from which timely help could have been sent. In this case, officials of various ranks can at most be accused of a failure to predict events and of lacking resolve to impose punitive measures on the rioters. There is no evidence that they in any way consciously instigated or tolerated the disorder.[20]

Efforts have been made to link the outbreak of pogroms, as well as the participation of Lithuanians in the Holocaust, to long-established religious Judeophobia. There is no doubt that such traditional anti-Judaism was characteristic of Lithuanian peasants. We see here the penetration from the West of the traditional Roman Catholic myth that Jews kidnapped Christian children and used their blood for their religious needs. But the existence of traditional anti-Judaism as a form of "cultural code" cannot explain why ethnic tensions intensified at a particular moment and grew into pogroms. One approach to the history of antisemitism suggests a strict delineation between "traditional xenophobia" and "modern antisemitism." In the case of Lithuania, we find this interpretation somewhat oversimplified, given that traditional religious elements have adapted easily to modern conditions by modifying their external form. For example, the aforementioned superstition about the Jews using Christian blood was tenacious in Lithuania not only in the nineteenth century (and, of course, before that) but also in the twentieth. There are reports of many incidents (in

1861, 1900, 1905, and the 1930s) when the disappearance of a child in some Lithuanian village triggered anti-Jewish unrest because the Jews were accused of committing this crime for religious reasons.[21]

During the interwar period, Catholicism was one of the most important criteria defining Lithuanian identity. Therefore, it was ultimately no accident that some Lithuanian–Jewish clashes, like the one in Leipalingis, transpired immediately after religious services. In other words, we need to identify those societal changes that transformed long-established, passive xenophobia into collective violence.

Was Lithuanian nationalism such a factor? Nationalism, in the form of an ideology and social movement that seeks to create a nation-state, is often capable of generating ethnic tensions and conflicts. But the relations between Lithuanians and Jews in this regard were more complicated. Antisemitism never existed as an organized movement in Lithuania, although there were certain tendencies and auguries. For example, in the second half of 1905 an appeal was circulated calling for the founding of a "Lithuanian antisemitic newspaper" directed at opposing the "economic and political domination" of the Jews, said to have already been achieved on a global scale. Evidently, there were similar attempts during the interwar period but they received little support.

The orientation of Lithuanian nationalism to objective ethnocultural, primarily ethnolinguistic, values has determined the relations of the modern Lithuanian nation with other national communities, including Jews. In theory, this national model—based on such objective values as the centrality of the Lithuanian language and culture—should have complicated the civic integration of other national communities. In reality, the ethnolinguistic situation at the turn of the century was hardly favorable for the creation of a mono-ethnic Lithuanian state. It suffices to note that, according to the All-Russian census of 1897, Vilnius, which was to become the capital of an independent Lithuania, had a Lithuanian-speaking population of only about 2 percent. In a struggle against both Russians and Poles over the possibility of freely nurturing their ethnoculture and later creating a nation-state, the Lithuanians were forced to look for allies. This was a role that could be played by Jews, for example, in elections to the Russian State Duma[22] or in the subsequent dispute with the Poles over control of Vilnius.

The governments of interwar Lithuania, especially that of President Antanas Smetona, put an end to any manifestations of antisemitism.[23] Paradoxically, it is possible to say that toleration of the Jews was connected to the goal of strengthening the Republic of Lithuania as a nation-state. In this case, the principle of "an enemy of my enemy is my friend" held true. It was precisely this context that explains why the Lithuanian authorities so strongly condemned the anti-Jewish pogroms in Vilnius when it was controlled by Poland.[24]

The claim has been made that in the autumn of 1939 (31 October–1 November) Lithuanian authorities incited Poles against Jews in Vilnius, which had just been reclaimed from the defeated Polish Republic.[25] Protests in the city against the Lithuanian authorities and high prices began on 29 October. At first, these were organized and directed by Poles. The Lithuanian police intervened and the demonstrators were dispersed. Over the next two days, Jews became the main target of unrest, based on rumors that the hoarding of foodstuffs by Jewish traders was causing a dramatic rise in bread prices. A pogrom broke out on 31 October in which Jewish shops were robbed, homes attacked, and Jews beaten in the streets. The Lithuanian police initially did nothing to deter the pogrom and later were unable to suppress it. By the end of the day, when Soviet army units intervened to stop the pogrom, twenty-two Jews had been severely injured. Dozens of the perpetrators, evidently all Poles, were arrested.

Conflicting explanations emerged about how this demonstration against authorities descended into a pogrom within a couple of days. According to reports from the Lithuanian State Security Service in 1939, the pogrom was organized by members of Polish paramilitary organizations and Polish soldiers. The security service also reported that local Jews suspected that "Lithuanian spies and fascists" were guilty of inciting the Poles of Vilnius against them. A number of factors argue against this interpretation. As mentioned, the large Jewish population of Vilnius was a logical choice for Lithuanian authorities as allies in bringing the city, with its sizeable Polish population, under their control. Furthermore, the inability of Lithuanian authorities to establish order quickly and efficiently, as exemplified by a pogrom, worked against their own moral authority. (Archival documentation reveals that the government viewed the pogrom as a blow to its authority.)[26] Moreover, the pogroms grew out of unrest that was directed not only against higher prices but also against the Lithuanian authorities. Finally, in terms of topography, Vilnius was foreign territory for the Lithuanian police, which would have been hard-pressed to organize any sort of response in unfamiliar streets and neighborhoods.[27]

As it secured postwar independence, the so-called Second Republic of Lithuania was a "nationalizing state," in the words of Rogers Brubaker.[28] Consequently, its educational and cultural policies were directed at the creation of a mono-ethnic Lithuanian state. It is thus not surprising that among the young generation and rightist opposition groups the idea of a Lithuanian nation acquired more radical forms. It was, therefore, no accident that representatives of organized nationalist groups, such as the Riflemen (Lith., Šauliai) in Leipalingis, actively participated in some disorders.[29] The defacing of signs that were not in Lithuanian was perhaps the public anti-Jewish action most clearly related to ethnonationalistic thinking.

Precisely the violation of the ideals of a "nationalizing state" at the beginning of the first Soviet occupation, rather than external influences, strongly influenced Lithuanian anti-Jewish sentiment. Although no antisemitic laws had existed in independent Lithuania, such as the introduction of a *numerus clausus* in education, Jews nevertheless had been essentially eliminated from the governing of the state, either as civil servants or elected officials. At the beginning of the Soviet occupation, local Jews were given the opportunity to occupy various public positions, and they eagerly responded to the offer. A large part of Lithuanian society was angered precisely by the Jews' integration into administrative structures and political life. Nevertheless, the new regime was not judged negatively as a consequence. Rather, some antisemitic appeals were at the same time pro-Soviet.[30]

An intensification of ethnic tensions, as historical research has shown, is frequently linked to economic and social circumstances. Research on the reasons behind the pogroms in southern Russia has noted that roots of the pogroms lay deep in the urban environment. In parallel to rapid urbanization and industrial growth, in 1880–1881 there was a crisis of unemployment (some of the unemployed were migrants from other areas of the empire), exacerbated by a poor harvest.[31] These phenomena were less pronounced in the "backward" northwest region where Jews and Lithuanians essentially lived separately from one another and industry was developing at a slower rate.[32] Although Lithuanian peasants did not consider anyone who pursued a trade or engaged in commerce as worthy of social respect, they did not necessarily have a negative view of the Jews' role as intermediaries. The clergy, in particular, urged peasants to protect themselves from the Jews (and especially the Jewish tavern) and not to allow themselves to be "exploited" and to differentiate between "useful" and "useless" Jews.[33] Nevertheless, Jews were indispensable as intermediaries, not only in selling alcohol and other products, but also in helping illegal emigrants and handling illegal printed works and contraband (and thus cheaper) goods.

During the period when modern Lithuanian nationalism took shape, the economic situation on the ground changed only slightly. The degree of change was magnified in the work of nationalists, in, for example, the writings of Vincas Kudirka in the illegal Lithuanian press at the turn of the nineteenth century. There, Jews were frequently portrayed as competitors who prevented Lithuanians from establishing themselves in the urban economy.[34] Even with these signs of change in nationalist literature, the real occupational structures of Lithuanians and Jews changed very little before 1917. Consequently, there was not much economic competition between the communities. This may have been one of the more important reasons behind the relatively low level of collective violence directed against the Jews in Lithuania compared to other, more modernizing, regions of the empire.

The creation of a Lithuanian nation-state in 1918 was accompanied by a desire to create a "national economy" that would dominate commerce and an emergent industry, not just agriculture. In the 1920s and especially the 1930s, Lithuanians rapidly gained a foothold in commerce and industry,[35] with Jews remaining their principal competitors. Thus, it is not surprising that perhaps the strongest antisemitic publication of interwar Lithuania was the *Verslas* (Business) of the Lithuanian Businessmen's Union.[36] It is not easy to find a direct connection between economic competition and collective violence. However, the founding of the Seira agricultural cooperative in 1938 by peasants in Leipalingis was accompanied by "business-oriented nationalistic propaganda with clear antisemitic aspects," and in 1939 the aforementioned pogroms occurred.[37] One can also find an economic aspect to perhaps the most radical antisemitic appeals of the late 1930s, which already unambiguously mentioned the possible expulsion of the Jews. A leaflet from 1939, titled "Lietuvi darbininke" (Lithuanian worker), declared: "Enough of our pulling the heavy Jewish yoke. Let us drive these tiresome and capricious tenants out of our cities and our lands. Enough is enough; their time among us is now at an end." A leaflet from Kretinga in July 1939 urged, "If you are worried about your future, then strike the Jews. Drive them out of your homeland, Lithuania. Boycott them, buy nothing from the Jews."[38]

There was also competition over workplaces, which, in the opinion of agents of the State Security Department, was already leading to Lithuanian–Jewish clashes. One example cited in reports was the conflict between Lithuanian and Jewish workers in Šiauliai in 1935, where the Lithuanians' discontent was aroused by members of the Zionist *He-halutz* (Hebrew, pioneer) movement, who were learning various professions in special courses prior to immigrating to Palestine. It was natural that while these *halutzim* were studying, they occupied the workplaces of Lithuanians.[39]

In addition to economic factors, another important precondition for the intensification of ethnic tension was the *crisis* of authority, especially that of the central government. A reasonable hypothesis suggests that pogroms that began in the south of the Russian Empire in 1881 were triggered by the chaos following the assassination of Tsar Alexander II. Significantly, the government censor at the time issued strict instructions that the death of the tsar was not to be discussed, apparently for fear that a regime that could not protect its own leader would appear weak. During the revolution of 1905, Russian prestige was considerably weakened in Lithuania, for example in Kaunas Province, where a massive purge of Russian teachers and other officials took place. It was thus possible for Lithuanians to impose their own order, which, in their mind, necessitated putting the Jews in their place.

World War I and the struggles for independence that followed it in the territories controlled by both the Lithuanian and Polish armies and authorities created conditions more conducive than before for anti-Jewish pogroms. Perhaps the very obvious decline in the authority of the government influenced ethnic conflicts in Lithuania in the late 1930s. We have already mentioned that in its struggle with the Poles, Lithuania's political elite was forced to conclude a "political pact" with the Jews. A number of crises significantly weakened the status of the interwar government. These included the economic difficulties in the 1930s, exemplified by the farmers' strike in Suvalkija in 1935–1936, and even more the political crisis when Lithuania was forced in 1938 and 1939 to accede to two ultimatums from Poland and Germany. Poland's ultimatum, which demanded the establishment of diplomatic relations, was especially painful.

The forced concession to Poland created the impression that the struggle for Vilnius was over. (Rumors claimed that those Lithuanian authorities who "were under the influence of the Polish element" had long awaited the restoration of diplomatic relations with Poland and had requested that the Poles supply the necessary pretext through diplomatic pressure.)[40] Thus, the authorities, who had for many years made the recovery of Vilnius their most important political goal, revealed themselves to be completely powerless. When the authorities lost their power, the situation of their Jewish "partners" also changed. The way in which Jews could be made culpable along with the ruling nationalists was clearly reflected in one contemporary appeal: "Because of the devious policy of the Jews abroad, we had to foreswear Vilnius and abandon Klaipėda since they know that an economically pressured nation is good soil for their dirty affairs."[41]

Blaming Jews for the loss of Klaipėda to Germany might appear entirely illogical in light of the Third Reich's antisemitic policy, but it becomes entirely understandable (albeit not justifiable) in the context of the "pact" between the authorities and the Jews: As "allies," the Jews were equally culpable for "sins." Consequently, the cry went up that "relations with the Jews had to be regulated." We see a direct relationship between the decline of the government's authority and the rise of anti-Jewish sentiments in the aforementioned Leipalingis pogrom. In the course of the disorders, the authorities were openly challenged, with both stones and insults hurled at the police. Agitators urged the crowd on, assuring them that the police would offer no resistance; for example, they would not use firearms.[42]

The Soviet government formed in 1940 gradually lost whatever authority it ever had had in the public's eyes. At the same time, however, anti-Jewish incidents in the public sphere (whether shouted in the streets or publicized in the press) declined compared to the period of the independent republic. This change was, of course, caused by the fairly effective Soviet repressive apparatus. Latent forms of antisemitism still remained. But at the same time, the Soviet repressive system "demonstrated" that it could "solve" political problems with radical measures. Thus, Gediminas Bašinskas's hypothesis seems credible, wherein the Soviet repressive system, which was attractive to at least a segment of society, could become a model for solving political or other problems.[43]

*   *   *

We have argued here that there is apparently no *single* cause that can explain the instances of anti-Jewish collective violence in the northwest region of tsarist Russia or in the independent Republic of Lithuania. The existence of Judeophobia as a "cultural code" does not justify the emergence of anti-Jewish riots. Lithuanian nationalism, which was oriented toward a model of a mono-ethnic state, was, of course, an important factor in shaping anti-Jewish sentiments. People of a rival nationality were an obstacle to the creation of such a state. There was little hope of Lithuanianizing Jews, while such a hope could apply to Poles. It is, therefore, inappropriate to look for the sources of anti-Jewish sentiments and excesses solely in Lithuanian ethnocentrism. Rather, at the beginning of the twentieth century the leaders of the Lithuanian national movement sought allies in the struggle against their principal enemy, the Poles. Toward this end, they concluded informal "pacts" with the Jews in elections to the Russian Duma and in the political struggle over Vilnius.

A more careful look at specific conflicts shows the role of "external influences." These included the knowledge about pogroms in 1881–1882 in the south of the Russian Empire, the echoes of resurgent European antisemitism in the 1930s, and the different geopolitical orientations of Lithuanians and Jews, especially in regard to Germany and the Soviet Union in 1940. Economic transformation also played a role: the more Lithuanians engaged in nonagricultural activities, the more the competition between the two national groups increased. Besides this, the political crises (the assassination of Alexander II, the 1905 revolution, etc.) prompted anti-Jewish acts of violence. The effect of a political crisis was patently clear in the late 1930s when the regime, which had always suppressed antisemitism, lost its authority.

In sum, it is possible to explain the relatively limited occurrence of ethnic violence against Jews in Lithuania prior to 1941 by the slow pace of economic modernization, the political circumstances (the aforementioned "pact" against the Poles), and the efforts of the authorities (of both tsarist Russia and the Republic of Lithuania) to prevent pogroms.

Notes

1. Liudas Truska, "The Crisis of Lithuanian and Jewish Relations (June 1940–June 1941)," in *The Preconditions for the Holocaust: Anti-Semitism in Lithuania (Second Half of the 19th Century—June 1941)*, ed. Liudas Truska and Vygantas Vareikis (Vilnius: Margi raštai, 2004), 201–202.

2. Dov Levin, *The Litvaks: A Short History of the Jews of Lithuania* (Jerusalem: Yad Vashem, 2000).

3. Hans Rogger, "Conclusion and Overview," in *Pogroms: Anti-Jewish Violence in Modern Russian History,* ed. John D. Klier and Shlomo Lambroza (Cambridge: Cambridge University Press, 1992), 316.

4. Liudmila Gatagova, "Iudofobiia: summa zol," http://www.dartmouth.edu/~crn/crn_papers/Gatagova3.pdf (4 September 2009).

5. "Pogromy," in *Kratkaia evreiskaia entsiklopediia* (Jerusalem: Obshchestvo po issledovaniiu evreiskikh obshchin; Evreiskii universitet v Ierusalime, 1992), 6: 562.

6. David Vital, *A People Apart: A Political History of the Jews in Europe, 1789–1939* (New York: Oxford University Press, 1999), 285.

7. Roger D. Petersen, *Understanding Ethnic Violence: Fear, Hatred, and Resentment in Twentieth-Century Eastern Europe* (Cambridge: Cambridge University Press, 2002), 17–32.

8. Darius Staliūnas, "Anti-Jewish Disturbances in the North-Western Provinces in the Early 1880s," *East European Jewish Affairs* 2 (2004): 126.

9. Vilma Žaltauskaitė, "Smurtas prieš žydus Šiaurės Lietuvoje 1900 m. įvykiai ir interpretacijos," in *Kai ksenofobija virsta prievarta: lietuvių ir žydų santykių dinamika XIX a.–XX a. pirmojoje pusėje,* ed. Vladas Sirutavičius and Darius Staliūnas (Vilnius: Lietuvos istorijos instituto leidykla, 2005), 84–85.

10. On this episode, see file "Po prosh.[eniiu] Chegisa i dr.[ugikh] obv.[iniaemykh] v pogrome v m.[estechke] Dusiatakh, *Rossiiskii gosudarstvennyi istoricheskii arkhiv* (Russian State Historical Archive, St. Petersburg), f. 1405, op. 108, d. 6519.

11. Šarūnas Liekis, Lidia Miliakova, and Antony Polonsky, "1919 m. antižydiški ekscesai Lenkijoje ir Lietuvoje," in *Kai ksenofobija,* 213–245.

12. Liudas Truska, "Tikros ir primestos kaltės. Žydai ir lietuviai pirmuoju soviet-mečiu 1940–1941," *Darbai ir dienos* 34 (2003): 298.

13. Staliūnas, "Anti-Jewish Disturbances," 121.

14. Vaidotas Kuprelis, *Lietuvių-žydų buitiniai santykiai XX a. 4-ame dešimtmetyje* (unpublished manuscript), 4.

15. Algimantas Kasparavičius, "Lietuviai ir žydai katastrofos išvakarėse: iššūkiai ir įvaizdžiai," in *Kai ksenofobija*, 146–147.

16. Truska, "Tikros ir primestos kaltės," 286–320.

17. Jan Tomasz Gross, *Sąsiedzi. Historia zagłady żydowskiego miasteczka* (Sejny: Pogranicze, 2001).

18. Zita Medišauskienė, " 'Ottalkivaiushchii, no bez nego ne oboitis': evrei kak alter ego litovskogo dvorianstva serediny XIX v.," *Ab Imperio* 4 (2003): 93–114.

19. Shmuel M. Galai, "Evreiskie pogromy i rospusk I Gosudarstvennoi dumy v 1906 godu," *Voprosy istorii* 9 (2004): 23–42.

20. Staliūnas, "Anti-Jewish Disturbances," 127–131.

21. Vladas Sirutavičius, "Kaip prietarai tampa prievarta: kaltinimai žydams vartojant krikščionių kraują. Kelių atvejų Lietuvoje analizė," in *Kai ksenofobija*, 104–116.

22. Darius Staliūnas, "Rinkimai į I Rusijos Dūmą Lietuvoje," *Lietuvos istorijos metraštis 1992* (Vilnius, 1994): 45–46.

23. Liudas Truska, *Antanas Smetona ir jo laikai* (Vilnius: Valstybinis leidybos centras, 1996), 296–305.

24. Saulius Sužiedėlis, "The Historical Sources for Antisemitism in Lithuania and Jewish-Lithuanian Relations during the 1930s," in *The Vanished World of Lithuanian Jews*, ed. Avydas Nikžentaitis, Stefan Schreiner, and Darius Staliūnas (Amsterdam: Rodopi Publishers, 2004), 131–133.

25. For more information on this claim, see Regina Žepkaitė, *Vilniaus istorijos atkarpa 1939 m. spalio 27–1940 m. birželio 15 d.* (Vilnius: Mokslas, 1990), 68; Vygantas Vareikis, "Žydų ir lietuvių susidūrimai bei konfliktai tarpukario Lietuvoje," in *Kai ksenofobija*, 179.

26. Žepkaitė, *Vilniaus istorijos atkarpa*, 68.

27. Žepkaitė, *Vilniaus istorijos atkarpa*, 66–70.

28. Rogers Brubaker, "Mify i zabluzhdeniia v izuchenii natsionalizma," *Ab Imperio* 1 (2000): 157.

29. Dangiras Mačiulis, "Žvilgsnis į vieno pogromo anatomiją tarpukario Lietuvoje," in *Kai ksenofobija*, 192–194.

30. G. Bašinskas cites an appeal found in Rokiškis, which proposed not voting for those "Smetona-supporting leeches, the Jews," and ends with the call, "Long live the true people's Seimas, free of Jews. Long live our comrade Stalin. Long live the Red Army." Gediminas Bašinskas, "Lietuvių-žydų konfliktai sovietinės okupacijos pradžioje 1940 metų vasarą: tęstinumai ar lūžiai," in *Kai ksenofobija*, 205. Liudas Truska cites another appeal: "Dear fellow Lithuanian countryman or countrywoman, stop and think about where you are going," in which was written: ". . . Remember how many times [the Jews] have wronged you. Do you want to stand in the honourable ranks of Communism together with Jewish exploiters? . . . We demand Jewish capital be expropriated, . . . we demand all the Jewish houses in the cities be expropriated. . . . We want to see those rich Jews working beside us, performing the physical labor, which they have avoided and feared all their lives." See Truska, "Tikros ir primestos kaltės," 299.

31. See I. Michael Aronson, *Troubled Waters: The Origins of the 1881 Anti-Jewish Pogroms in Russia* (Pittsburgh: University of Pittsburgh Press, 1991), 217–235.

32. Staliūnas, "Anti-Jewish Disturbances," 131–132.

33. Vladas Sirutavičius, "Notes on the Origin and Development of Modern Lithuanian Antisemitism in the Second Half of the Nineteenth Century and at the Beginning
of the Twentieth Century," in *The Vanished World*, 66.

34. Vladas Sirutavičius, "Vincas Kudiska's Programme for Modernizing Society and
the Problems of Forming a National Intelligentsia," *Lithuanian Historical Studies* 5 (2000):
109–112.

35. According to the data presented by Saulius Sužiedėlis, in 1923, 83 percent of
commercial enterprises were in Jewish hands and 13 percent in Lithuanian hands. In
1936, 43 percent of such enterprises were owned by Lithuanians. At the end of the
interwar period, Lithuanians controlled 60 percent of the industries and workshops and
Jews 32 percent (actually, Jewish enterprises were usually larger). According to Liudas
Truska, the large urban demographic increase of the 1930s was caused by the large
influx of Lithuanians, a steep decline in emigration, and the completion of the land
reform.

36. Liudas Truska, "Lietuvių verslininkų sąjunga ir verslų 'atlietuvinimo' sąjūdis
(1930–1940 m.)," *Istorija* 58 (2003): 39–51; Algimantas Kasparavičius, Lietuviai ir žydai
katastrofos išvakarėse: iššūkiai ir įvaizdžiai, in *Kai ksenofobija*, 127–130.

37. Mačiulis, "Žvilgsnis į vieno pogromo anatomiją," 190.

38. Kuprelis, *Lietuvių-žydų buitiniai santykiai*, 87–88. It is nevertheless necessary to
say that the "tenant" metaphor is closer to the mark for the national discourse. Very
frequently nationalistic discourses used the "home is national property" metaphor,
meaning that people from other nations can also live here but only with the rights of a
renter or, in other words, a "tenant."

39. Kuprelis, *Lietuvių-žydų buitiniai santykiai*, 87–88.

40. Gediminas Rudis, "Jungtinis antismetoninės opozicijos sąjūdis 1938–1939
metais," *Lietuvos istorijos metraštis* 1996 (Vilnius, 1997): 185.

41. Kuprelis, *Lietuvių-žydų buitiniai santykiai*, 81. The historian Zenonas Ivinskis,
who was famous at that time, mentioned in his diary the rumors about the Jews having
bought an estate for Smetona in Palestine, meaning that Smetona was very pro-Jewish
(Mačiulis, "Žvilgsnis į vieno pogromo anatomiją," 184).

42. Mačiulis, "Žvilgsnis į vieno pogromo anatomiją," 182.

43. Bašinskas, "Lietuvių-žydų konfliktai," 209.

~ 9 ~

The Missing Pogroms of Belorussia, 1881–1882: Conditions and Motives of an Absence of Violence

CLAIRE LE FOLL

The presumed absence of violence in the provinces of historic Lithuania and Belorussia/Belarus played a very important role in the formation of the classic interpretations of anti-Jewish pogroms of 1881–1882. The quiet and order that reigned in the region was attributed to the determined stance of Eduard I. Totleben, the governor-general of the northwest region of the Russian Empire (the provinces of Vilna, Grodno, and Kovno). Totleben's behavior indicated to his subordinates that pogroms would not be tolerated—and none occurred. His actions were compared unfavorably against those of officials such as Aleksandr R. Drentel'n, the governor-general of the southwest region (the provinces of Kiev, Podolia, and Volhynia), where pogroms were rife. Drentel'n's well-known Judeophobia and alleged inactivity permitted pogroms to erupt, intensify, and spread. Historians such as Simon M. Dubnov, seeking to attribute culpability for the pogroms to Judeophobic authorities in the provinces, claimed that resolute action was sufficient to stop pogroms, as demonstrated by the example of the northwest.[1]

Subsequent research has challenged this interpretation. On the one hand, the briefest examination of published archival materials reveals that Drentel'n, and other authorities, were just as active as Totleben in issuing anti-pogrom warnings, and in taking the usual police and military precautions.[2] On the other hand, Darius Staliūnas has shown that the Lithuanian provinces were not as free of anti-Jewish violence as is often assumed, even if it never reached the level of the urban pogroms in Elizavetgrad, Kiev, or Balta.[3]

This latest scholarly investigation of the pogroms prompts an obvious question: if violence was a possibility, and if the activity of tsarist officialdom does not explain the absence of major violence, why was the northwest spared the mass violence that wracked the southwestern provinces of the Russian Empire between 1881 and 1882? This essay will attempt to answer this question with reference to the provinces of historic Belorussia/ Belarus, primarily Minsk, Vitebsk, and Mogilev. It will show that the "northwest exception" casts light on the mechanisms of interethnic relations in the Russian Empire during the second half of the nineteenth century and also illustrates the local differences relating to the social, economic, cultural, and political development of each region in the Pale of Settlement.

In addition to the disorders noted by Darius Staliūnas, Jewish communities, panicked by events in Ukraine, reported to the authorities a number of insults, threats, or rumors about pogroms said to be in the planning stages.[4] Drunken peasants called upon their fellows to "beat the Jews like in the province of Kiev." The police gave the provincial administration accounts of growing agitation in railway stations (Novogrudok, Pinsk, Minsk, Stolin), and of rows in taverns, for example in Novogrudok and Rechitsa (Minsk province) in the summer of 1882.[5] In the provinces of Mogilev and Minsk, adjoining the pogrom-ridden province of Chernigov where pogroms took place, some conflicts occurred.[6] This rise of interethnic tensions threatened worse but nothing more happened. Globally, the situation was calm, as the police repeated in its reports,[7] and the sporadic disorders that did occur were immediately stopped.[8] In a collective letter, the Jewish community of Dokshitsy even thanked the authorities and the local *ispravnik* (district police officer) for their vigilance and energy.[9] The success of the local police in preventing pogroms was generally regarded as linked to the decisive action of Governor-General Totleben. Yet it primarily benefited from the fact that the violence it had to control was far weaker and less serious than in the southwestern provinces. The thesis of this article is that the "absence" of pogroms—collective attacks on the Jewish population and its goods in Belorussia—resulted from the persistence of the ancient semi-feudal economic system and thus from the perpetuation of existing social and interethnic relations. We will scrutinize how this historical specificity developed and manifested itself in the realm of socioeconomic organization, anti-Jewish stereotypes, and interethnic relations.

Socioeconomic Stagnation

Three socioeconomic factors—industrialization, urbanization, and economic competition between Jews and non-Jews—have been identified in recent historiography as decisive for the pogroms in the southwest provinces of the empire. These were all weakly developed on the eve of the 1881–1882 wave of pogroms.[10]

I. Michael Aronson argued that many of the *pogromshchiki* were Great Russian workers, wandering in the industrialized regions of Ukraine in search of jobs or, in desperation, of free vodka. The situation was different in Belorussia. In the 1820s, when industry began to develop in parts of the Russian Empire under the promptings of the government, the Belorussian provinces of Mogilev, Vitebsk, and Minsk (all part of the Pale of Settlement) had very few factories.[11] The two main industrial regions were the provinces of Grodno and Volhynia, where more than 70 percent of the Jewish textile factories in the Pale were concentrated. At the end of the 1840s, a new sector became dominant in the industry of the Pale: the sugar-beet industry. The centers of this industry were not Volhynia or Grodno but the Ukrainian agricultural regions where the beets were grown. While the textile industry declined in provinces such as Volhynia, it continued to grow in Grodno province and the northwest in general. That production was centered in small, barely mechanized shops, which were unable to provide jobs to the many Jews deprived of work by the reforms of the 1840s. These new laws restricted Jews' participation in the production and commerce of alcohol. The economic situation among Jews declined again following the emancipation of the serfs in 1861, which incited landlords to manage their estates by themselves and to progressively do without Jewish middlemen. As a consequence of the above, a disproportionately large number of Jewish craftsmen labored in small-scale, unmechanized workshops.[12]

The industrialization of Belorussia began only in the 1880s and exploded in the 1890s, thanks primarily to the creation of railway lines. Before 1881, the development of capitalism in Belorussia was slow and sporadic. At best, nobles and other landlords established small manufacturing establishments on their estates in the years following emancipation of the serfs. These sites specialized in the production and commercialization of agricultural products (cereals, alcohol, leather, flax, and wood). But the persistence of the feudal social and economic structure slowed the process of industrialization and the modernization of agriculture. If in the Minsk and Grodno provinces some landowners acquired a number of machines for their factories, the level of industrialization remained very low in the regions of Mogilev and Vitebsk, where small factories situated in the countryside predominated.[13] The provincial governors repeatedly complained about the fragility of industry in Vitebsk province.[14] Jews played an important role in the higher ranks of these factories; few of them were simple laborers.[15] Then, the bad conditions and the scarcity of work in the handicraft and industry of Belorussia created a socioeconomic context less conducive to pogroms, which were partly provoked by the homeless and alienated proletariat converging on an industrialized region in search of employment.

Aronson further emphasizes that the pogroms of 1881–1882 were primarily an urban phenomenon, ignited in towns and spreading from there to the countryside. The fact that the urbanization of Belorussia was relatively weak and incomplete is thus crucial.[16] This region presented many conditions favorable to urbanization: the rate of demographic growth was high, the construction of railways began in the 1860s, technological progress was incremental, and the Belorussian provinces possessed a large number of villages (*mestechko*), a potential basis for the evolution of modern towns. But urbanization in Belorussia never really took off. The rural character of the region and weak industrialization slowed the arrival of peasants in the towns. The lack of mineral resources and the limitation of the local production of foodstuffs restricted exports. Consequently, Belorussia lacked local sources of capital and was financially dependent on external resources. Moreover, the survival of patriarchal relationships between landowners, peasants, and Jews was not favorable to the development of trade, industry, and towns. This was manifest in the persistence of feudal rules and habits in agriculture, the lack of banks and credit institutions, and the dependence of Jewish middlemen on landlords.

In addition to these factors, tsarist policy intentionally slowed urbanization in the western provinces. After the Polish insurrection of 1863, the tsarist government was obsessed by the Polish influence in these provinces and was afraid that the growth of small towns would particularly profit Polish nobles and Jewish entrepreneurs. The tsarist strategy was to transform the multiethnic small villages of the Pale of Settlement into large towns, as in Russia. Therefore, not a single town was created in Belorussia on the basis of the existing *mestechko* (in the Jewish case, the shtetls), some of which were as developed as, and, from an economic and commercial point of view, even more developed than, district centers and provincial capitals.[17]

Given the limited urbanization and industrialization of Belorussia, in contrast to the Ukrainian provinces, there was no influx of proletarianized peasants into towns. Instead, there was an influx of Jews, who eventually came to dominate urban economic life. The density of the Jewish population was very high in the Belorussian towns. Given the generally poor quality of land in Belorussia, many recently emancipated Belorussian peasants preferred to engage in *otkhod* (seasonal migration), seeking jobs in other provinces or even emigrating and settling in Siberia. The combined result of the repeated expulsions of Jews from the villages, together with the slow urbanization and the migration of Belorussian peasants, led to the demographic domination of the Jewish population in towns. Consequently, Jews represented more than 50 percent of the population, sometimes up to 70 or 80 percent in most Belorussian towns, and even more in the shtetls.[18] The numerical superiority of Jews in Belorussian towns certainly made the pogroms more difficult to organize than in Ukrainian towns, where the Jewish population was less concentrated. Dense Jewish settlement in the towns also helped to expedite the formation and work of self-defense organizations.[19]

Another consequence of these related phenomena was far less aggressive economic competition between Jews and non-Jews in Belorussia. First, the lesser industrial dynamism of the Belorussian provinces rendered the region less attractive for the numerous displaced peasants coming from Russia or Ukraine, and avoided an influx of unemployed and uprooted workers. Second, the survival of a semi-feudal economic system in Belorussia promoted continuity in interethnic and interclass relationships. "Alienation" associated with rapid social change was not a serious factor. The supposed "emancipation of the serfs" by Tsar Alexander II hardly changed the situation of the peasants in practice. The Belorussian provinces stayed mostly under the control of the landlords who sold very little land to the emancipated peasants, whose own land was usually of poor quality. The latter were therefore forced to keep working on seigniorial estates until they could afford to purchase additional holdings.[20] The maintenance of quasi-feudal relationships also meant that Belorussia was relatively free of the landlord–peasant antipathy that marked the settlement elsewhere. Thus, the old order prevailed: peasants tilled the soil, while Jews served as the main conduit to the marketplace and the source of the limited supply of manufactured goods.

Most ethnographers and memoirists, although reporting antipathy on the part of some noblemen and bureaucrats against "Jewish hegemony," acknowledged that the economic status quo was generally accepted on all sides.[21] Finally, the lack of opportunity for rapid economic advancement in Belorussia meant that the region lacked upwardly mobile Jewish entrepreneurs who were a feature of Moscow and St. Petersburg or financial centers like Kiev and Odessa. Moreover, there were no wealthy Jewish businessmen in Belorussia to excite the jealousy and envy of non-Jews, as, for example, Kiev sugar magnate Lazar' Brodsky in the case of Ukraine. The peasants of Belorussia were poor, but so, in the main, were their Jewish neighbors. Hence, the economic backwardness of Belorussia and the high density of Jews in towns worked in favor of the Jewish community during the wave of pogroms. Relative social equality and the proximity in daily life of Jews and non-Jews thereby limited the risks of interclass violence. More concentrated, more traditional, and better organized than in Ukraine, the Jewish communities of Belorussia succeeded in alerting local authorities and protecting themselves from pogroms.

The Feudal Stereotype of the Belorussian Jew: Exploiter and Fanatic

Stability in the socioeconomic structure and feudal ties did not mean that relations between Jews and non-Jews were always quiet and free of anti-Jewish prejudices. The historical archive of Minsk contains numerous documents testifying to daily violence against Jews, principally from Polish noblemen and landowners. This took the form of antisemitic talk, robbery, blows, and even torture, as when a glazier of Lepel was seized, robbed, and beaten for three days by a nobleman and his friends.[22] But this violence of the seigniorial class is better seen as a vestige of the arbitrary relationship between the landlord and his leaseholder in a feudal economic system than as an act of modern, interethnic violence. Individual caprice was very different from the collective attacks against Jews from the urban classes and the peasantry, which exploded in Ukraine and Poland during 1881–1882. Given the claim that the administration played a decisive role in preventing pogroms, its actions should be explored in greater depth. In particular, was their attitude more tolerant toward Jews than in other parts of the Pale of Settlement? And, more generally, how did non-Jews perceive Jews? In other words, was Belorussia also spared the emergence of the modern, ethnic antisemitism that gradually grew in the Russian Empire?[23]

The encounter of the tsarist government with the Jews of Belorussia dates back to the end of the eighteenth century. From the time of the first comprehensive investigation of this region in 1800 by the poet and senator Gavril Derzhavin, authorities branded Jews as exploiters of the peasantry.[24] Derzhavin's report, part of an investigation of the endemic poverty of the region, established the culpability of the Jews in the poverty of the Belorussian peasantry. This allegation, accepted by the central government, culminated in efforts to expel Jews from residence in peasant villages in Belorussia, beginning in 1804, and continuing for the remainder of the reign of Tsar Alexander I. The assumption that the Jews were "the exploiters of the Belorussian peasantry" became a generally accepted assumption throughout the nineteenth century, and efforts were undertaken to correct the situation.

From documents emanating from the local police and the administration during the decades preceding the pogroms, it is obvious that these stereotypes were completely absorbed by officials of lower rank as well as by provincial governors. In reports responding to a governmental inquiry in 1846 about the "fanaticism of the Jews," rural police chiefs systematically and conscientiously repeated the same clichés about Jewish parasitism.[25] They also enumerated the "fanatical" customs that were supposed to be harmful to Christians and that made all attempts to promote the merging (*sliianie*) of Jews with the native population impossible: *kashrut* (dietary laws), Sabbath rules, the complicated rituals for holidays, education in the *heder* (religious schools), and the abuses of burial societies. One official more zealous and imaginative than his colleagues offered an explanation for some of the strange customs of the Jews. He affirmed, for instance, that the *kippa* (a ritual head covering used by Jewish men) was a consequence of messianic expectation: Jews wear a hat because they "must live as if they were always on their way; because of that, when they have lunch or dinner, they wear a hat in order to seem to be on the road and not at home."[26] He declared that it was time for European Jews to realize that the *kippa*, which he claimed had been prescribed for them in order to protect their heads from the sun of Asia, was not necessary in Europe.[27]

Police reports dedicated to the investigation of Jewish sects in 1852 give further evidence of the deep ignorance and misconceptions about Jewish culture prevalent among local bureaucrats.[28] In attempting to explain the distinctive features of ultra-Orthodox Hasidim, the police characterized such Jews as "Leviters," or descendants of the Tribe of Levi. The police encountered problems even finding a name for the sect, variously calling its adherents *Skakuny* (from the Russian verb *skakat'*, to jump), *Kitaiovtsy* (from the Hebrew *kita*, sect), or *Khassidy*. One policeman said they were descended from the Pharisees; another called them followers of an "Asiatic ritual"; and a Minsk policeman believed that they prayed like those in an "Oriental synagogue (*sfard*)."[29] Nor could police agree on the character of the Hasidim. Seen as "calm and silent" by the police of Nesvizh, they were judged harmful by the police of Minsk, which had noticed that "they pronounce prayers constantly, shout loudly, and jump."[30]

It is evident from these documents that the local Belorussian administration regarded Belorussian Jews on the whole as exploiters and harmful fanatics. It is striking that the local bureaucracy was likewise disinclined to go beyond stereotypes, even when the "Jewish question" became a public issue, and the Jews of Belorussia were the subject of a polemic in St. Petersburg. In Ukraine, Poland, and Russia during the 1860s and 1870s, intellectuals and ethnographers debated the "Jewish question" and thought about the place of Jews in the wider society.[31] In general, the debaters were more concerned with developing and discussing the policies that came to be known as "Russification."[32]

It is true that ethnographers of Belorussia and the publicists in the official local press expressed real interest in, and curiosity about, the Jewish population. Illarion Zelenski, for example, an ethnographer who in 1864 published a major study of Minsk province,[33] made an attempt to find rational answers, based on statistical and economic material, to questions related to Jewish poverty, their supposed "parasitism and idleness," and their aversion to agriculture. But his position was an exception. No other ethnographer of the Belorussian provinces criticized the deeply rooted prejudices against the Jews. On the contrary, they confirmed and gave weight to assertions about the dirtiness, avidity, and wealth of the Jews. Thus, an ethnographer of the Vitebsk province justified the hostility of the "simple Russian people" by asserting the insolent prosperity of the Jews and their coarseness.[34] Aleksandr Dembovetskii, a specialist on Mogilev province, despite some erudite and acute remarks on the historical fate and contemporary material life of the Jews (diet, habitation, rituals), based his paragraph dedicated to the "character of the Jewish life" on Iakov Brafman's notorious Judeophobic work, The Book of the Kahal (Kniga kagala).[35] He attacked with equal fervor the idleness of the Jews, their lack of patriotism, their exploitation of "human weakness," the kahal[36] and the Talmud, the heder and its teachers (melamdim), the St. Petersburg-based Society for the Spread of Enlightenment among the Jews of Russia (OPE), and the French Alliance Israélite Universelle. Dembovetskii criticized the latter two as organs of an "International Jewish Union."

The work of the Ukrainian ethnographer Pavel Chubinskii can be considered philosemitic by comparison.[37] He also used Brafman's work about the kahal, but in a balanced manner stripped of fantasies about an international Jewish plot. Instead, Chubinskii turned out to be a defender of the Jewish people and an advocate of emancipation. If Jews still constituted a state within the state, he argued, it was due to past persecutions and to the inability of official Russian policies to merge the Jewish with non-Jewish populations. Chubinskii's opinion on the "Jewish question" became even more atypical for his time, as he took up the defense of the Jewish exploiter par excellence—the tavern-keeper—who, he affirmed, was often honest and sincere. Furthermore, Chubinskii refuted the generally accepted opinion about Jewish artisans, merchants, and middlemen by emphasizing their honesty and usefulness.

The publicists and writers of the official provincial press (the *gubernskie vedomosti*), like local ethnographers, showed a certain curiosity about the Jewish popular or religious customs. But they popularized Judeophobic prejudices and seemed indifferent to the public debate on the Jewish question. Some articles tried to familiarize the readers of the newspapers *Vitebskie gubernskie vedomosti* and *Mogilevskie gubernskie vedomosti* with the Jewish calendar, the customs of the Jewish New Year, and Jewish religious life in general. But more often, the reader received information about the fanaticism of the Jews, their backwardness in regard to education, morality, or hygiene, and other echoes of Brafman's prose. The Jewish intelligentsia and its efforts toward assimilation were denounced as a stratagem to obtain rights and riches and to ruin the Russian state.

The bureaucracy, intelligentsia, and press of Belorussia were generally ill-disposed toward Jews in the decades preceding the pogroms of 1881. The persistence, and even legitimization, of the most common religious, moral, and economic prejudices against Jews indicates the conservatism of a region isolated from contemporary political debates about the possible abolition of the Pale of Settlement and the prospect of extending equal rights to Jews.[38]

Relations between Belorussians and Jews: The Status Quo

Some observers and historians have considered "backwardness" a reason for the absence of pogroms in Belorussia. Aronson echoed the assumptions of contemporary Russian observers that the absence of pogroms could be explained by the apathy and patience of the local population resulting from their lack of political and cultural enlightenment. The Belorussian national historical narrative addresses this issue in a more positive way, claiming that the Belorussian people are tolerant by nature, and never initiated pogroms (an assertion, incidentally, that only holds true for 1881–1882). The scarcity of documents in the National Historical Archives of Belarus reporting acts of violence in the daily life of peasants and Jews tends to confirm these assumptions. Another approach, not usually employed by scholars, is to examine these relationships through the agency of literary, pictorial, and ethnographic works. These will help to refine the rather stereotypical image of the passive and apathetic Belorussian peasant. These documents are undoubtedly a product of intellectual discourse but can nonetheless provide some understanding of the place that Belorussian society assigned to Jews.

The Jewish archetype in Belorussian literature was neither as positive as Adam Mickiewicz's patriotic tavern-keeper, Jankiel (in his epic poem, *Pan Tadeusz*), nor as negative as the Jewish go-between in Cossack chronicles from Ukraine.[39] The traditional image of the Jew in Belorussian literature has its roots in the puppet-theater, *batleika*, where the Jew is one of the comic characters. Caricatured as wealthy, a seller of alcohol, cunning, and greedy, he is often beaten by the rude and brutal Cossack, or even killed and taken away by the Devil. The burlesque aspects of puppet-theater violence, and the comic accent invariably employed by the "Jew," were a source of merriment for the audience. To take one example from analogous, but "higher" culture, the Jewish character in the play *Komedia* by Gaetan Marasheŭski (1787) also belongs to the category of the rude liquor seller and pawnbroker, but he becomes the occasional ally of the peasant in his attempt to deceive the Devil, who symbolizes the *pan*, or Polish lord.[40]

At the beginning of what is considered "modern" Belorussian literature (written, actually, mainly in Polish), during the first half of the nineteenth century, the Jew as an active character was virtually absent. The most common representation of the Jew was still the greedy and mocked tavern-keeper or leaseholder. But he rarely played a role in the plot. For example, in Ian Barsheŭski's poem *Bunt khlopaŭ* (1812) on the insurrection of peasants against their landowners, the tavern is only the place where peasants come to drink, talk, and lament. The (unquestionably Jewish) tavern-keeper is invisible.

With the emergence of ethnography and the appearance of a *savant* interest in Jewish culture from the 1840s, Jewish people again became visible but with a different image. In his travel accounts, the Belorussian ethnographer Pavel Shpilevskii, for example, emphasized the great number of Jews in all Belorussian towns and stressed their useful, and even indispensable, professional skills for Belorussian towns and villages.[41] Belorussian paintings of the time also show this familiar and beneficial presence: Konstantin Kukevich created ethnographic and very detailed portraits of Jewish booksellers and hat sellers. His lithograph, *Inn of the Suburbs*, portrayed a Jewish tavern-keeper talking amicably with peasants. "Such passing references, which assume that the audience will immediately grasp the author's intention, establish the Jew as a regular feature of the Belorussian sociological landscape," a specialist of Belorussian literature has observed.[42]

In the Belorussian works of playwright Vintsent Dunin-Martsinkevich, the Jew at first conforms to the traditional stereotype of the tavern-keeper: Itska argues with a peasant who cannot pay for his vodka (*Idylia;* 1842–1844).[43] But in later plays, the Jewish character engages directly in the action (*Hapon;* 1855) or is very far from the stereotype of the tavern-keeper (*Zalioty;* Gallantries, 1870). In *Hapon,* the "aliandar" (lease holder) reveals the secret marriage plans of the peasants Hapon and Katsiaryna to the overseer, who plans to take his revenge on Hapon, his rival, by sending him to the army. But the Jew does so without malice, without seeking to harm, and merely confesses to the overseer that he has extended credit to the young peasants for their marriage. The Jewish tavern-keeper emerges as a humane, kind, and naïve character. In *Zalioty,* Dunin-Martsinkevich inverts all stereotypes: the greedy and crooked rich man is not the Jew but the nobleman Sabkovich. The Jewish character of the play, Mordka, is a naïve artisan, whom Sabkovich dupes and humiliates. Here, the Jew personifies morality and honesty.

This brief survey of Belorussian literature before 1881 shows that Belorussian writers treated Jewish characters with no special emphasis. No more than a participant in the daily life of the village, he appeared rarely, played little role in the plot of the story and seldom rose above a psychological and social caricature. Jews were not a focus of hatred as in Ukrainian literature, which preserved the traditions of the old Cossack chronicles with their glorification of the Chmielnicki era.

The difference in approach of Belorussians and Ukrainians toward the "Jewish question" is also noticeable in the historical development of their respective national identities. Whereas Ukrainian nationalists thought about the place of the Jewish element in a future independent Ukraine and participated in heated debates in the Russian and Ukrainian press on the "Jewish question" during the 1860s and 1870s, the embryonic Belorussian movement was silent about Jews. In his letters to the peasants (*Muzhytskaia praùda*), published in 1862–1863, Kastus Kalinoùski, the leader of Belorussian peasantry during the Polish insurrection, who was crowned a national hero after the independence of Belarus in 1991, did not pay special attention to Jews.

In contrast, Ukrainian nationalists held, at best, an ambiguous position about Jews.[44] Idealizing the Cossack nation and Chmielnicki, the theorists of Ukrainian nationalism saw Jews as traditional allies of the Polish nobility in exploiting the peasantry. Still, some intellectuals favored the emancipation of Jews until the nascent Ukrainophile movement clashed with representatives of Russified Jewish intellectuals during the Osnova/Sion debate of 1861. The affair began when a Jewish intellectual, Benjamin Portugalov, reproached the Ukrainian journal *Osnova* for using the term *zhyd*, which he branded as insulting. This generated a controversy during which Panteleimon Kulish, a prominent Ukrainian writer, decried the "blind national egotism" of leading Jews. The polemic marked the beginning of the degradation of relations between Ukrainian and Jewish intellectuals. Ukrainian leaders, who officially expressed hope that Jews would be granted full civil rights, reproached them for not supporting the Ukrainian movement, and refusing "Ukrainization."

Mikhail Dragomanov's position toward Jews deserves special attention. Dragomanov, one of the most respected Ukrainian activists and the partisan of a federation of national communities in Ukraine, advocated a sort of "mixed marriage" between Jews and Ukrainians as a solution for the "Jewish question." He even called for the use of Yiddish in socialist propaganda, in a brochure published in Geneva in 1880 aimed at Jewish socialists, and wished for the Jewish proletariat to become an ally of Christians against tsarism. After the pogroms, however, he was reluctant to criticize the Ukrainian people and adopted a Judeophobic position, like most Ukrainophiles. Nonetheless, this brief survey shows that Ukrainian leaders debated the "Jewish question," and offered a number of solutions to it.[45]

The Belorussian movement, not yet politically developed but in early stages, had no such expectations from Jews. The silence about Jews on the part of the most popular leader of the Belorussian peasantry, and from most nationalist writers, indicates that Belorussians were indifferent to the "Jewish question." In Belorussia it was not yet a question, nor a subject of thought or debate as it was in Russia, Poland, and Ukraine. If Kalinoŭski did not choose to make Jews a political and economical target in his propaganda, it therefore seems that he considered tsarism the only real enemy of Belorussians. If the recurrent adversary of the peasant in Belorussian literature was the Polish landowner, it stands to reason that the Jewish go-between or tavern-keeper was not perceived by the intelligentsia (if not by its audience) to be as harmful as the imperial bureaucracy suggested. If the place of Jews in the publications of Belorussian intellectuals was minor in relation to their actual place in society, it seems reasonable to believe that Jews were not a major topic of interest to Belorussians.

Apparently unconcerned with the debates around the "Jewish question," Belorussian society preserved a traditional xenophobia based on a religious and feudal Judeophobia, as yet untouched by the innovations of antisemitism in the modern age. Even five years after the pogroms of 1881, a number of Belorussian peasants failed in their attempt to organize pogroms in the region of Lepel (Vitebsk province) that mimicked previous disorders in Vilna province.[46] These attempts, which were thwarted by communal vigilance, the actions of the police, and the absence of leadership, indicate that at least some elements of Belorussian society harbored anti-Jewish feelings. But this hostility was still pre-modern. It resulted occasionally in agrarian uprisings against landlords and their Jewish leaseholders but did not lead to massive ethnic violence. Paradoxically then, the Belorussian provinces were spared pogroms thanks to their isolated positions, cultural and economic backwardness, and delayed political modernization. This observation confirms the analysis of the pogroms published in 1881 by the proto-Zionist Moses Leib Lilienblum. As summarized by Jonathan Frankel, Lilienblum argued:

> In Eastern Europe for centuries the [Jews] had served as an intermediate stratum between the nobles and peasants. But when the caste barriers began to break down as society became more fluid and complex, so the Jews increasingly found themselves in direct competition with members of the majority nationality. Competition produced resentments and resentments provided fertile soil for antisemitism. . . . To be useful at any level meant to be successful and success was dangerous. . . . To follow this logic was to conclude that the greater the emancipation, the greater the danger; the more the modern world advanced, the less secure the situation of the Jews.[47]

Notes

1. Simon Dubnov, *Noveishaia istoriia evreiskogo naroda*, t. 3 (Moscow and Jerusalem, Mosty Kultury-Gesharim, 2002), 96–97.

2. See Grigori Krasnyi-Admoni, ed., *Materialy dlia istorii antievreiskikh pogromov v Rossii*. II: Vos'midesiatye gody [15 aprelia 1881 g.–29 fevralia 1882 g.] (Moscow and Petrograd, Gosudarstvennoe izdatel'stvo, 1923).

3. Darius Staliūnas, "Anti-Jewish Disturbances in the North-Western Provinces in the Early 1880s," *East European Jewish Affairs* 34, no. 2 (Winter 2004): 121–126. See also the chapter by Staliūnas and Vladas Sirutavičius in this volume.

4. *Natsional'ny istoricheski arkhiv Belarusi* (National Historical Archive of Belarus) (NIAB), f. 295, op. 1, d. 3660.

5. NIAB, f. 295, op. 1, d. 3660, ll. 226–231, 263, 264.

6. Staliūnas, "Anti-Jewish Disturbances," 124.

7. NIAB, f. 295, op. 1, d. 3660. See the reports of the commissars (*ispravniki*) of Minsk (l. 250), Borisov (l. 252), Slutsk (l. 253), and Pinsk (l. 258).

8. NIAB, f. 295, op. 1, d. 3660, ll. 79, 154, 231, 264, 313.

9. Ibid., l. 296.

10. See Irwin Michael Aronson, *Troubled Waters: The Origins of the 1881 Anti-Jewish Pogroms in Russia* (Pittsburgh: University of Pittsburgh Press, 1990), chap. 7, and Aronson, "Geographical and Socioeconomic Factors in the 1881 Anti-Jewish Pogroms in Russia," *Russian Review* 39, no. 1 (January 1980): 18–31.

11. See Abraham Yuditski, *Yidishe burzhuazye un yidisher proletariat in ershter helft XIX y.h.* ([Kiev]: Melukhe-farlag "Proletar," n.d.).

12. Ezra Mendelsohn, *Class Struggle in the Pale* (Cambridge: Cambridge University Press, 1970), 14–15.

13. See Simon Dubnov, "Evrei v Mogilevskoi gubernii," *Voskhod* 10 (1886): 9–10.

14. Memorandum of the governor of Vitebsk published in *Khrestomatiïa po istorii Belarusi* (Minsk: BGU, 1977), 233, 300.

15. According to Dubnov, Jews owned one-third of the factories in the Mogilev province and managed another third.

16. Zakhar Shybeka, *Harady Belarusi* (Minsk: Eùroforum, 1997).

17. Ibid., 41–45.

18. See, for example, the description of Mogilev and the little towns of the province in Aleksandr Dembovetski, *Opyt opisaniia Mogilevskoi guberni*, kn. 2 (Mogilev, 1884). In Vitebsk in 1881, the Jewish population represented 50 percent of the total population; see Aleksei Sapunov, *Vitebskaia Starina*, t. 1, (Vitebsk, 1883), 452. In the Minsk province in 1857, the Jewish population already represented 72 percent of the urban population; see Illarion Zelenskii, *Materialy dlia geografii i statistiki Rossii. Minskaia guberniia*, t. 1 (St. Petersburg: Pechatno v Voennoi tip., 1864), 587.

19. See Vladimir Levin's article in this volume.

20. Iaùhen Novik and Henadz Martsul, *Historyia Belarusi u dvukh chastkakh*, t. 1 (Minsk: Universitetskae, 1998), 320.

21. Abraham Paperna, "Iz Nikolaevskoï epokhi," in *Evrei v Rossii. XIX vek* (Moscow: Novoe literaturnoe obozrenie, 2000), 33–34; Lev Levanda quoted by Zelenskii, t. 1: 590; Saul Ginzburg, "Iz davnego proshlogo," *Mishpokha* 11 (2002): 30.

22. NIAB, f. 1297, op. 1, d. 23706 (1853).

23. On racism and antisemitism in Russia, see Eugene M. Avrutin, "Racial Categories and the Politics of (Jewish) Difference in Late Imperial Russia," *Kritika* 8, no. 1 (Winter 2007): 13–40.

24. Gavril Derzhavin, "Mnenie ob otvrashchenii v Belorussii goloda i ustroistve byta evreev," in *Sochineniia Derzhavina*, VII (St. Petersburg: Izdanie imperatorskoi Akademii nauk, 1872), 229–332. See also John D. Klier, *Russia Gathers Her Jews: The Origins of the Jewish Question, 1772–1825* (DeKalb: Northern Illinois University Press, 1986).

25. NIAB, f. 1430, op. 1, d. 12959.

26. Ibid., l. 10.

27. Ibid., ll. 10ob, 11.

28. NIAB, f. 295, op. 1, d. 1151.

29. Ibid., l. 76.

30. Ibid., l. 51.

31. See John D. Klier, *Imperial Russia's Jewish Question, 1855–1881* (Cambridge: Cambridge University Press, 1995).

32. See Theodore R. Weeks, *Nation and State in Late Imperial Russia: Nationalism and Russification on the Western Frontier, 1863–1914* (DeKalb: Northern Illinois University Prerss, 1996); Mikhail Dolbilov, "Russification and the Bureaucratic Mind in the Russian Empire's Northwestern Region in the 1860s," *Kritika* 5, no. 2 (Spring 2004):

245–271; John D. Klier, "The Polish Revolt of 1863 and the Birth of Russification: Bad for the Jews?" *Polin* 1 (1986): 96–110; Aleksei Miller, *Imperiia Romanovykh i natsionalizm* (Moscow: Novoe literaturnoe obozrenie, 2006), 96–146.

33. Zelenskii, *Materialy*, 581–584, 650.

34. Aleksandr Sementovskii, *Etnograficheskii obzor Vitebskoi gubernii* (St. Petersburg: Khana, 1872), 66.

35. Aleksandr Dembovetskii, *Opyt opisaniia Mogilevskoi gubernii*, kn. 1 (Mogilev, Gubernskoe pravlenie, 1882), 694–782. On Brafman's domination of Russian public opinion, see John D. Klier, "The Pogrom Paradigm in Russian History," in *Pogroms: Anti-Jewish Violence in Modern Russian History*, ed. John D. Klier and S. Lambroza (Cambridge University Press, 1992), 20–21.

36. The *kahal* was the Jewish communal board.

37. Pavel Chubinskii, *Trudy etnografichesko-statisticheskoi ekspeditsii v zapadno-russkii krai. Iugo-zapadnyi otdel. Materialy i issledovanie*, 7 (St. Petersburg: Imperatorskoe russkoe geograficheskoe obshchestvo, 1872), 1–211.

38. On the debates about emancipation and assimilation in the 1850s and 1860s, see Benjamin Nathans, *Beyond the Pale: The Jewish Encounter with Late Imperial Russia* (Berkeley: University of California Press, 2002), 50–79.

39. See Israel Bartal and Magdalena Opalski, *Poles and Jews: A Failed Brotherhood* (Hanover, N.H.: University Press of New England, 1992), 19–20, and Zenon E. Kohut, "The Image of Jews in Ukraine's Intellectual Tradition: the Role of *Istoriia Rusov*," in *Cultures and Nations of Central and Eastern Europe: Essays in Honor of Roman Szporluk*, ed. Zvi Gitelman et al. (Cambridge: Ukrainian Research Institute, Harvard University, 2000), 343–358.

40. The play was written in 1787 by the Dominican monk Gaetan Marasheuski, who taught rhetoric and poetics at the monastery of Zabelsk. Two versions of the play were published: a short but bilingual (Belorussian and Polish) version in *Vypisy z belaruskae litaratury*, vol. 1 (Moscow-Leningrad: Dziarzh. vyd-va Belarusi, 1925); and an unabridged Belorussian version in *Khrestamatyia pa historyi belaruskaha teatra i dramaturhii*, t. 1 (Minsk: V'idavetstva V'isheishaia shkola, 1975), 49–98.

41. Pavel Shpilevskii, *Puteshestvie po Poles'iu i belorusskomu kraiu* (Minsk: Polymïa, 1992), 142, 148 (first published in *Sovremennik*, St. Petersburg, 1853–1855).

42. Vera Rich, *The Image of the Jew in Soviet Literature: The Post-Stalin Period* (New York: Ktav Publishing House, 1984), 115.

43. Vintsent Dunin-Marsinkevich, *Vybranyïa tvory* (Minsk: Mastatskaïa litaratura, 2001).

44. On Ukrainian attitudes toward Jews, see Klier, *Imperial Russia's Jewish Question*, chapter 9.

45. Klier, *Imperial Russia's Jewish Question*, 204–221.

46. NIAB, f. 1430, op. 1, d. 53133.

47. Jonathan Frankel, *Prophecy and Politics: Socialism, Nationalism and the Russian Jews, 1862–1917* (Cambridge University Press, 1981), 86. Lilienblum's article was titled "The General Jewish Question and Palestine," *Razsvet* (9 October 1881).

～ 10 ～

Ethnic Conflict and Modernization
in the Interwar Period:
The Case of Soviet Belorussia

ARKADI ZELTSER

The tempo of modernization in the Soviet Union during the 1920s and 1930s was rapid in both the social and family spheres. This tempo led to increased interethnic hostility, with ethnic intolerance being manifest both on the part of non-Jews toward Jews and that of Jews toward non-Jews. However, the former hostility predominated and, in general, actions by non-Jews tended to be more violent. Despite regional differences, the case of Belorussia was typical for all of the former Pale of Settlement.

Ethnic stereotypes held by groups living in Belorussia were based not only on traditional ideas formed over the long period of time when the different ethnic groups lived side by side, but also on values formed after the Bolshevik Revolution. In the prerevolutionary years, many traditional prejudices (religious, ethnic, and social) that often led to conflict were strengthened due to the influence of hostile attitudes toward the Jews of the tsarist bureaucracy and allied conservative circles that included part of the intelligentsia. Such views were spread by the right-wing press and by history texts for schoolchildren.[1]

Traditional prejudices about Jews were particularly characteristic of farmers, who comprised the most conservative stratum of the population. This group projected onto the Jews their opposition to the city as Jews in Belorussia began to be viewed as a symbol of the urban way of life. For Belorussian peasants, the Jew was the incarnation of the foreigner: he spoke a different language, followed a different religion, acted differently in daily life, and was engaged in different, "unnatural" types of labor. Such a view was based on individual and collective experience, largely from the frequent contact of peasants with Jews in the economic sphere either as partners or competitors. Before the revolutions of 1917, tsarist legislation that imposed restrictions on Jews exacerbated such differences.

It was not always possible to completely separate traditional stereotypes from new ones, since under the impact of Soviet policies, traditional stereotypes were altered and took on specific Soviet features. The interaction between the city and the countryside grew stronger during the period of mass migration—from the early 1920s until the end of 1932—when compulsory registration of all Soviet citizens came into force. While new migrants to urban areas retained their peasant mentality, some attitudes of the city dwellers, including attitudes toward Jews, were transmitted to farmers. Relations between urban dwellers and Jews, to a greater extent than those between rural dwellers and Jews, were affected by social gaps, ethnic self-identity, and the pace of modernization. In the cities and towns, the role of a person's character was much more important, and affected an individual's economic situation and living conditions. In the Soviet period, one of the main sources of interethnic tension was the rapid breakdown of stable concepts of the different social roles that were firmly associated with the many ethnic groups in the population. All those factors that undermined usual views —i.e., stereotypes about the "other"—aroused suspicion between non-Jews and Jews.

New ethnic stereotypes emerged largely as a result of the rapid social advancement of the Jews, which became possible once civil rights were granted to them as an outcome of the revolution of February 1917. The principle of ethnic equality was adopted by the Bolshevik Revolution, whose leaders made it a cornerstone of their nationality policy in the interwar period. The Soviet authorities wanted to create conditions that would eliminate the backwardness of ethnic minorities (in comparison to the Russian people) that had existed in the prerevolutionary period. A feeling of guilt on the part of ethnic Russians for persecuting and discriminating against the other peoples of the Russian Empire affected the Soviet attitude toward non-Russian peoples until the mid-1930s.[2] Jews were among the ethnic minorities that made use of the opportunities for social mobility granted them by Soviet policy. During the interwar years, Jews occupied important positions at the national level and in the republics, not only in the Soviet economy, but also in administration, science, the armed forces, and in the secret police (OGPU/NKVD). All of these areas had been closed to them during tsarist times.[3]

Concern regarding increasing Jewish influence was felt among all segments of the population, regardless of the level of education. For example, during the years of revolution and civil war, Trotsky was considered a symbol of Jewish success at the highest level. After the death of Lenin in January 1924, one often heard among Belorussian peasants of Gomel *guberniia* (province) remarks such as "The Russian Orthodox Tsar is dead, the Jewish one remains."[4] Often, even the advancement of Jews to middling positions was seen as an indication of increasing Jewish upward mobility.

Like the Jews, many Belorussians suffered during the difficult process of urbanization. Indeed, the reactions of members of both groups to the multiple changes affecting them were in many respects similar. There were differences, however. On the whole, the integration of Jews from the shtetls (towns) into urban life was more successful than that of the former peasants. The latter, who were often less literate, were newer in the towns, lacked experience in urban professions, and encountered greater difficulties, which caused dissatisfaction and engendered in them the feeling of being outsiders. The combination of their failure to find a place in their new urban environment and their lack of willingness to reconsider their prejudices about Jews often resulted in contradictory attitudes.

Belorussians considered Jews to be parasites for not working at productive, physical labor. The former peasants projected onto Jews their preconceptions about "real" and "parasitical" work. Any social advancement of Jews, no matter how modest, was often perceived as evidence that Jews were different. As one Belorussian worker remarked in 1932 about a Jewish instructor at her factory, "He is [obviously] a former speculator because all kikes were speculators and now they are our bosses."[5] (In this woman's view, both speculators and bosses belonged to the "parasitic" part of the population.)

The belief in Jewish "infiltration" (i.e., overrepresentation) into prestigious professions, good jobs, and the like, reflected the deep conflict that existed in general between the population, on the one hand, and the government and party elite, on the other. In these cases, non-Jews, in their opposition toward "others," combined ethnic with social and political factors. For example, at one end, workers found an enemy in communists, Jews, and professionals ("specialists") while, at another end, members of the intelligentsia and officials found their enemies among communists and Jews, between whom they often had no desire to distinguish.[6]

The antagonism of former peasants toward Jews was largely emotional—as mentioned, they did not want to see any change in Jewish employment patterns. For example, in the mid-1920s officials of peasant origin expressed doubt about the ability of Jews to engage in agriculture and, somewhat malignantly, noted that their specialty was commerce. At the same time, they complained that Jewish shtetls were full of speculators and money-grubbing merchants. Such officials often took the side of peasants in the latter's conflicts with Jews. The existence of special programs to make Jews more productive, particularly by encouraging them to become farmers, aroused dissatisfaction among non-Jews: "The Jews are being given land and money and we are getting nothing."[7] It was commonly assumed that only Belorussian peasants, as the "legitimate" heirs to farmlands formerly owned by the gentry, had the right to cultivate this land. The view that Jews should stick to their involvement in commerce was held mainly by workers, particularly in those enterprises where few or no Jews had been employed. Urban workers protested that "Jewish women are lazy workers. They shouldn't be allowed into factories. Let them sell herring, they're good at that."[8]

Mutual distrust was reinforced by the rapid introduction of some terms into the officially sponsored phraseology of the day. One manifestation of this attitude reflected distrust of the sincerity of members of other ethnic or social groups regarding their adaptation to progressive Soviet reality (e.g., the transition from the private to the state sector). Thus, non-Jews viewed Jews as former businessmen, or "NEP-men" (those who capitalized on the private enterprise made possible through the New Economic Policy instituted by the Soviet regime), who took up factory work in order to hide their alien class origin. For their part, Jews viewed non-Jews as former "kulaks" who were fleeing to the city in order to escape "dekulakization."[9] Some Jews believed that former peasants were underdeveloped both professionally and educationally, and, hence, were unsuitable for fulfilling contemporary social demands. In some cases, they used derogatory phrases to describe non-Jews, for example, *"Hmm, boy mit zey sotsializm"* ("Well, go ahead, try to build socialism with such as these").[10] Both Jews and Belorussians were quite dissatisfied with the social advancement of the "others" and were convinced that it resulted from ethnic favoritism.[11]

Soviet ethnic policy during the 1920s and 1930s envisaged the creation of fundamentally new relations between members of different ethnic groups. The sphere of ethnic relations provided one of the main indicators of the success of Soviet modernization. The authorities assumed that inter-ethnic suspicion and the nationalism of ethnic minorities could be overcome via the establishment of real equality, by means of comprehensive support for ethnic identity in various forms (such as the establishment of ethno-territorial units, encouragement of national cultures and languages, and the like).[12] Another means used to diminish ethnic tensions was the attempt to reduce gaps between ethnic groups in the public sphere, including in the workplace (via "internationalization"; i.e., ethnic mixing at workplaces). In the towns, this entailed the liquidation of vocational specializations that had developed among the various ethnic communities.

For example, Jews had become preponderant in the sewing, shoemaking, and tobacco industries, whereas Poles were overrepresented in the glass industry, and Belorussians in the textile industry. In agriculture, this resulted in the "internationalization" of Jewish agricultural *artels* when many Belorussian peasants joined, thereby making the Jews an insignificant minority in these rural cooperatives.[13]

The issue of identity was less urgent for Belorussians than for Jews. In general, Jews knew how much they differed from the surrounding population. For its part, the nationally oriented Jewish intelligentsia in the USSR was less concerned with creating a national identity per se than with developing a modern Yiddish culture that they considered an efficient tool to save this identity.[14] For Belorussians, it was important to know, and for their intelligentsia to confirm, that they formed a separate people with a culture of their own. They did not want to be considered indigenous residents (*tuteishie*) who spoke the "language of the simple folk" (*prostaia mova*), in contrast to the language of the aristocrats (*panskaia mova*). The latter were Russian-speakers in Soviet Belorussia and Polish-speakers in Western Belorussia.

Notwithstanding their differences, the two ethnic groups competed against each other to enter the Soviet middle class. In Belorussia, the development and use of Belorussian and Yiddish increased ethnic tensions. For Jews and Belorussians alike, the possibility of using their native language in various contexts was an indicator of their touted equality with other groups. Both were highly sensitive to situations where reality did not match this promise. Although formally Belorussian and Yiddish (together with Russian and Polish) had the status of official languages in the republic, Belorussian was considered the primary language and was obligatory in regard to education for a significant part of the population, particularly in the workplace and in schools. Jews viewed this situation as discriminatory. Even a Jewish worker who was not officially required to learn Belorussian wrote to *Pravda* in 1926:

> The Soviet regime, which in all regards and all rights granted Jewish workers equality with the workers of other nations and which gives Jews the possibility of developing their culture, the Soviet regime, I say, is trampling the rights of the latter when it forces them to study the Belorussian language that they do not understand. We, laboring Jews, have the right to ask why we have to learn by heart the [Belorussian] grammar of Iazep Lesik while the Iazep Lesiks have the right not to know Yiddish. After all, according to the Constitution, the latter is also an official language.[15]

At the same time, the introduction of Yiddish as one of the languages in government institutions sometimes had a negative effect on those speaking other languages. Thus, Belorussian workers reacted angrily to the use of Yiddish at general factory and trade union meetings. The mere fact that people were speaking in a language they didn't understand caused some non-Jews to assume that Jews must be speaking about them![16]

One of the main aims of the ethnic Belorussian elite was to decrease the attractiveness of the Russian language to Jews, given the conflict between Belorussian and Russian culture and the less prestigious status of the former vis-à-vis the latter. This was attempted by providing support for Jewish schooling in Yiddish, and alternatively, by trying to attract Jews to Belorussian culture.[17] In the mid-1920s, however, a new phenomenon emerged. Part of the radical, or more nationalistically oriented, Belorussian intelligentsia began to view Belorussian culture as exclusively a national one, closed to the participation of others. Thus, despite the opposition of the administration of the Vitebsk Jewish Pedagogical Seminary (*pedtekhni-kum*) where he worked, a Jewish teacher of the Belorussian language was fired and replaced by an ethnic Belorussian, at the insistence of Belorussian authorities in Minsk. During a discussion of this episode, it was stressed that "it is precisely in the Jewish *pedtekhnikum* that a native Belorussian, not a Jew, is needed to teach Belorussian subjects."[18] In another case, a teacher in a Belorussian school publicly expressed dissatisfaction that a Jew had been sent to work with the members of the "Pioneer" Communist children's group, and remarked that only Belorussians should be working in a Belorussian school.[19]

The rapid, nationwide growth in the number of industrial laborers during the second half of the 1920s and in the 1930s, and the influx of people without any previous factory or even crafts experience, led to tensions between "old" and "new" workers.[20] It is hardly surprising, therefore, that social pressures often surfaced in the sensitive ethnic sphere. When a small number of people from one ethnicity worked at a factory where the majority belonged to another group, the former tended to encounter all sorts of ethnic stereotypes. This was aggravated by the fact that at enterprises where the majority were members of another ethnic group, "internationalization" brought in people who had arrived in the town from villages, and were often poorly educated and intellectually undeveloped. The result was that social and ethnic prejudices reinforced each other among such a population. The most dramatic incidents of antisemitism at factories took place at enterprises where Jews were in the minority and troublemakers were confident that they would not be punished. At the same time,

Jews cruelly mocked and insulted their Belorussians coworkers at factories where Jews constituted the majority.[21]

Ethnic conflict fluctuated during the interwar period. Increased anti-semitism in the second half of the 1920s was first manifest in the booming Soviet metropolises of Moscow and Leningrad. This evidently came from significant cohorts of educated people who were more inclined than their cousins outside the two capitals to make generalizations about trends in the country. Such people were dissatisfied with Soviet social policy and were upset about growing competition from Jews, as well as by the general process of urban modernization, which occurred much more rapidly than in the provinces.[22] However, by the late 1920s, modernization also began to take hold in provincial areas.

After 1917, Soviet cities experienced considerable deviation from what had previously been considered appropriate behavior. The causes were many: changing attitudes toward property; new views about the position of women in society, marriage, and the family; severe economic crises; housing shortages; and severe unemployment. The deteriorating social environment brought increases in prostitution, drunkenness, and fighting.[23] Such behavior reflected a decline in respect for other people which affected large segments of the population, including the new Soviet elite, workers, and employees, particularly newcomers from the countryside. Deviations from traditional behavioral norms were so frequent in 1926 that the authorities felt compelled to launch a mass campaign against drunkenness and "hooliganism," which had become serious social problems.[24] At this time, hooliganism often had an ethnic aspect, as it was stirred up by, and expressed, increased interethnic tension.

A wave of dissatisfaction was caused by destabilization in the country in the late 1920s. The destabilization was three-fold: economic, social, and psychological. Economically, it related to declining standards of living and a lack of food and commodities. Socially, it related to restrictions of basic economic freedoms, including limits on private property.[25] Psychologically, it reflected disillusionment with traditional values, war hysteria in the Soviet press during the second half of the 1920s, and the confusion caused by rapid modernization. People, especially in the countryside, found the guilty parties in middlemen who exploited the difficult food situation and in bureaucrats who ignored the needs of the population. Belorussians largely tended to associate these two groups with Jews, who historically were employed in business or who had advanced rapidly in government or Communist Party service.

It is widely known that the general population was shocked by the cruelty with which the authorities pursued collectivization, the anti-kulak campaign, as well as the confiscations, searches, and arrests of the petty urban bourgeoisie from late 1929 until 1932.[26] People were increasingly inclined to cast the blame for what was happening on the Soviet regime and bureaucrats, who did not share the difficult living conditions of the people. The traditional Russian belief that the top rulers of the country were not responsible for what was happening began to wane.

The wave of antisemitism in 1928–1929 foreshadowed an overall increase in xenophobia in Soviet society. In addition to increasing social pressures and the crisis of traditional values, the mass influx of non-Slavic and non-Christian people (primarily Muslims) into the cities and to the new industrial centers of the Five-Year Plan significantly aggravated interethnic tensions.[27] Most probably, the fact that increased antisemitism preceded other forms of ethnic conflict was related to the more visible social achievements of many Jews in comparison with those of other groups.

Although popular antisemitism was manifest in Belorussia throughout the 1930s, denunciations received by the NKVD that reported popular sentiments indicate that in the second half of the decade the Jews were not among the main targets of dissatisfaction, as they probably had been in the late 1920s. There were several reasons for this change in attitude:

1) After the population recovered from the initial shock over the serious shortages of food and commodities, people were more concerned with physical survival and adaptation to the difficult situation than with finding guilty parties. Under such conditions, hostility toward Jews became more passive than active. Furthermore, old stereotypes gave way as people of all ethnicities in the city and countryside were forced to engage in "speculation" (unofficial or illegal business) and, thus, could no longer easily condemn such activity as "Jewish."

2) Industrialization—despite the limitations on mobility caused by the introduction of internal passports and residence restrictions in 1932—led to a reduction in unemployment. The population of the new Soviet industrial centers, located primarily in the Russian Federation and Ukraine, grew quickly with newcomers from the countryside, people fleeing the newly collectivized farms, and refugees from dekulakization.

3) In the second half of the 1930s, Soviet propaganda created a new category of national threat, consisting of spies and so-called "enemies of the people." Consequently, Jews lost their relative centrality as objects of hostility.

4) It is also possible that migrants from the countryside began to feel less alienated and threatened when they arrived in the cities because of the increasing presence of former peasants who had already settled there in previous years.

5) The increasing threat of punishment for expressing ethnic intolerance may have been a deterring factor in the 1930s. Employees in the state sector (both non-Jews and Jews) risked losing their jobs for manifestations of "nationalist" behavior. A non-Jewish resident of Vitebsk told his wife, "Don't argue with these lousy people and don't even curse them because if you use the word 'kike' you might pay dearly and I might too, because of you."[28]

It is difficult to evaluate the effectiveness of administrative and criminal measures in lessening interethnic conflict in Belorussia. Nonetheless, it is clear that people tended, at least in public, to refrain from expressing ethnic insults and that this helped reduce ethnic confrontations. In contrast to the 1880s, when modernization was a main cause for pogroms,[29] almost no pogroms targeted Jews or Jewish symbols (such as synagogues, Torah scrolls, etc.) in the USSR. The authorities prosecuted all collective manifestations of disorder, including mob attacks against ethnic minorities. In the Belorussian town of Liozno, a "mobilization" (or "conscription") pogrom occurred in 1924. It resembled, to a degree, the 1904 pogroms that had broken out during the mobilization for the Russo-Japanese War.[30] Draftees in Liozno broke into the synagogue, desecrated Torah scrolls, and prepared to attack Jews when they came to defend their sacred objects. For unknown reasons, the Jews did not come to the synagogue and, therefore, no one was harmed. When the local police were unable to stop the *pogromshchiki,* an armored vehicle was summoned from Vitebsk; the authorities restored order and arrested those who had attacked the synagogue.[31] As a result of Soviet policy, anti-Jewish actions like the Liozno incident did not spread. Starting in the period of the civil war, strict punishment (including dismissal from work, arrest, or even execution) was meted out to perpetrators of ethnic violence. News about these punishments was disseminated among broad segments of the population through the national and local press, as well as by lecturers and educators at various local venues.[32]

In this regard, the actions of Soviet authorities differed radically from that of tsarist officials. Before the 1917 Revolution, the authorities were reluctant to conduct mass propaganda against antisemitism by means of the press, meetings, or school education. Tsarist officials often made no effort at all to convey to the population that strict measures would immediately and inevitably be taken against perpetrators of pogroms. In short, the tsarist regime had encouraged in a variety of ways the growth of antisemitic attitudes among the population in its empire. Not so the Soviets.

*　*　*

The rapid and intensive modernization of Soviet society during the 1920s and 1930s, along with its urbanization and industrialization, became key factors in the increase of interethnic tensions. The mass migration of peasants to the city—far larger than the parallel flow of migrants from shtetls—led to a breakdown of traditional ideas among large groups of the population. Many of them suffered dearly from their inability to adapt quickly to the new conditions of life and were unprepared for the redistribution of the previous social roles between various ethnic groups. This dissatisfaction was further aggravated by the social success of Jews. By giving broad support for ethnic minorities, the Soviet nationalities policy made this Jewish success seem even larger among those groups that experienced less upward mobility than the Jews. Furthermore, this contrasted markedly with the prerevolutionary legal inequality of the Jews and with the tsarist bureaucracy's political support for antisemitism.

The popular discontent fed by modernization led to heightened anger and aggressiveness among large segments of the population. This belligerence often manifested itself in the sensitive ethnic sphere. Therefore, the case of interwar Belorussia suggests that the rises and falls in interethnic tension in Soviet society correlated with shifts in the level of general social tension.

Notes

1. Robert Edelman, *Gentry Politics on the Eve of the Russian Revolution: The Nationalist Party, 1907–1917* (New Brunswick: Rutgers University Press, 1980), 65–101; Hans Rogger, *Jewish Policies and Right-Wing Politics in Imperial Russia* (London: Macmillan, 1985), 25–39; Vladlen Izmozik, "Jews in 19th and 20th Century Russian History Textbooks," *Jews in Eastern Europe*, no. 1–2 (38–39) 1999: 44–73.

2. On Soviet policy toward ethnic minorities, see Terry Martin, *The Affirmative Action Empire: Nations and Nationalism in the Soviet Union, 1923–1939* (Ithaca, N.Y.: Cornell University Press, 2001); Terry Martin, "An Affirmative Action Empire: The Soviet Union as Highest Form of Imperialism," in *A State of Nations: Empire and*

Nation-Making in the Age of Lenin and Stalin, ed. Ronald G. Suny and Terry Martin (Oxford: Oxford University Press, 2001), 67–89; Yuri Slezkine, "The USSR as a Communal Apartment, or How a Socialist State Promoted Ethnic Particularism," *Slavic Review* 53, no. 2 (Summer 2004): 424.

3. Mordechai Altshuler, *Soviet Jewry on the Eve of the Holocaust: A Social and Demographic Profile* (Jerusalem: The Centre for Research of East European Jewry, 1998), 133–184.

4. *Natsional'nyi arkhiv Respubliki Belarus'* (National Archive of the Republic of Belarus) (NARB), f. 4, op. 10, d. 3, l. 4, copy in the Central Archives of the History of Jewish People, Jerusalem (CAHJP), inventory no. 7732. The idea of Jewish leaders replacing the deceased (murdered) Russian Orthodox tsar was apparently widespread. See, for example, Nikolai Teptsov, "Monarkhiia pogibla, a antisemitizm ostalsia (Dokumenty Informatsionnogo otdela OGPU 1920-kh gg.)," *Neizvestnaia Rossiia. XX vek* (Moscow: Istoricheskoe nasledie, 1993): 353. This indicates the weakness of a sense of ethnic consciousness among Belorussian peasants, who confused ethnic and religious ideas.

5. Menachem Nadel, " 'Sher un ayzn,' perek al itonut yehudit be-mifalei taasiya sovietiyim," *Asupoth* 2 (n.s.) (1971): 83–84.

6. Sarah Davies, *Popular Opinion in Stalin's Russia: Terror, Propaganda and Dissent, 1934–1941* (Cambridge: Cambridge University Press, 1997), 84, 136–137; Vladimir N. Brovkin, *Russia after Lenin: Politics, Culture and Society, 1921–1929* (London: Routledge, 1998), 186–187.

7. *Oktiabr',* 20 June 1929: 2.

8. Ibid., 24 November 1928: 4.

9. *Gosudarstvennyi arkhiv Vitebskoi oblasti* (State Archive of Vitebsk Oblast') (GAVO), f. 102, op. 1, d. 159, l. 97.

10. *Sher un ayzn,* 16 May 1929: 2.

11. GAVO, f. 10051, op. 1, d. 746, l. 364; *Vitsebski praletary,* December 18, 1929: 3.

12. Slezkine, "The USSR as a Communal Apartment," 424; Martin, "An Affirmative Action Empire," 72–73.

13. Khone Shmeruk, *Ha-kibuts ha-yehudi veha-hityashvut ha-hakla'it ha-yehudit be-belorusyah ha-sovietit, 1918–1932* (Ph.D. diss., Hebrew University of Jerusalem, 1961), 130–135.

14. On the formative period of Soviet Yiddish culture, see David Shneer, *Yiddish and the Creation of Soviet Jewish Culture 1918–1930* (New York: Cambridge University Press, 2004).

15. *Pravda,* 14 July 1926: 4.

16. *Oktiabr',* 29 November 1928: 3.

17. Mordechai Altshuler, *Ha-yevsektsiya bi-vrit ha-moatsot, 1918–1930* (Tel Aviv: Sifriat Poalim, 1980), 144, 169, 171.

18. NARB, f. 42, op. 1, d. 1472, ll. 22–23, 51, copy CAHJP, HMF 470.2.

19. GAVO, f. 10051, op. 1, d. 705.

20. See, for example, Hiroaki Kuromiya, *Stalin's Industrial Revolution: Politics and Workers, 1928–1932* (Cambridge: Cambridge University Press, 1988), 87–99.

21. NARB, f. 11, d. 120, l. 87; *Der emes,* October 28, 1930: 2.

22. For more on the growth of antisemitism in Leningrad, see Michael Beizer, *Evrei Leningrada: Natsional'naia zhizn' i sovetizatsiia* (Jerusalem-Moscow: Gesharim-Mosty Kul'tury, 1999), 102–111.

23. On deviant behavior in the USSR during the 1920s, see Nataliia B. Lebina, *Povsednevnaia zhizn' Sovetskogo goroda: normy i anomalii, 1920–1930 gody* (St. Petersburg:

Zhurnal "Neva"—Letnii Dom, 1999), 19–98: idem, "Tenevye storony zhizni sovetskogo goroda 20–30-kh godov," *Voprosy istorii*, 2, 1994: 30–41; Sheila Fitzpatrick, *Everyday Stalinism: Ordinary Life in Extraordinary Times, Soviet Russia in the 1930s* (New York: Oxford University Press, 1999), 52–53; idem, *The Cultural Front: Power and Culture in Revolutionary Russia* (Ithaca, N.Y.: Cornell University Press, 1992), 65–90.

24. Lebina, *Povsednevnaia zhizn' Sovetskogo goroda*, 36–98.

25. Elena A. Osokina, "V tiskakh sotsialisticheskoi torgovli," in Sergei A. Pavliuchenkov, *Rossiia nepovskaia* (Moscow: Novyi Khronograf, 2002), 403–418.

26. For Soviet restrictions on the Jewish population at the end of the 1920s and the beginning of 1930s, see Arkadi Zeltser, "The *Shtetl* During the 'Great Watershed' of 1929–1931: The Case of Vitebsk Region," *Jews in Eastern Europe* 3 [46] (2001): 5–33.

27. Solomon Shvarts, *Antisemitizm v Sovetskom Soiuze* (New York: Izdatel'stvo imeni Chekhova, 1952): 105–107; Gennadii Kostyrchenko, *Tainaia politika Stalina. Vlast' i antisemitizm* (Moscow: Mezhdunarodnye otnosheniia, 2001), 108.

28. GAVO, f. 10051, op. 1, d. 746, l. 366.

29. Michael Aronson, "The Anti-Jewish Pogroms in Russia in 1881," in *Pogroms: Anti-Jewish Violence in Modern Russian History*, ed. John D. Klier and Shlomo Lambroza (Cambridge University Press, 1992), 46.

30. Shlomo Lambroza, "The Pogroms of 1903–1906," in Klier and Lambroza, *Pogroms*, 212–219.

31. NARB, f. 4, op. 10, d. 5, l. 73.

32. For details about the strict Soviet policy toward antisemitism in the 1920s and 1930s, see Solomon M. Schwarz, *The Jews in the Soviet Union* (Syracuse, N.Y.: Syracuse University Press, 1951), 274–291; Shmuel Etinger, "Rusiya veha-yehudim—nisayon shel sikum histori," *Gesher*, no. 1 (66), 1971: 17–18; Matthias Vetter, *Antisemiten und Bolschewiki: Zum Verhaltnis von Sowietsystem und Judenfeindschaft, 1917–1939* (Berlin: Metropol, 1995); Beizer, *Evrei Leningrada*, 102–111.

❧ 11 ❧

Defusing the Ethnic Bomb: Resolving Local Conflict through Philanthropy in the Interwar USSR

JONATHAN DEKEL-CHEN

At first glance, this essay may seem a bit oddly placed in a volume dedicated to a reappraisal of the forces behind, and the realities of, anti-Jewish violence in Eastern Europe. After all, it often seems that the history of Jewish relations with non-Jewish neighbors can be understood mainly through an interpretive prism of when, how, and why the former inevitably were targeted and victimized by the latter. Or is Jewish history better understood through the looking-glass of when, how, and why governments—be they autocratic, dictatorial, hypernationalist, fascist, or otherwise—repressed their Jews? Such questions are most common in reference to the fate of Jews in Eastern Europe.

While not discounting the importance of anti-Jewish violence, intriguing work in recent years from scholars like Benjamin Nathans and Yuri Slezkine has begun to reconsider Jewish "otherness" in this region of the world. Such scholarship suggests patterns of Jewish integration and acculturation (and not just assimilation) into the home societies that are comparable, if not always equal in importance, to trends of anti-Jewish behavior and violence "from above" and "from below."[1] At the very least, this recent scholarship suggests a recalibration of the historiographic balance between what was done to Jews from outside forces versus what Jews (both "great" and "small") themselves did in their daily lives and how they maneuvered within the often treacherous waters of late Imperial Russia and the early Soviet Union.

The successes and failures of coexistence can be instructive on multiple levels. Obviously, this should be a productive method for grasping what transpired between Jews and their neighbors in various historical milieus. Beyond this, specific cases of coexistence in an otherwise tense political environment may also be helpful in handling potential trouble spots for ethnic conflict in the contemporary world. Academics and the wider public must never ignore the sources or dangers of antisemitism. But this does not absolve us from pondering another question: should not our investigation of interethnic dynamics in the past do more to seek out probable formulas for coexistence in the present and future, even if perfect harmony between Jews and non-Jews is rarely, if ever, achieved?

This paper studies a relatively unknown and fascinating case of interaction between Jews and non-Jews in interwar Soviet southern Ukraine and Crimea. The axis of this interaction was the development of organized Jewish agricultural settlement in the region. Most of the discussion will focus on Crimea, which had an unusually diverse ethnic composition at the time. This episode in the interwar Soviet Union did not just reflect the complex workings of interethnic tensions, but also how external intervention can serve to enflame and/or calm hostility. On its surface, this case study deals with events in the Soviet countryside—internal migration, colonization, rural development, and interaction. No less, however, it deals with what did *not* happen in this time and place—namely, interethnic violence—despite the explosive environment created by the arrival of tens of thousands of Jewish newcomers laying claim to relatively scare resources at a time of undergovernance in the Soviet periphery.[2] A variety of factors averted this gloomy scenario. While the outcomes in Crimea and southern Ukraine cannot be categorized as an ethnic "garden of Eden," they can inform us about the creation of a modus vivendi in such potential hotspots.

Organized Jewish agricultural settlement in the USSR began in 1924 and 1925, following the signing of settlement contracts between the Soviet government and three western Jewish philanthropies (the American Jewish Joint Distribution Committee in New York [JDC], the ORT-Farband in Berlin, and the Jewish Colonization Society in Paris).[3] The target region was the northern Crimean peninsula and southern Ukraine, in the regions surrounding Odessa, Kherson, and Dnepropetrovsk. The Joint Distribution Committee was the most active of these organizations in the resettlement of Jews to the agricultural colonies. The vast majority of the new colonists were resettled around the Black Sea from the traditional towns in the former Pale of Settlement. The JDC created a sub-unit called "Agro-Joint" to support this enterprise and supplied the colonies with high-quality housing, low-interest loans, medical and educational facilities, as well as state-of-the-art agricultural equipment and expertise.[4] This aid package bore crucial importance for interethnic relations because the Soviet countryside was still very primitive at that time.[5] The Bolshevik state contributed to the resettlement project through the creation of agencies

(Komzet and Ozet) for the support of Jewish colonization and launched a major propaganda campaign for this purpose.[6] Publicity on behalf of Jewish land settlement was part of a wider Soviet campaign of the era to popularize positive images of ethnic minorities.[7] The Soviets also supplied logistical support and other benefits to the settlers and philanthropic organizations. For lack of space, this paper foregoes other Jewish settlement episodes elsewhere in the USSR during the interwar era.[8]

At its zenith, the project around the Black Sea encompassed hundreds of thousands of acres, approximately 250 colonies, and a total of some 200,000 settlers. Tens of thousands of Jewish colonists from the traditional areas of the former Pale virtually "parachuted" into Crimea from 1922 until 1941. Until the early 1920s, Jews had been a relatively small urban phenomenon in the peninsula. Suddenly, large blocs of Jewish settlements sprouted all over the rural landscape with the blessing of the Kremlin. These blocs contained, and were surrounded by, non-Jewish villages inhabited by Tatars, ethnic Germans, ethnic Swiss, Russians, Ukrainians, and others. Agro-Joint saw the development of the colonies in relatively compact blocs as means for efficient delivery of its aid. It also saw blocs with clear Jewish majorities as a guarantor for the safety of the colonists from unfriendly forces. The foreign philanthropic organizations left the USSR by 1938 but the settlements survived until they were overrun by Hitler's armies in 1941.

The ethnic mosaic that characterized Crimea until 1941 was laden with tension before the arrival of the first Jewish colonists in the early 1920s. Ruled by a new nationalistic Tatar-communist regime, relations were fractious among the many ethnicities of the peninsula; even individual Muslim Tatar communities competed against one another. The latter were a minority in Crimea, constituting approximately one-quarter of the population. Nonetheless, the Tatar-communist leadership claimed much of the land appropriated by the Soviet state for Jewish agricultural colonies. From the standpoint of these Tatar leaders, this part of northern Crimea was most desired for the resettlement of Tatar returnees from abroad or to satisfy the land-hunger of Tatars living in the arid central mountain region of the Crimean peninsula. The ethnic powder keg was further sensitized by the fact that most of the other indigenous peoples in the northern half of the peninsula—including Lutheran Germans, Mennonite Swiss, Estonians, Greeks, and Bulgars—were suspect in the Kremlin and among the local Tatar-communist rulers of Crimea. Caught in the middle of this center-periphery conflict, the intrusion of a new, uninvited population could have easily ignited an explosion of hatred that would consume the Jewish colonists.

Making matters worse, the central authority in Moscow had unilaterally granted state lands to Jews that until then had been leased (or "squatted" on) by many of these indigenous peoples for grazing or farming. The new Jewish occupants refused, in some cases, to rent these lands to the former leasers, even if the Jews themselves did not use them for farming. This created a temporary land shortage in the northern Crimean peninsula because internal migration in these years by Jews and, to a lesser extent, other ethnic groups soaked up much of the free land that had been staples of previous rental arrangements. Therefore, colonization sparked quick, grassroots reactions against the perceived injustice of the state's "affirmative action" on behalf of Jews.[9] Embittered German colonists wondered why the government did not provide them with equipment equal to that given to the Jewish newcomers by Agro-Joint.[10]

Herein was the two-headed core of potential conflict: on the one hand, non-Jewish farmers and shepherds had used this land before the arrival of the Jewish colonists and still believed it to be theirs, regardless of what the Kremlin had decided; on the other hand, the new local communist rulers of Crimea had very different ambitions for this land. Added to these sources of tension, talk radiating out from Moscow in the mid-1920s about the creation of a Jewish republic in Crimea sparked anger among the non-Jewish population who sensed that their own newfound autonomy might be at risk. In response to these and other considerations, the Tatar-communist leadership in Crimea acted to obstruct Jewish colonization.

A host of negative rumors about the settlement project, both in the former Pale and nearer to the colonies, added to these points of friction. Some rumors claimed that Jewish settlers around the Black Sea received the best land and did not work. Other rumors attributed the settlement contracts between the JDC and the Soviet government to a "deal" cut by the Bolsheviks to repay debts to unnamed "Americans" from before the 1917 revolution. Others, especially local German colonists, often lashed out against their new neighbors, sure that they were conspiring with a supposedly Jewish-controlled Kremlin to evict them from marginal and leased parcels. Popular rumors in Ukraine charged that Jewish farmers were lazy and therefore employed hired, non-Jewish labor.[11] The local Soviet secret police recorded rumors that the regime allowed rabbis and Tatar mullahs to operate freely while it persecuted Russian Orthodox clerics.[12] In still other cases, local peasants heard that the Jewish newcomers had stolen their land and pumped resources out of it (*vykachivayut iz nee*) to Palestine.[13]

At first glance, such rumors seemed likely to stir popular antisemitism. Scandalous stories and stereotypes about Jews as speculators of land had circulated for decades in Russia's officialdom and populace.[14] Some recent scholarship has reinforced this dark picture by assuming that any hopes for interethnic harmony vanished with the waves of political turmoil and economic revolution that came with nationwide collectivization, industrialization, and purges from the late 1920s into the 1930s.[15] And as other recent scholarship shows, Judaism (but not Jews) was a valid target for vilification at this time.[16] At a theoretical level, the high incidence of rumors in this scenario seems to fit Donald Horowitz's paradigm for the outbreak of interethnic violence.[17]

How were these doubts, fears, and very real, albeit sporadic, attacks against the colonists overcome? For its part, the state helped through stiff and swift administrative and legal action. Local Soviet authorities believed these measures necessary to protect Jewish colonists and, perhaps more importantly, rural order.[18] Some colonists responded to the threats on their own through modest self-defense efforts.[19] In hindsight, such actions explain only part of the process of rural integration. Punishment and deterrence could, at best, impede future hostility against the Jewish newcomers but cannot explain why these colonies became a respected part of the rural landscape within a few years. Moreover, the Soviet state simply did not have enough coercive force available on a daily basis in the periphery during these years; simply stated, all imagery aside, the Kremlin did not have the power to eradicate attacks. It did, however, have more influence than mere brute force. For example, the anti-antisemitic environment created by the Soviet regime's publicity campaign in the Russian, and other indigenous, languages should not be taken for granted; for reasons not always the most benign, the Bolsheviks from 1917 on radically changed the tone and content of the official position toward Jews. It must be remembered, however, that the application of Soviet mandates was never total. Rather, Soviet citizens often circumvented policy and mistrusted new images promoted by the regime.[20]

Traditional racial stereotypes among the Jewish settlers at times made them as much a part of the formation of the interethnic problem as a part of its solution. Some Jewish colonists regarded their neighbors with condescension and contempt. Indeed, most bore from their shtetls in the Pale of Settlement a long-standing disdain for "Russian" peasants and at first refused to learn from their experience. Patronization of rural Tatars was perhaps even worse. A well-known Polish Jewish author met colonists who thought their Tatar neighbors kind people, "satisfied with what they have and do not look further. They just needed strong coffee, shish kebab, and a song."[21]

All of these factors notwithstanding, ground-level relations warmed quite rapidly, although not universally. In retrospect, it appears that mutual benefit, beyond all else, pushed the majority of the surrounding villagers closer to the Jewish colonists. The newcomers needed help beyond that which Agro-Joint agronomists could provide in their visits to the new colonies once or twice a week. Therefore, the new Jewish farmers had to also depend on (grudgingly or not) the advice of more experienced German, Tatar, or Russian peasants. The individual non-Jewish neighbors pragmatically gauged the situation; more often than not they accepted the Jewish colonists, despite grievances. We shall shortly see what drew the indigenous peoples to the Jews.

Despite some nationalistic tensions caused by the aforementioned resistance from the Tatar-communist authorities in the capital city of Simferopol, relations between Jews and local Tatars were generally the most positive among all of the non-Jewish neighbors. Before 1924, Tatars in the areas of colonization had rarely encountered urban, ethnic European Jews.[22] Such unfamiliarity meant that there was little preexisting prejudice to impede fraternity; cordiality and commercial ties quickly developed, with violence occurring relatively rarely.[23] At the other end of the ethnic spectrum, by the end of the 1920s Germans and Jews stood to gain the most from each other because of their status as the two most advanced farming communities. According to archival and other records, good relations usually began with humanitarian gestures that gradually evolved into mutual respect based on professional accomplishments.[24]

Interethnic relations in Crimea in the first half of the 1930s can be characterized overall as halting acceptance, not limitless affection. In almost all of the Soviet-era literature that dealt with Jewish colonization, a common formula described the genesis of relations with the neighboring peasants. As depicted there, the surrounding villages came to respect and depend upon the Jewish colonists, particularly for their tractors. Evidently, these conditions compared favorably to interethnic tensions elsewhere in the Soviet Union, where state-sponsored affirmative action programs on behalf of specific ethnic groups often exacerbated tensions with others.[25] At the same time, it is possible that the official campaign to popularize a more positive and productive image of Jews had achieved a measure of success in the public mind. In 1932, the state significantly defused any residual tensions over land tenure questions when it increased the land holdings of non-Jewish *kolkhozy* in Crimea.[26] We shall explore shortly the narrow areas in which interethnic conflicts nonetheless persisted into the 1930s.

The Role of Philanthropic Aid

The JDC embarked in 1924 on a massive and multilayered project involving a range of interests, possible plans of action, and all sorts of dangers. Its scale and boldness was unlike anything attempted in the world of Jewish philanthropy until that time. The impact of philanthropic aid was felt not just by the Jewish settlers themselves, but also by the neighboring peasants. Given the perceived sparseness of the population and its non-Russian character, the JDC felt that interethnic harmony could be achieved in and around the settlement tracts. While individual colonies or settlers made some inroads, philanthropy from abroad systematically accelerated interethnic relations.[27]

More than the other foreign philanthropies, the efforts of Agro-Joint had multiple, positive effects on interethnic relations. Direct assistance from the JDC to non-Jews commenced even before Agro-Joint began formal operations. This included famine relief with Herbert Hoover's American Relief Administration (ARA) in 1921–1922[28] and the admission of non-Jewish children into schools built by the Joint.[29] The organization and individual colonists employed some non-Jewish laborers, mostly to compensate for manpower deficits or gaps in agricultural skills.[30] This proved a mixed blessing, however; by the late 1920s, agricultural machines imported by Agro-Joint from the United States started to replace these workers, thereby putting new stresses on interethnic relations. Indirect aid fostered other forms of interaction. Among these was the supply to neighboring settlements of inexpensive processed items from Agro-Joint workshops in the Jewish colonies.[31]

At a most basic level, the organization warmed the local environment by distributing modern equipment and expertise. During the 1920s, and in some cases well into the 1930s, Agro-Joint delivered to non-Jewish villages supplies and services unavailable from any other source, or at much greater expense.[32] As a case in point, water disputes eased greatly from the late 1920s once Agro-Joint drilled artesian wells for its Jewish colonies *and* for neighboring villages. It increased goodwill still further through the supply of tractors: between nine and thirteen of its ninety-five tractors in service in Crimea were given to local Tatars, and Agro-Joint regularly offered low-cost services from its large tractor teams to neighboring villages.[33] This was not happenstance. Rather, the JDC thought from the outset of its colonization work about how to assist non-Jewish neighbors and sent special envoys to calm local Tatars and Russians in Crimea.[34] In the words of its director in 1923, looking back upon its last two years of work under the ARA,

> it was understood that the economic recovery must be general if the Jewish population were to get any permanent benefit from the help given and therefore the reconstruction work, no less than the relief work, was done on a non-sectarian basis. The figures which are now available demonstrate quite conclusively, how non-sectarian the activities of the JDC have been to date. Of 100,000 acres plowed, at least 70% belonged to Russian peasants. Of 50,000 families on the land receiving agricultural aid, more than half were non-Jewish. That the work was appreciated by the non-Jewish population and by the government itself is plain from the fact that, hundreds of telegrams and letters of thanks for the reconstruction work done, have been received and that the Departments of Agriculture in Moscow and Kharkov have asked the JDC to continue its work.[35]

Agro-Joint did, however, have its stipulations. In the words of the director:

> Although we did the work for non-Jewish as well as Jewish farmers, we made it a rule that no plowing was to be done for any villages which participated in pogroms [during the Russian Civil War]. From many of these villages we had petitions asking us to do some plowing for them, and expressing regret for the criminal activities of some of their villagers.[36]

Even if it touched comparatively few indigenous villagers, Agro-Joint projects deeply affected specific cases. In 1926 alone, it supplied 300 Tatar families with 150 oxen, 60 wheel-bases, building materials, and cash. In the same year Agro-Joint spent approximately 150,000 rubles, or 30 percent of its local budget, on non-Jewish neighbors of the colonies. The JDC helped more than 15,000 non-Jewish, peasant households before 1929 and 80,000 families by 1937. Health care and education were another aspect of Agro-Joint aid to the neighboring population, where non-Jews constituted as many as 60 percent of the patients treated at its local infirmaries. As early as 1925, non-Jewish children comprised one-third of all students in Agro-Joint schools in the settlement areas. By 1929, their enrollment ranged from 20 to 64 percent of the total student population.[37] In return, Tatars and other indigenous peasants openly thanked Agro-Joint and its colonists for bringing the gifts of modernity.[38]

What other factors led indigenous peoples to welcome the outstretched hand of Agro-Joint? For local peasants, the international status of the JDC was inconsequential. As with anyone hovering around subsistence, their sentiments hinged on what was to be gained or lost at home.[39] Beyond the material aid supplied by Agro-Joint, its agronomists were a key to understanding how the local environment coalesced. The formula was simple: Agro-Joint agronomists and agricultural instructors compared favorably to the inadequate supply of unqualified and politicized Soviet agronomists of the period. The separateness of these Agro-Joint employees from the state apparatus, and their proven ability to improve crop yields, made them a very valued part of the aid delivered to the local neighbors.[40] Local peasants had no obvious reason to resist help from foreign philanthropies. In contrast to power-conscious and politically problematic government officials of all ranks who did not want to surrender any authority or status to the "locals," indigenous farmers seemed to have nothing to lose in the 1920s by welcoming these myriad forms of aid from "the Americans."

Lastly, the conscious inclusion of non-Jewish peasants into agricultural and industrial cooperatives created or underwritten by Agro-Joint added to the positive local dynamic. Such cooperative ventures could be quite large, encompassing several villages of different nationalities where the equipment and expertise of Agro-Joint became common property. These took shape as cooperative dairies, winter workshops, or grain mills. Evidently, there was also an outward ripple effect from the Jewish colonies—where cooperatives were the rule—to the surrounding villages.[41] Business and social links between the Jewish and non-Jewish *kolkhozy* remained intact in the three and a half years between the exit of Agro-Joint and the German conquest of the region—an indication of the lasting strength of the interethnic bridges constructed until then.

Who's to Say? Everyday Rural Cruelties or Anti-Jewish Violence

Up to this point, we have described and assessed details of the case in interwar Soviet Crimea. What might they mean from a wider perspective? Whether we study anti-Jewish violence as scholars, community leaders, or interested citizens, a first order of business is to clarify the nature of the beast. A most common explanation for violence is, of course, rooted in the existence and influence of antisemitism. But this may at times miss the mark. Are we always talking about "anti-Jewish violence" or perhaps do we mean "violence against Jews"? This interpretive dilemma is hardly unique to the interwar Soviet Union. As Helmut Walser Smith and Chris Clark concluded a number of years ago, the historiography of Wilhelmine

Germany tends too often to portray Jews as hapless victims of a monolithic "gentile" culture or of clear-cut antisemitism.[42] In the case of Jewish settlement in Crimea and southern Ukraine, both the contemporary philanthropist-activist and the modern historian can have trouble discerning the line between normal interethnic relations in the countryside and evidence of modern antisemitism fostered by states, hostile media, or transnational movements. Accordingly, there might be one interpretation or solution pertinent for antisemitic attacks and others for less racially driven violence.

What was the norm of hostility in and around the Jewish colonies of Crimea in the early years of settlement? Multiple sources reported that non-Jewish neighbors stole and destroyed the colonists' equipment, livestock, and seeds; unlawfully used their wells and pastures; encroached on arable lands; resorted to physical violence; and even forced some Jewish settlers to flee.[43] It appears that the abuse heaped upon the newcomers was aggravated by widening gaps between the general rural squalor among many of the indigenous peoples and the emerging prosperity in the Jewish settlements.[44] These gaps, as we now know, were narrowed by the work of the philanthropic organizations.

What appeared at first glance to be antisemitic violence usually turned out to be, upon further consideration, something else. Attacks against Jewish colonists at this time should be seen more as a fairly generic form of rural hooliganism, which was endemic to the interwar Soviet Union. Some Agro-Joint agronomists immediately recognized the attacks as such.[45] In a representative example, settlers in the Freidorf colony realized in 1928–1929 that the boorish and violent behavior of a neighboring non-Jewish family was not antisemitism. Rather, it was the same antisocial, rural hooliganism that these people had brought with them from their former region of residence.[46] By the early 1930s, attacks against Agro-Joint or the colonists were clearly a function of petty criminal activity and not nationalism or antisemitism. For example, when local thieves raided an Agro-Joint warehouse in the autumn of 1934, this reflected the nationwide economic crisis caused by the "total" collectivization of agriculture, not a surge of Judeophobia.[47]

Violence against colonists was also an expression of anger against the state, which seemed to be using these foreigners to evict indigenous farmers from their leased lands. While threats to "slaughter all the 'zhidy'" accompanied some attacks, hostility to those perceived as unwanted interlopers—regardless of ethnicity—was the dominant dynamic.[48] Therefore, assaults against Jews represented first and foremost a counterattack against the center of power in Moscow in defense of land tenure arrangements that preceded the arrival of Jewish settlers in Crimea. Other attackers targeted Jewish colonists who seemed to present a convenient opportunity for quick and easy profits in the periphery.

Another persistent dilemma in the assessment of violence against Jews is weighing the accounts of the Jewish participants in a given episode against later assessments by scholars, activists, or public officials. A modern researcher may consider a specific act in the past against Jews as a heinous crime that signaled or symbolized wider anti-Jewish patterns. A contemporary participant in (or observer of) the event, however, may have seen things quite differently. For most colonists, in fact, by the late 1920s the level of government taxation on farm produce had become a much greater daily burden than the specter of unpleasantries inflicted by non-Jewish neighbors.[49] We must also seriously consider the possibility that Jewish settlers manipulated to some degree the official Soviet propaganda campaign against antisemitism. In other words, Jewish colonists may have purposely invoked exaggerated cries of antisemitism in attempts to elicit a stronger response on their behalf from the authorities. We now know that some of these incidents were probably no more than normal rural fights over land and stray livestock.[50] In this way, the regime might be mobilized to the defense of Jewish interests more expeditiously, and with greater force, than if the issue had been merely the product of "normal" disagreements among neighbors in the countryside.

* * *

When conceptualizing interaction between Jews and their neighbors based on the record in interwar Crimea, we should avoid "black or white" rubrics. Must the complete absence of interethnic tension be an analytical sine qua non for concluding that reasonable relations existed with neighboring populations? Whether in the interwar Soviet countryside or in other complex interethnic environments, it seems that a degree of friction almost always accompanies relations between Jews and non-Jews. At times, ethnic or nationalistic friction feed the hostility. At other times, rather banal, nonethnic, nonsectarian economic issues underpin intercommunal stress.

Conversely, the mere presence of tension should not be, in and of itself, a single indicator of crisis when viewed in an historical perspective. Why? Above all, the outcome of social and/or economic friction is not always violence. Secondly, tensions are a nearly inevitable part of Jewish "differentness" in some local scenarios. In the end, understanding the real quality of Jewish life in Eastern Europe calls for a delicate tallying of the cooperation and rancor that merged in everyday life wherever Jews interacted with non-Jews.[51]

Taken together with the findings in Natan Meir's article in this volume, it seems that anti-Jewish violence was just as often in the background as in the foreground of Jewish life in Eastern Europe from the second half of the nineteenth century until the eve of World War II. To draw a parallel with Meir's term from the urban scene, there was a "larger fabric of relations between Jews and non-Jews" in the Crimean countryside than simple interpretations of violence would lead us to conclude. The case of interwar agricultural settlement in the USSR also allows us to observe how the neighboring population modified its behavior toward Jews in accordance with changing situations; people who treated Jews harshly yesterday in the countryside (or as Meir found, in the city) could be swayed tomorrow. Moreover, the process of modernization "from above," when applied with reasonable equity, could improve relations between Jews and their neighbors. Skeptics of my arguments might point to an apparent hole in the above conclusion. After all, as they could say, local Crimeans collaborated with the conquering Nazi army in the extermination of those Jewish colonists who had not evacuated the peninsula in advance of the invasion. The historical record, as it currently stands, suggests that levels of collaboration in Crimea were similar to those in most other parts of Nazi-occupied Eastern Europe.[52] Understanding the wartime behavior of non-Jewish civilians toward Jews—in the Soviet Union and elsewhere—is among the many painful questions that await definitive answers from scholars of the Holocaust and is far beyond the scope of this article.

It seems that the biggest single factor in the relatively positive ethnic outcomes in interwar Crimea lies in the thoughtful and thorough work of Agro-Joint. It eased jealousies and fears in the peninsula by raising the living standards of the neighbors at a pace comparable to that of the Jewish colonists. By spreading modernity to all residents of the regions where it worked, Agro-Joint did much to neutralize the root causes of envy and distrust on the part of local population and thereby "defused" what could have developed into a much hotter ethnic conflict. I suspect that civil relations would have emerged even without the Agro-Joint, but its work increased the pace of the process exponentially.

All this being said, the conscious and systematic actions of Jewish philanthropic organizations were (and are) not a "cure-all" for ethnic strife. Generally speaking, the longer interethnic tension exists, the harder it is to reduce. Therefore, much is to be said for an argument that philanthropic "medicine" worked well in around the Black Sea precisely because much of the indigenous populations had little or no prior exposure to Jews before the settlers arrived on the land. What we do know, however, is that foreign economic support—augmented by the deterrent effect of Soviet legal muscle—encouraged local harmony. The case of Crimea suggests that such support works best when there is an ample supply of skilled officials from the philanthropic organization on the ground to administer the programs.

Finally, this episode suggests what can be achieved when nongovernmental organizations remain cognizant of interethnic issues and take active steps to offset tensions between their target beneficiaries and the surrounding populations. Perhaps most interesting, the case of interwar Soviet Russia shows that such things can be accomplished in the context of a state—in this case, Stalin's Soviet Union—that had dictatorial intentions, if not always dictatorial results. Cannot a wider range of action for philanthropic work to ease ethnic tensions exist in more liberal states and societies?

Notes

1. Benjamin Nathans, *Beyond the Pale: The Jewish Encounter with Late Imperial Russia* (Berkeley: University of California Press, 2002); Yuri Slezkine, *The Jewish Century* (Princeton, N.J.:: Princeton University Press, 2004).

2. A number of studies have discussed this. For example, see James Hughes, *Stalin, Siberia and the Crisis of the NEP* (Cambridge: Cambridge University Press, 1991); Sheila Fitzpatrick, *Stalin's Peasants: Resistance and Survival in the Russian Village after Collectivization* (Oxford University Press, 1994); and Neil Weissman, "Policing the NEP Countryside," in *Russia in the Era of NEP*, ed. Sheila Fitzpatrick, Alexander Rabinowitch, and Richard Stites (Bloomington: Indiana University Press, 1991), 174–191.

3. For accounts of the activities of the Jewish Colonization Association in Soviet-era colonization, see *Evreiskoe Kolonizatsionnoe Obshchestvo, Dva goda raboty EKO v oblasti pereseleniia* (Moscow: EKO, 1928); idem, *Piat' let raboty evreiskogo kolonizatsionnogo obshchestva v SSSR, 1923–1927* (Moscow: EKO, 1928); Theodore Norman, *An Outstretched Arm: A History of the Jewish Colonization Association* (London: Routledge, 1985). The activity of ORT-Farband is described in Aryeh Munitz, *Irgunei "ORT" be-Brit ha-moatsot be-shanim 1917–1938* (Tel Aviv: Tel Aviv University, 1981); Leon Shapiro, *The History of ORT: A Jewish Movement for Social Change* (New York: Schocken, 1980); Jack Rader, *By the Skill of Their Hands: The Story of ORT* (Geneva: ORT, 1970).

4. For an account of the JDC's work and the entirety of the project around the Black Sea, see my *Farming the Red Land: Jewish Agricultural Colonization and Local Soviet Power, 1924–1941* (New Haven, Conn.: Yale University Press, 2005).

5. For details, see R. W. Davies, *Soviet Economic Development from Lenin to Khrushchev* (Cambridge: Cambridge University Press, 1998), 23–31.

6. *Komzet* was the acronym for *Komitet po zemel'nomu ustroistvu trudiashchikhsia evreev pri Prezidiume Soveta Natsional'nostei Tsentral'nyogo Ispolitel'nogo Komiteta SSSR*

(Committee for the Settlement of Jewish Laborers on the Land under the Council of Soviet Nationalities for the Central Executive Committee of the USSR). *Ozet* was the acronym for *Obshchestvo po zemel'nomu ustroistvu trudiashchikhsia evreev* (The Society for the Settlement of Jewish Toilers on the Land). Both were liquidated by the Soviet government in 1937–1938.

7. For details, see my " 'New' Jews of the Agricultural Kind: A Case of Soviet Interwar Propaganda," *Russian Review* 66 (July 2007): 424–450.

8. For details on interwar Jewish agricultural settlement throughout the USSR, see Antje Kuchenbecker, *Zionismus ohne Zion. Birobidžan: Idee und Geschichte eines jüdischen Staates in Sowjet-Fernost* (Berlin: Metropol, 2000); Robert Weinberg, *Stalin's Forgotten Zion: Birobidzhan and the Making of the Soviet Jewish Homeland* (Berkeley: University of California Press, 1998); Yaacov Levavi, *Ha-hityashvut ha-yehudit be-Birobizhan* (Jerusalem: Israel Historical Society, 1965); Chone Shmeruk, "Ha-kibutz ha-yehudi veha-hityashvut ha-haklait be-belorusyah ha-sovietit, 1918–32" (Ph.D. diss., Hebrew University of Jerusalem, 1961); Allan L. Kagedan, *Soviet Zion: The Quest for a Russian Jewish Homeland* (New York: St. Martin's, 1994); Solomon Lifshitz, *Istoriia evreiskogo kolkhoza v Sibiri, 1926–1934*, Soviet Institutions series, no. 4 (Hebrew University of Jerusalem, 1975).

9. *Gosudarstvennyi arkhiv pri Sovete Ministrov Avtonomnoi Respubliki Krym* (State Archive of the Council of Ministers of the Autonomous Republic of Crimea) (GAARK), f. r-515, op. 1, d. 14, l. 23 (Martens to Gashek, 17 October 1927). A German land association protested to the Crimean Central Committee against a new Jewish colony that refused to rent excess land. This colony sat on land previously cultivated, under rent, by farmers in the German association. The Crimean Commissariat of Agriculture allocated 8,000 desiatins to Komzet in January 1925, all taken from excess holdings of German colonists. See Archive of the YIVO Institute for Jewish Research, New York, RG 358/224, p. 3 (statistical report on the Jewish collectives on rented land, 1 January 1926). Evidently, the Jewish colonists hesitated to lease unused land to local peasants for fear that such a practice would be condemned as bourgeois by the Soviet authorities.

10. United States National Archives and Records Administration, Washington, D.C. (NARA), RG 59, Decimal file, 1910–29, 861.5017, Living Conditions/109, pp. 2, 5 (Coleman to the State Department, 13 November 1929); GAARK, f. p-1, op. 1, d. 477, l. 58 (Loit to Petropavlovskii, 31 May 1926), d. 830, l. 6 (Gurevich to Takser, 1 January 1928), d. 917, l. 2 (Evsektsiia agitpropotdel report on antisemitism, 1929).

11. Joshua A. Sanborn, *Drafting the Russian Nation: Military Conscription, Total War, and Mass Politics 1905–1925* (DeKalb: Northern Illinois University Press, 2003), 126–127.

12. F. Fal'ko, "V gostiakh u evreev-krest'ian," *Tribuna* 8 (1927): 10–11; I. Dobrushin, "U Krymskikh Pereselentsev," *Tribuna* 8 (1927): 5–8; GAARK, f. r-515, op. 1 d. 14, l. 23 (Martens to Gashek, 17 October 1926); GAARK, f. p.-1, op. 1, d. 830, l. 7 (Gurevich to Tasker, 1 January 1928), d. 917, l. 2 (Agitpropotdel Evsektsiia report on antisemitism, 1929).

13. GAARK, f. p-1, op.1, d. 830, l. 66 (Gurevich's report, 13 January 1928). These and other rumors about supposed Jewish deceit regarding Crimea persist, even today. See Jonathan Dekel-Chen, "Crimea 2008: A Lesson about Uses and Misuses of History," *East European Jewish Affairs* 39, no. 1 (April 2009): 101–105.

14. P.S. Korshunov, *Evreiskoe pereselenie v Krymu: mogut li evrei rabotat' na zemle* (Simferopol: Krymgosisdat, 1929), 4–5; Georgii Reitanovskii, *Na kolkhoznoi zemle: evrei-pereselentsy v Krymu* (Simferopol: Krymgosizdat, 1933), 19; Yehezkiel Keren, *Ha-hityashvut ha-haklait ha-yehudit be-hatzi ha-i Krim* (Jerusalem: Zak, 1973), 165–166; Livne-Liberman, *Ikarim yehudim be-Rusyah*, 119–120.

15. Derek J. Penslar, *Shylock's Children: Economics and Jewish Identity in Modern Europe* (Berkeley: University of California Press), 251.

16. Robert Weinberg, "Demonizing Judaism in the Soviet Union during the 1920s," *Slavic Review* 67, no. 1 (2008): 120–153.

17. This paradigm is presented in Donald L. Horowitz, *Ethnic Groups in Conflict* (Berkeley: University of California, 2000) and idem, *The Deadly Ethnic Riot* (Berkeley: University of California, 2000).

18. GAARK, f. r-515, op. 1, d. 78, l. 94 (Dashkovskii to Agro-Joint, 5 June 1928), l. 91 (Korchiniv and Shchur to Dzhankoi Raizo, 5 September 1928), l. 49 (Dashkovskii to Agro-Joint, 18 July 1928), l. 61 (Grinshtein to Fridman, 21 May 1928); GAARK, f. p-1, op. 1, d. 557, l. 7 (Lobovokii's report, 1 October 1926), d. 477, l. 70 (Gulov to Guliaeva, ca. 1926), d. 917, l. 8 (Evsektsiia report, 1929); S. Epshtein, *Po evreiskam poselkam: putevye zametki* (Kharkov: UkrOzet, 1928), 39–40.

19. GAARK, f. r-515, op. 1, d. 78, l. 65 (Fridman to GPU Crimea, 28 September 1928); GAARK, f. p-1, op. 1, d. 990, l. 144 (GPU report, 27 December 1930); *Gosudarstvennyi arkhiv Rossiiskoi Federatsii* (State Archive of the Russian Federation) (GARF), f. r-7746, op. 3, d. 46, ll. 22–23 (questionnaire on relations, 1928); V. Sotnichenko, "Evreiskaia sel'skokhoziaistvennaia kolonizatsiia na Ukraine v seredine 20-kh godov XX veka," *Vestnik Evreiskogo Universiteta v Moskve*, 1997, no. 3: 54; Viktor Fink, *Evrei na zemle* (Moscow: Gosudarstvennoe izdatel'stvo, 1929), 56.

20. For examples of peasant circumvention and manipulation of Soviet authority, see Fitzpatrick, *Stalin's Peasants*, 5–7, 11, 16.

21. Israel Yehoshua Zinger, *Nay-Rusland: bilder fun a rayze* (Vilna: Klatskin, 1928), 161–162; YIVO, RG 358/195, p. 4 (Fabrikant's inspection of Crimean collectives, 18 February 1925).

22. American Jewish Archives, Cincinnati (AJA), W(arburg) P(apers), Box 222/4, pp. 7, 12 (Kahn's report from Russia, 1925); GAARK, f. p-1, op. 1, d. 557, l. 8 (Lobovokii's report, 1 October 1926). Anti-colonization rhetoric from the Tatar communists had the heaviest effect among the mountain Tatars—those to whom Simferopol had promised steppe tracts that the Soviet government actually had allotted for Jewish settlement. Steppe Tatars (neighbors of the Jewish colonists) showed the lowest rates of antisemitism of all ethnic groups in Crimea; see S. V. Fatuev, "K probleme natsional'no-gosudarstvennogo stroitel'stva v Krymskoi ASSR," *Problemy otechestvennoi istorii: sbornik nauchnykh statei aspirantov i soiskatelei* 3 (Moscow: Rossiiskaia Akademiia Uprav. Gumanitarnyi Tsentr, 1994), 209–210.

23. American Jewish Joint Distribution Committee Archive, New York (JDC), Agro-Joint Archive, collection AR 21/32, 530 (notes of Hyman interview, 15 December 1928); GAARK, f. p-1, op. 1, d. 990, l. 144 (GPU report, 27 December 1930); GARF, f. r-7541, op. 1, d. 626, l. 44 (Shapiro's report, 2 May 1934); Benjamin Vest and Miriam Shtarkman, *He-halutz be-Rusyah* (Tel Aviv: Hehalutz, 1931), 69; "Memoir from Mishmar," 8 (Lavon Institute, Vest Collection, IV-104).

24. Early colonist-envoys [*khodoki*] and land associations often lived in German villages and colonies adjacent to proposed Jewish settlement tracts. Although Jewish colonists occupied some of their land, Germans in many instances provided them with water and fodder. See YIVO, RG 358/150, p. 3 (report on the staff meeting, January 1926); M. Bregman, "Puti evreiskogo zemledeniia," in: *Protiv antisemitizma*, Gleb Alekseev, et al. eds. (Moscow: Zhizn' i znanie, 1930), 204; GAARK, f. p-1, op. 1, d. 557, l. 7 (Lobovokii's report, October 1, 1926); GARF, f. r-7746, op. 3, d. 46, ll. 23–24 (questionnaire on relations, 1928).

25. From 1923 to 1937, the official nationalities policy of the USSR was called "indigenization" (in Russian: *korenizatsiia*). It allowed for the development of cultural

autonomy within ethnically based Soviet republics and lesser territorial units. For discussions of indigenization, see Ronald Suny and Terry Martin, *A State of Nations: Empire and Nation-Making in the Age of Lenin and Stalin* (New York: Oxford University Press, 2001), 11; and Terry Martin, *Affirmative Action Empire: Nations and Nationalism in the Soviet Union, 1923–1939* (Ithaca, N.Y.: Cornell University Press, 2001), 72–74. For examples of contemporary commentary on Jewish rural integration, see "Rasskaz kolonista: *na s'ezde v Belorussii,*" in: *Protiv antisemitizma,* ed. Gleb Alekseev, Konstantin Bol'shakov, Sergei Budantsev (Leningrad: Zhizn' i znanie, 1930), 247–248; M. Gorev, *Protiv antisemitov: ocherki i zarisovki* (Moscow: Gosudarstvennoe izdatel'stvo, 1928), 160; and Edwin Embree, "Jews on the Steppes," *Survey Graphic* 24, no. 1 (1935): 15.

26. *Rossiisski gosudarstvennyi arkhiv ekonomiki* (Russian State Archive of the Economy) (RGAE), f. 7486, op. 19, d. 126, ll. 30–31 (Smidovich to Grin'ko, 19 May 1930); Yaacov Levavi, "Atudat ha-karka le-tsorkhei ha-hityashvut ha-haklait ha-yehudit be-Krim" *Shvut* 9 (1982): 67; Korshunov, *Evreiskoe pereselenie,* 3.

27. Examples of Jewish colonies that did not need Agro-Joint for this purpose can be found in "Memoir from Mishmar," 8; Keren, *Ha-hityashvut,* 59.

28. For more on the ARA and the JDC's role in it, see Bertrand M. Patenaude, *The Big Show in Bololand: The American Relief Expedition to Soviet Russia in the Famine of 1921* (Stanford, Calif.: Stanford University Press, 2002); and, Zoşa Szajkowski, *The Mirage of American Jewish Aid in Soviet Russia, 1917–1939* (New York: privately printed, 1977).

29. JDC 455, pp. 8, 16 (memorandum of meeting with Belenky, 6 January 1925). As early as 1925, non-Jews comprised one-third of all children in Agro-Joint schools. By 1929, their enrollment ranged from 20 to 64 percent. See B. B. Berezhanskaia, "Evreiskie kolkhozy v Krymu," in *Evrei Kryma,* ed. E. Solomnik (Simferopol: Mosty, 1997), 76; GARF, f. r-7746, op. 1, d. 278, l. 29 (visit from the Timiriazev Academy, 1929).

30. YIVO, RG 358/151, p. 2 (Surdutovich's account, October 30, 1926); YIVO, RG 358/200, p. 5 (report of the Crimean group, 1926–1927). Hired labor peaked in the summer of 1928, with the arrival of flocks of unemployed Ukrainians in Crimea. Hired labor proved unprofitable because the workers' draught animals had to be fed. See Yaacov Levavi (Babitsky), *Haklaim yehudim b'arvot Krim: perek be-toledot ha-yehadut ha-sovietit, 1918–1948* (unpublished manuscript, Hebrew University of Jerusalem, 1984), chapter 16, p. 8. The author thanks Prof. Mordechai Altshuler for permission to use this manuscript. See also Zinger, *Nay-Rusland,* 158–159; S. Epshtein, *Novymi putiami* (Moscow: Ozet, 1931), 14.

31. Fink, *Evrei na zemle,* 142–143; JDC 541, p. 1 (Rosenberg to Warburg, Baerwald, 29 October 1931); Aleksandr Merezhin, *O sploshnoi kollektivizatsii i likvidatsii ku-lachestva u evreiskikh pereselentsev* (Moscow: Ozet, 1930), 42.

32. Junius Wood, "Jews Return to the Soil: A Story of Thriving Agricultural Colonies in Soviet Russia" (*Chicago Daily News,* 1927. *Chicago Daily News* reprint, no. 32), 6.

33. Levavi, *Haklaim yehudim,* chapter 16, p. 2.

34. JDC 483 (Rosen to JDC, 10 February 1923); Dan Pines, *He-halutz be-kur ha-mahapechah* (Tel Aviv: Devar, 1937), 211. Immediately upon its arrival in the region, Agro-Joint also provided much-welcomed tractor service to the neighboring non-Jewish farmers of the colonies in southern Ukraine. See JDC 455, pp. 8, 16 (meeting with Belenky, 6 January 1925).

35. JDC 454, p. 1 (Rosen's Report on JDC reconstruction work, 1923).

36. Ibid., p. 3.

37. Keren, *Ha-hityashvut,* 50, 88; "Pomoshch' Tatarskomu naseleniiu," *Evreiskii krest'ianin* 2 (1926), 249; AJA, WP, Box 222/4, p. 8 (Kahn's report, 1925); JDC 483 (Rosen to Rosenberg, January 25, 1928); JDC 516, p. 8 (minutes of informal meeting, 25 January 1937); Berezhanskaia, "Evreiskie kolkhozy," 76; JDC 457a, p. 17 (Becker, "Russia 1927");

GARF, f. r-7746, op. 1, d. 278, l. 29 (visit from the Timiriazev Academy, 1929). Some reports told of direct Agro-Joint support for 160 Tatar schools in Crimea; see Pines, *Hehalutz*, 253.

38. Bregman, "Puti evreiskogo zemledeniia," 207; Embree, "Jews on the Steppes," 15.

39. YIVO, RG 358/19, p. 11 (Fischer, "To the Soil Movement"); Pines, *Hehalutz*, 211; Keren, *Ha-hityashvut*, 25.

40. YIVO, RG 358/246, pp. 3, 9 (Zaichik to Lubarsky, 26 July 1926). For evidence of Agro-Joint's conscious attempts to distance itself from the state apparatus, see YIVO, RG 358/227 (protocol of conference at Sde Menucha, December 1925).

41. JDC 534, p. 7 (notes on Hyman's visit, 17 December 1928; JDC 483 (Rosen to JDC, 10 February 1923); JDC 455 (memorandum of meeting with Belenky, 6 January 1925); JDC 483 (Rosen to Rosenberg, 25 January 1928); JDC 509 (Boris Smolar interview for UJA Oral History, 22 June 1977); Levavi, *Haklaim yehudim*, chapter 18, p. 5; Embree, "Jews on the Steppes," 14; JDC 457a, p. 17 (Becker, "Russia 1927"); Bregman, "Puti evreiskogo zemledeniia," 207.

42. Helmut Walser Smith and Chris Clark, "The Fate of Nathan," in *Protestants, Catholics and Jews in Germany, 1800–1914*, ed. H. W. Smith (London: Berg, 2001), 11.

43. Fal'ko, "V gostiakh," 10–11; Emmanuil Feigin, "Direktor MTS," *Sovetskomu Krymu dvadtsat' let, 1920–1940* (Simferopol: Krymgosizdat, 1940), 281; Levavi, *Haklaim yehudim*, chapter 4, p. 1; GAARK, f. r-515, op. 1, d. 78, l. 61 (Grinshtein to Fridman, 21 May 1928); GAARK, f. r-1, op. 1, d. 990, l. 144 (GPU report, 27 December 1930); YIVO, RG 358/249, p. 26 (Zaichik's report on Kherson, 1925–1928).

44. While new, spacious homes sprouted in Jewish colonies, most indigenous villagers could construct, at best, one-room huts; see NARA, RG 59, Decimal File 1910–29, 861.52/92, p. 9 (Carlson to the Secretary of State, October 1928). Similar disparities arose in agriculture. By partially insulating Jewish farmers from famines in 1927–1928 and 1932–1933, modernization exacerbated tensions at moments of crisis; see Aryeh Munitz, "Haklaim yehudim be-Ukraina bi-tkufat ha-ra'av ha-gadol, 1932–1934," *Shvut* 11 (1985), 69. Thanks to tractors and agricultural instruction, Jewish colonies around Kherson harvested 125–135 pood per desiatin in 1926, their neighbors only 65–70. See JDC 62a, p. 15 (Billikopf's statements at press conference, 30 August 1926). Lewin found (in *Russian Peasants and Soviet Power* [Evanston, Ill.: Northwestern University Press, 1968], 30) that 2.1 of the 5.3 million peasant households in Ukraine in 1929 owned neither a horse nor an ox. Such cases were rare among Jewish colonists after one or two years of arrival in Crimea.

45. YIVO, RG 358/249, p. 25 (Zaichik's report on the Kherson Region, 1925–1928); YIVO RG 358/249, p. 26 (Zaichik's report on Agro-Joint work, 1925–1928). For general assessment of rural hooliganism, see Alexis Berelowitch and Viktor Danilov, eds., *Sovetskaia derevnia glazami OGPU* 2 (Moscow: Rosspen, 2000), 414–415; Neil Weissman, "Policing the NEP Countryside," in *Russia in the Era of NEP: Explorations in Soviet Society and Culture*, ed. Sheila Fitzpatrick, Alexander Rabinowitch, and Richard Stites (Bloomington: Indiana University Press, 1991), 186–188; Altrichter, "Insoluble Conflicts," in idem, 198; and Fitzpatrick, *Stalin's Peasants*, 235–236.

46. GAARK, f. r-515, op. 1, d. 78, l. 48 (residents of Freidorf to Komzet, 19 September 1929).

47. GAARK, f. r-515, op. 1, d. 414, l. 23 (Redkin to Komzet, 9 October 1934), l. 25 (Redkin to Director of Crimean militia, 5 October 1934), l. 60 (Komzet to Evpatoria Raikom, 15 June 1934), l. 59 (Komzet to militia, 16 June 1934). For the general picture of the rural crisis, see Elena Osokina, *Our Daily Bread: Socialist Distribution and the Art of Survival in Stalin's Russia, 1927–1941* (New York: Sharpe, 2001), 51. Similar debates

existed in early Mandatory Palestine about the causes for some Arab attacks against
Jewish settlements in the Galilee region. See Simon Schama, *Two Rothschilds and the
Land of Israel* (London: Collins, 1978), 220.

48. GAARK, f. r-515, op. 1, d. 78, l. 61 (Grinshtein to Fridman, 21 May 1928). *Zhid* is
a Russian pejorative applied to Jews.

49. GARF, f. r-7746, op. 1, d. 278, ll. 9–10 (visit by the Timiriazev academy, 1929).

50. GAARK, f. r.-515, op. 1, d. 78, l. 61 (Grinshtein to Fridman, 21 May 1928).

51. Margaret Lavinia Anderson's "Afterword: Living Apart and Together in
Germany" (in Smith, *Protestants, Catholics and Jews,* 319–332) sparked my initial
thoughts on this point.

52. For further discussion, see Jonathan Dekel-Chen, "Soviet Jewish Agricultural
Colonists, 1937–1945," *Jews in Eastern Europe* 3, no. 46 (Winter 2001): 34–58.

GLOSSARY

Agro-Joint—a unit of the American Jewish Joint Distribution Committee created to support Jewish agricultural settlement in the Soviet Union.

Black Hundreds (*Chernaia sotnia***)**—far-right political organization in the Russian Empire espousing extreme ethnic-Russian nationalism and antisemitism.

Cossacks—autonomous militaristic communities in southern Russia and Ukraine whose members often fought alongside regular units in the tsarist army.

desiatin (R.)—Russian measure of area, equal to approximately 2.7 acres.

Hasidim (H., Y.)—followers of the mystical-pietistic stream of Judaism that emerged in Eastern Europe in the eighteenth century.

heder (H.), Kheyder (Y.)—traditional Jewish elementary school teaching religious subjects such as Bible and Talmud, and sometimes secular subjects as well.

kahal (H., Y.)—governing body of the Jewish community.

kippa (H.)—head covering traditionally worn by Jewish men, also known as *yarmulke*.

kolkhoz (R.)—Soviet-era collective agricultural settlement.

Nestor Makhno—leader of the peasant-anarchist Revolutionary Insurrectionary Army of Ukraine ("Black Army") during the Russian Civil War.

Pogromshchik (pl. pogromshchiki) (R.)—perpetrator of pogroms.

Symon Petliura—Ukrainian politician and military leader and head of the Directorate (government) of the Ukrainian National (or People's) Republic during its brief independence after World War I.

pood, pud (R.)—Russian measure of weight, equal to approximately 36 pounds.

shtetl (Y.)—market town where Jews formed a substantial minority or even a majority of the population, usually in the territories identified with the Pale of Settlement and Congress Poland or adjacent regions. Sometimes identified with the Russian *mestechko*.

varta (U.)—Ukrainian "guards" or paramilitary organization.

zemstvo (R.)—system of local government introduced during Alexander II's Great Reforms. The zemstvo system was never implemented in the provinces of the Pale of Settlement or Congress Poland.

zhid (R.)—pejorative term for Jew, often translated as "Yid" or "kike."

CONTRIBUTORS

Israel Bartal is Dean of the Faculty of Humanities and Avraham Harman Chair in Jewish History at the Hebrew University of Jerusalem. Bartal was Academic Chair of the Leonid Nevzlin Research Center for Russian and East European Jewry at the Hebrew University of Jerusalem from 2003 to 2006. Among his books are *Poles and Jews: A Failed Brotherhood* (with Magdalena Opalski) and *The Jews of Eastern Europe, 1772–1881*.

Vladimir P. Buldakov currently serves in the Institute of Russian History of the Russian Academy of Sciences and is editor of *Soviet and Post-Soviet Review*. Among his books are *Krasnaya smuta: Priroda i posledstviya revolutsionnogo nasiliya* (Red Chaos: The Nature and Aftermath of Revolutionary Violence); and, *Quo Vadis. Krizisy v Rossii: Puti pereosmysleniya* (Quo vadis. Crises in Russia: Paths of Reconsideration).

Jonathan Dekel-Chen is a senior lecturer on modern history at the Hebrew University of Jerusalem and Academic Chair of its Leonid Nevzlin Research Center for Russian and East European Jewry. Dekel-Chen is author of *Farming the Red Land: Jewish Agricultural Colonization and Local Power in Soviet Russia, 1924–41*.

David Engel is Greenberg Professor of Holocaust Studies, Professor of Hebrew and Judaic Studies and Professor of History at New York University, and a fellow of the Goldstein-Goren Diaspora Research Center at Tel Aviv University.

David Gaunt is Professor of History at Södertörn University, Stockholm. He is author of *Massacres, Resistance, Protectors: Muslim–Christian Relations in Eastern Anatolia during World War I* and primary editor of *Collaboration and Resistance during the Holocaust: Belarus, Estonia, Latvia, Lithuania*.

Peter Holquist is Associate Professor of History at the University of Pennsylvania. He is author of *Making War, Forging Revolution: Russia's Continuum of Crisis, 1914–1921* and co-founder and co-editor of the journal *Kritika: Explorations in Russian and Eurasian History*.

Lilia Kalmina is a leading specialist at the Buryat Scientific Center, Siberian Branch of the Russian Academy of Sciences (Ulan-Ude). Her research focuses on the history of Siberian diasporas, including Jews. Professor Kalmina is author of approximately one hundred scholarly works, including seven books. Her landmark book is *Evrei vostochnoi sibiri: "dukhovnaia territoriia" (seredina XIX veka-1917 god)* [*The Jews of Eastern Siberia from the Mid-Nineteenth Century to February 1917*].

Claire Le Foll is a lecturer at the University of Southampton. Her research areas are the history of Jews in Belorussia before the Revolution of 1917 and the cultural history of Belorussia, Ukraine, and Lithuania in the first half of the twentieth century. Her book on the Vitebsk Art School was published in French and Russian.

Vladimir Levin received his Ph.D. from the Hebrew University of Jerusalem with a dissertation on "Jewish Politics in Russia in the Period of Reaction, 1907–1914." He was a Kreitman postdoctoral Fellow at Ben-Gurion University of the Negev, 2006–2009.

Eric Lohr is Associate Professor of History at American University. He is author of *Nationalizing the Russian Empire: The Campaign against Enemy Aliens during World War I* and *The Papers of Grigorii Nikolaevich Trubetskoi* and co-editor, with Marshall Poe, of *Military and Society in Russian History, 1450–1917.*

Natan M. Meir holds the Lorry I. Lokey Chair in Judaic Studies at Portland State University and is author of *Kiev, Jewish Metropolis: A History, 1859–1914* (Indiana University Press, 2010).

Vladas Sirutavičius is a senior research fellow at the Lithuanian Institute of History. His main interests are the history of modern Lithuania, ethnic conflicts, and Lithuanian–Polish relations. He is author (with Č. Laurinavičius) of *Lithuanian History: Sajūdis, from Perestroika to March 11.*

Darius Staliūnas is Deputy Director of the Lithuanian Institute of History. He is author of *Making Russians: Meaning and Practice of Russification in Lithuania and Belarus after 1863.*

Arkadi Zeltser is a researcher at the International Institute for Holocaust Research at Yad Vashem. He is author of *Evrei sovetskoi provintsii: Vitebsk i mestechki, 1917–1941* (The Jews of the Soviet provinces: Vitebsk and the shtetls, 1917–1941).

INDEX

Acculturation, Jewish, 186
Administrative measures, 56, 119, 182, 190
Affirmative action, 189, 191
Agitation: anti-Jewish, 74–77, 79, 82, 87,
   134, 160; Bolshevik, 75
Agriculture, 153, 166, 176–177, 178; aid for,
   192, 193, 201n34; modernization of, 161
Agro-Joint, 187–189, 191–194, 195, 197
Agronomists, 16, 191, 194, 195
Aleksandrovskoe Military School, 75
Alekseev, Mikhail, 44
Alexander I, 165
Alexander II, 28, 113, 124, 131, 163;
   assassination of, 4, 6, 10, 32, 115, 154,
   156
Alexander III, 32
Alienation, 162, 163, 182
Aliens, 80, 82, 148, 177. *See also* Enemy
   aliens
Alliance Israélite Universelle, 166
American Jewish Joint Distribution
   Committee (JDC), 187, 189, 192–193. *See*
   also Agro-Joint
American Relief Administration (ARA),
   192, 193
Anarchists, 10
Anglo-Russian Agreement, 12
Anti-defamation, 12–13
Anti-Jewish accusations, 113–114
Anti-Jewish action, 117–118, 137, 152, 155,
   182
Anti-Jewish sentiment, 48, 76, 113–114,
   117, 124, 125, 152, 155
Anti-Jewish violence, 19, 82, 122, 186, 197;
   causes of, 7, 14, 55, 58, 68, 138, 148,
   154, 156; characteristics of, 3, 5–6, 16,
   26, 29–30, 31, 35, 46, 133–134, 194;
   comparisons of, 41; context for, 8, 74,
   111, 125; extent of, 8–9, 16, 22, 145–147;
   external factors in, 147, 148, 155;
   legitimization of, 11; periodization of,
   26; prevention of, 34, 96, 103, 106.
   See also Pogroms
Anti-Judaism, 3, 141, 149

Antisemitism, 81, 111, 147, 148, 164, 187,
   194–195; agrarian, 80; appeals regarding, 152, 153, 157n30; and attitudes, 9,
   14, 74, 133, 141; efforts to counter, 11,
   12–13, 96, 103–104, 105, 106; extent of,
   149, 200n22; growth of, 74, 147–148,
   156, 180, 181, 183; latent, 155; official,
   4, 10, 181; organization of, 105, 150;
   popular, 181, 189; program of, 9, 52–54,
   58, 61, 64; revolutionary, 74, 77, 79;
   urban, 76, 80, 81–82; wartime, 141
Antonescu, Ion, 34
Armenians, 59
Army command, Russian, 42–43, 67, 79
Aronson, I. Michael, 161, 162, 167
Artels, 178
Assimilation, Jewish, 3, 5, 10, 104–105,
   136, 165, 186; government policies for,
   166–167; narratives of, 131
Atrocities: purported Austrian, 53, 63, 64,
   65, 72n53; Ukrainian, 84
Austria, 22–23, 63, 64, 65, 112
Authority, 32, 35, 154, 155, 156; moral,
   140, 151
Autonomy: of non-Jewish Crimean
   population, 189; within Soviet
   republics, 200n25

Backwardness, 116, 152, 164, 167, 171, 175
Balkan Wars, 62
Balta, 22, 159
Baltics, 44, 48
Barguzin, 137
Bark, Petr L'vovich, 44
Barnaul, 133
Barsheŭski, Ian, 168
Bašinska, Gediminas, 155
Bavaria, 31
Bazili, Nikolai, 58
Behavior: antisemitic, 80, 186; deviant,
   180, 184n23; genocidal, 4; Jewish, 33,
   106; nationalist, 182; threatening, 8; of
   victims, 24; violent, 21, 30, 145, 195;
   wartime, 197

Ethnic groups, 35, 78, 177, 183, 191

Ethnic relations, 16, 23, 111, 138, 163, 187, 190–192, 194–195, 197, 198; traditional, 160

Ethnic tensions, 46, 48, 116, 117, 145–147, 149, 160, 174, 177, 178, 179–180, 187, 188, 196, 197; causes of, 152–154; factors affecting, 14, 16, 175, 181–183

Ethnocentrism, 155

Evert, General Aleksei Ermolaevich, 59

Everyday life, 111, 116–118, 120, 122, 164, 169, 186, 196–197

Executions, 33, 56, 63, 65

Exiles, 131–132, 133, 137, 138

Exploitation, 10, 125, 131, 157n30, 164–165, 166; economic, 13

Expropriation. *See* Property, expropriation of

Expulsions: from army, 44; Jewish, 2, 13, 31, 42, 59, 61–67, 112–115, 118–119, 125, 153, 163–165; policies of mass civilian, 8–9, 43–44, 45, 46–47, 49, 61, 62, 65–66, 67. *See also* Deportations

Extermination, 59, 197

Extortion, 42, 43

Factories, 161, 179

Famine, 192, 202n44. *See also* American Relief Administration

Fanaticism, 15, 57, 131, 165–166, 167

Far East, 4

Fascism, 147

Fastov, 84, 86

Feudalism, 160, 161, 162, 163, 164, 171

Finland, 44

Five-Year Plan, 181

Foreigners, 43, 44, 49, 195; Jews as symbol of, 174

France, 23

Frankel, Jonathan, 3, 119, 120, 171

Frenkel' family, 123

Fridland, Ben-Zion, 100

Frontier society, 133

Frysztak, 22

Fuller, William C., 44

Funerals, 135, 140, 141

Galant, Ilia, 105

Gal'perin family, 123

Galicia, 9, 19, 54, 61, 64, 65, 66; occupation of, 52–57, 58, 60; retreat from, 67, 79

Gelezinis viklas (Iron Wolf) organization, 147

Gell-Mann, Murray, 25

General Headquarters, 58, 60–61, 63; antisemitism in, 53, 59; Diplomatic Chancellery of, 64

General Jewish Workers Union. *See* Bund (General Jewish Workers Union of Lithuania, Poland and Russia)

General Staff, Russian Army, 9, 57

Genocide, 2, 4, 6, 8, 68; Armenian, 59; Nazi, 5 (*see also* Holocaust)

Germans, 55, 57, 65, 191, 199n9, 200n24; and property, 47; violence against, 41, 45, 46, 48–49; violence by, 53, 56, 86

Germany, 154, 156, 194–195; anti-Jewish violence in, 22–23, 31; Nazi, 34, 61, 144, 147, 148, 154, 197

Getz, Faivel Meir, 105–106

Gintsburg, Baron Horace, 97

Glukhov, 10, 84

Goebbels, Josef, 34

Gogol, I. Ia., 83

Gogolevo, 84

Gololobov, Jacob Georgievich, 139–140

Gomel, 11, 85, 95, 99, 175

Government authorities, 8, 145, 183; Lithuanian, 146, 151, 156; local, 119, 165–166; Polish, 20; role of 24, 25–26, 149. *See also* Russian government; Soviet authorities; State, modern

Grabar', Vladimir, 53, 54, 57, 59, 63

Great Britain, 12, 19, 20; medieval, 27

Great Retreat, 67, 68

Grints, 85

Grodno province, 159, 161

Groza (newspaper), 76

Haidamaks, 81, 84, 114

Ha-melits (newspaper), 115, 117

Hamm, Michael, 121

Hasidim, 56, 165

Health care, 193

He-halutz (Pioneer) movement, 153

Hep! Hep! riots, 23, 31

Himmler, Heinrich, 34

Hindus, 23

Holocaust, 1, 5, 14, 144, 148, 149, 197

www.ingramcontent.com/pod-product-compliance
Lightning Source LLC
Chambersburg PA
CBHW020816300326
41914CB00051B/296